THE MAKING AND REMAKING
OF CHRISTIAN DOCTRINE

MAURICE WILES

The Making and Remaking of Christian Doctrine

ESSAYS IN HONOUR OF MAURICE WILES

Edited by
SARAH COAKLEY
and
DAVID A. PAILIN

CLARENDON PRESS · OXFORD
1993

Oxford University Press, Walton Street, Oxford OX2 6DP
Oxford New York Toronto
Delhi Bombay Calcutta Madras Karachi
Kuala Lumpur Singapore Hong Kong Tokyo
Nairobi Dar es Salaam Cape Town
Melbourne Auckland Madrid

and associated companies in
Berlin Ibadan

Oxford is a trade mark of Oxford University Press

Published in the United States
by Oxford University Press Inc., New York

British Library Cataloguing in Publication Data
Data available

Library of Congress Cataloging in Publication Data
The Making and remaking of Christian doctrine: essays in honour of
Maurice Wiles / edited by Sarah Coakley and David A. Pailin.
Includes bibliographical references.
1. Theology, Doctrinal. 2. Theology, Doctrinal—History.
3. Wiles, Maurice F. I. Coakley, Sarah, 1951– . II. Pailin,
David A. (David Arthur), 1936–
BR50.M244 1993   230—dc20   92–42790
ISBN 0–19–826739–8

1 3 5 7 9 10 8 6 4 2

Typeset by J&L Composition Ltd., Filey, North Yorkshire
Printed in Great Britain
on acid-free paper by
Biddles, Ltd., Guildford and King's Lynn

Preface

This collection of essays is offered to Maurice Wiles with affection and gratitude. Throughout his distinguished career he has been a staunch supporter of a liberal approach to Christian theological understanding. These essays, which span a wide range of opinions, reflect his dual interests in the making and remaking of Christian doctrine.

Maurice Wiles was educated at Tonbridge School, Christ's College, Cambridge, and Ridley Hall, Cambridge. He served for two years as curate at St George's in Stockport and then returned to Cambridge in 1952 to be Chaplain at Ridley Hall. From 1955 to 1959 he was Lecturer in New Testament Studies at Ibadan, Nigeria. In 1959 he became Lecturer in Divinity and Dean of Clare College in Cambridge, leaving in 1967 to be Professor of Christian Doctrine at King's College, London. Three years later he was appointed the Regius Professor of Divinity at Oxford, from which position he retired in 1991.

Those who know Maurice Wiles as a person, teacher, and writer are impressed by his generous open-mindedness, critical awareness, and perceptive understanding. In investigating questions about the structure and content of the Christian faith, he combines careful scholarship and rigorous honesty with enlightening insights. Although his probing studies have not always won him approval from some less willing to consider disturbing critical questions, he has not flinched from seeking to establish positive responses to the profound challenges posed to traditional beliefs by contemporary thought. A person whom many are delighted to have as a friend, he has been generous in his support of younger scholars. It is with gratitude for his personal as well as for his scholarly example that these essays are presented to him to celebrate his seventieth birthday.

SARAH COAKLEY
DAVID A. PAILIN

Contents

List of Contributors

JAMES BARR is Professor of Hebrew Bible at Vanderbilt University, Nashville, Tennessee and was formerly Regius Professor of Hebrew at Oxford University. His latest books include his Gifford Lectures, *Biblical Faith and Natural Theology*, and his Read-Tuckwell Lectures, *The Garden of Eden and the Hope of Immortality*.

HENRY CHADWICK is Emeritus Professor and was Master of Peterhouse, Cambridge. His books include *The Early Church*, *Boethius*, *Augustine*, *Augustine's Confessions*, *Early Christian Thought and the Classical Tradition*, and *Lessing's Theological Writings*; and his papers include studies of problems in ecumenical dialogue.

SARAH COAKLEY is Professor of Christian Theology at Harvard University. She was previously Tutorial Fellow and University Lecturer in Theology at Oriel College, Oxford. She is author of *Christ without Absolutes: A Study of the Christology of Ernst Troeltsch*, and is currently editing a book on *Religion and the Body*.

JOHN HICK is Danforth Professor Emeritus of the Philosophy of Religion at the Claremont Graduate School, California, and a Fellow of the Institute for Advanced Research in the Humanities at Birmingham University, England. His most recent publications include *An Interpretation of Religion* and *Disputed Questions in Theology and the Philosophy of Religion*.

MORNA D. HOOKER is the Lady Margaret's Professor of Divinity in the University of Cambridge and a Fellow of Robinson College. Her latest books include *Continuity and Discontinuity*, *From Adam to Christ*, and *A Commentary on St Mark*.

GORDON D. KAUFMAN is Mallinckrodt Professor of Divinity in Harvard University. His most recent publications include *An Essay on Theological Method*, *The Theological Imagination*, *Theology for a Nuclear Age*, and *In the Face of Mystery: A Constructive Theology*. His essay included in this volume is taken from his latest book, and is used with permission of Harvard University Press.

ANDREW LOUTH is Professor of Cultural History at Goldsmith's College in the University of London. His several publications include *The Origins of the Christian Mystical Tradition: Plato to Denys* and *Denys the Areopagite*.

REBECCA LYMAN is Associate Professor of Early Church History at the Church Divinity School of the Pacific, Berkeley, California. She is the author of *Christology and Cosmology: Models of Divine Activity in Origen, Eusebius and Athanasius* and *Origen as Theologian: A Critical Introduction*.

SALLIE MCFAGUE is the Carpenter Professor of Theology at Vanderbilt University, Nashville, Tennessee. She is the author of *Metaphorical Theology* and *Models of God*, books that deal with religious language and ecological theology.

JOHN MACQUARRIE is Lady Margaret Professor Emeritus of Divinity in the University of Oxford. His most recent publications include *Jesus Christ in Modern Thought* (awarded the Harper Collins Religious Book Prize) and *Mary for All Christians*.

BASIL MITCHELL was Nolloth Professor of the Philosophy of the Christian Religion at Oxford University from 1968 to 1984. His publications include *Law, Morality and Religion*, *The Justification of Religious Belief*, and *Morality: Religious and Secular*. He is a Fellow of the British Academy.

SCHUBERT M. OGDEN is University Distinguished Professor of Theology at Southern Methodist University, Dallas. Author of *The Reality of God and Other Essays*, *The Point of Christology*, and *On Theology*, his most recent book is *Is There Only One True Religion or Are There Many?*.

DAVID A. PAILIN is Reader in the Philosophy of Religion at the University of Manchester. His books include *Groundwork of Philosophy of Religion*, *God and the Processes of Reality*, *The Anthropological Character of Theology*, and *A Gentle Touch: From a Theology of Handicap to a Theology of Human Being*.

ROWAN WILLIAMS is Bishop of Monmouth and was formerly Lady Margaret Professor of Divinity at Oxford. He has written on historical and systematic theology, and on the frontiers of theology and spirituality. His books include *Arius: Heresy and Tradition* and *Teresa of Avila*.

FRANCES M. YOUNG is Edward Cadbury Professor of Theology in the University of Birmingham. She is known for *From Nicaea to*

Chalcedon and her recent publications include *The Art of Performance* and *The Making of the Creeds*.

Throughout the text of this book the editors have decided not to try to impose uniformity in relation to the use of upper and lower case for words like Church/church and Christology/christology, since the authors contributing to the volume not only vary in their practice, but intend by their usage theological nuances that an imposed uniformity would obscure.

Divine Action and Hebrew Wisdom

JAMES BARR

At an early stage in his Bampton Lectures, *God's Action in the World*, Maurice Wiles mentioned the familiar emphasis of the Old Testament on the 'acts of God' and the way in which this was exploited in the 'Biblical Theology Movement' earlier this century (Wiles 1986: 8). He recognized this, and rightly, as a primary feature of the biblical writings. He then went on to mention two qualifications. The first was that this feature was by no means as distinctive a characteristic as had often been supposed: and with the passage of time this qualification has come to be stronger and more widely recognized. 'Does he [God], like Zeus, send out thunderbolts in his displeasure?', Wiles asks (Wiles 1986: 1), hinting at an awareness that the 'God who acts' in this drastic sense belongs to the pagan, mythological world rather than to the biblical and Christian. The second qualification was that, even in recognizing the importance of the 'mighty acts of God' for the Old Testament, he added, in his own words, 'even if one finds it a little difficult to know what to do with the Wisdom literature'. The Wisdom literature, he thus suggested, was sparing or restrained in its mention of the mighty acts of God, and difficult to fit into any scheme dominated by 'acts' of that kind.

By putting it in this way, he was understating rather than exaggerating. It was always recognized that the Wisdom literature constituted something of an exception to the general Old Testament emphasis on God's actions in the world. Even George Ernest Wright in his *God Who Acts* conceded this (cf. Barr 1966: 73). He coped with it by admitting that Hebrew Wisdom was theologically deficient. Though it had 'radically shifted' the theological base of international wisdom and subjected it to the peculiarly Israelite principle of 'the fear of Yahweh', it had not gone far enough in this

direction. It was imperfectly removed from ethnic religion: 'In this
respect Proverbs remains near the pagan source of wisdom in
which society and the Divine work in history played no real role'
(Wright 1952: 103–4). And he goes on to point out, quite justifiably,
the criticisms of the wise and their counsel which various prophets
set forth. In any case, one way or the other, he accepted that the
Wisdom literature did not fit fully and positively into his scheme;
only partially, and mainly as a negative example, could it be
integrated.

In the event, however, things went the other way. The emphasis
on 'the mighty acts of God' in biblical theology came in the
course of time to be severely qualified. On the one hand there
were philosophical criticisms which Professor Wiles rightly
mentions. He refrains, on the other hand, from pressing the other
side of the same shift of opinion, namely the striking turn of
biblical scholarship towards a positive emphasis on the Wisdom
literature.

For since that time—since, say, 1952, when *God Who Acts* was
published—the atmosphere in biblical scholarship has changed very
greatly in exactly this respect. Emphasis on the 'acts of God in
history' has been heavily reduced, and interest in the Wisdom
literature has flourished and expanded mightily. From being an
apparent backwater in the theology of the Old Testament, it began
to seem like a wide river, the currents of which bore all the rest
along. No longer isolated in the small group of distinctively
'Wisdom' books, Wisdom characteristics and Wisdom motifs
began to be found everywhere—not only in some Psalms, where
they had been identified long before, but now in the law, the
prophets, and the historical writings; and von Rad insisted that
apocalyptic, an important current of later Judaism and one that
forms an essential link with the New Testament, also derived in
essence from Wisdom and not from the prophets. He likewise had
interpreted the story of Joseph in Genesis as a characteristic
expression of the Wisdom ethos. Others followed along similar
paths, and clearly Wisdom was becoming eminent, in a way that
had, perhaps, never before been the case in all the history of biblical
interpretation (unless perhaps in the Greek Fathers). In a judicious
survey of scholarship on Hebrew Wisdom published in 1979, John
Emerton wrote: 'The wisdom literature has moved towards the

centre of interest of Old Testament scholars during the past quarter of a century' (Emerton 1979: 214). And some specialists in the New Testament appeared to be inclining in the same direction.

The change of atmosphere was felt not only in the more technical and specialized work of scholars but also in wider theological applications. By 1972 Walter Brueggemann, a widely known scholar with strong popular appeal, had published a study with the provocative title of *In Man We Trust: The Neglected Side of Biblical Faith*. And this was about Wisdom; indeed its essential basis lay in the one book of Proverbs. Describing himself as a 'son of neo-orthodoxy', Brueggemann enthusiastically embraced the fresh perspectives that this change of emphasis had brought him:

The man of Proverbs is not the servile, self-abasing figure often urged by our one-sided reading of Scripture in later Augustinian-Lutheran theo-logical tradition. Rather he is an able, self-reliant, caring, involved, strong person who has a significant influence over the course of his own life and over the lives of his fellows . . . Proverbs . . . has no patience for a god who only saves sinners and judges sins. The God affirmed here trusts man, believes in him, risks his world with him, and stays with him in his failures. (Brueggemann 1972: 118)

Jesus himself was coming to be caught up in the movement. 'The theology of the wisdom teachers', Brueggemann declared, 'is consistent with the major thrust of Jesus' teaching'. Conventional terms of incarnation and atonement are not adequate for the fullness of his person and work. Rather, Jesus

embodies . . . the teaching of the wise men about how one lives as a life-bringer . . . He is the manifestation in a human life of the kind of style the wise urged upon people. He also enables people to attain that style . . . Jesus of Nazareth may be the culmination of other traditions but he is no less the culmination of the wisdom tradition. (Brueggemann 1972: 120–1)

Clearly, substantial changes were taking place. Indeed, the advance was so rapid that some felt a cautionary application of the brakes to be advisable. James Crenshaw, then of Vanderbilt, and one of the major specialists in the field, spoke to restrain the enthusiasm with which the influence of Wisdom had been expanded. 'Is the current emphasis on wisdom literature indicative of our inability to take revelation seriously any more?', he asked (Crenshaw 1970: 395). In an important article entitled 'Method in

determining Wisdom Influence upon "Historical" Literature' he
argued that attempts to spread the influence of Wisdom too widely
had often been based on loose definitions and inexact methods: thus
assertions that the stories of Joseph, of the Davidic succession, or
even of Esther (!) belonged to the Wisdom tradition were not to
be credited (Crenshaw 1969: 129–42; also Crenshaw 1976: 481–94).
Such attempts, he maintained in his Prolegomenon to a collection
of essays (Crenshaw 1976: 13), 'have not yet succeeded in breaking
out of circular reasoning': many of the arguments 'presuppose what
they attempt to demonstrate', and in the end they have the result
that 'wisdom has ceased to have any distinctive meaning'. He
wisely gave the common-sense advice that the definition and
delimitation of 'Wisdom' must be controlled by the recognized five
books: Proverbs, Job, and Qoheleth (Ecclesiastes) within the
Hebrew canon, plus ben Sira (Ecclesiasticus) and the Wisdom of
Solomon among the other books. Not all, however, are likely to
remain within these bounds. Even among the leading experts in
Hebrew Wisdom, therefore, there is some question about the scope
and extent of the phenomenon which they are so eagerly exploring
in our time.

Nevertheless the general impression given is clear: Wisdom is a
matter of first importance for any evaluation of the theological
meaning of the Old Testament. Just as there have in the past been
Old Testament theologies which seemed to take Deuteronomy as
their structural principle and paradigm, or the classical prophets,
or the Psalms, so it is only a matter of time, one supposes, until
someone publishes a theology which will say that Proverbs is the
core of the Old Testament and will take that book as the centre
and paradigm.

It is likely to be some time, however, before the consciousness
of this becomes widespread in the general theological and religious
public. Changes of fashion in scholarship take time to have a wide
effect. Moreover, in this case it will take time even to reach the
starting-point: for in the mind of the average Bible-reader the
Wisdom literature, apart perhaps from some parts of Job, does not
enjoy the highest priority. It is not central to familiar controversies.
Few such readers, one may suspect, are as quick to leap to the
support of its authority as they are to that of the Law of Moses,
the Gospels, or the letters of St Paul. They tacitly accept—
wrongly, if modern scholarly opinion is to be trusted—that its role

is a somewhat ancillary one. Moreover, and most important, although scholars are now largely united in emphasizing the importance of Wisdom, they themselves are far from united in the assessment of it or in the definition of the theological function they ascribe to it, so that the spread of their discussions to the wider public may be slow.

Paradoxically, however, in the Wisdom literature scholars may well be closer to the general public than they are in many other areas of their work. For in this field the operations of strict historical criticism, so much noted as a feature of biblical scholarship, have rather limited force. In a literature that contains very few historical statements, these operations seem to have little purchase. Once one has got the basic idea that Solomon himself did not actually write Proverbs and Ecclesiastes, and hence that Ecclesiastes is 'late', so also various parts of Proverbs, and Job somewhere from middling to late, not much more of great precision can be achieved. No one knows these dates within a century or two. The idea, often widespread in our time, that critical scholarship could never do anything without first attaining the most exact historical information about the earliest stages was always false in any case but was particularly untrue in respect of the Wisdom literature. In interpreting the meaning of these texts, one gets nowhere by asking such questions as 'what really happened?' or 'what historical events lay behind this?' Whole books on the subject, like von Rad's *Wisdom in Israel*, were written without bothering much about that sort of historical research. Technical scholarship has important resources in its linguistic knowledge, its acquaintance with Hebrew culture, and its means of access to the Wisdom materials of environing cultures; but for the wider question of evaluation it does not have any clear and decisive method in its possession. There is every reason to expect that an open conversation with theologians and philosophers will be fruitful.[1]

In all cases the problem is to know how the material hangs together: each Wisdom book within itself, each book with the rest of the Wisdom literature, and that with the rest of the Bible and the wider theological context of the synagogue and church. And on these large general issues we find a great variety of opinion, from those who hold that Wisdom, with its 'act-and-consequence sequence' (*Tun-Ergehen-Zusammenhang*, i.e. the idea that an action necessarily leads to a consequence, retribution or whatever it may be), is totally contrary to Christian faith and cannot be used in Christian preaching (cf. Preuss 1970: 393–417; Preuss 1974: 165–81) to those who think, with Brueggemann as cited above, that Jesus' entire teaching and life was fully in the spirit of Hebrew Wisdom. Some think that the older Wisdom of the Solomonic age was basically 'secular'; others that, even though drawn from experience and expressed in terms of it, it is still in essence religious. Some view its connections with the Wisdom of other lands (Egypt, Babylonia, later with Greek thought) with sympathy, others are anxious to show how it differentiated itself from these sources or contemporary parallels.

Again, one can often see underlying religious motivations behind the scholarly reasonings. Some, for instance, are moved by the consideration that the Wisdom books (or three of them) are in the canon of scripture: surely, the books would not be there if they did not have something positive to say to us? Others are unmoved by this: some other principle, perhaps justification by faith, is more important to them, and if Wisdom books are defective on this score they can be seen as 'an alien body in the world of the Old Testament' (Gese 1958: 2) or, as already mentioned, as imperfectly removed from their pagan background (Wright 1952: 104). There is thus a wide range of opinions, and the recent increase in the emphasis on Wisdom seems likely to leave it as a scarred theological battle-ground rather than a quiet flowered meadow. In other words, the Wisdom literature forms a very good area for conversation between Old Testament scholarship and ideas of modern constructive theology, such as Professor Wiles has put forward.

And yet the centre of all this seems to be largely agreed; indeed, if it is not always expressly stated, this is because it may generally be taken as implied. *In the Wisdom literature God seems not to act, or to act only little and in a muted or distant way.* And this is what brings the whole matter back to the arguments of Professor Wiles. For one has to consider that the Wisdom literature may be not only, negatively, a 'difficulty' for a view of God's revelatory action in history, but, positively, a serious biblical support for the sort of view of divine action which he himself proposes.

In a limited space we can touch only briefly on three of the more obvious aspects: (1) the absence, or limited presence, of mention of divine action in the world in the older Wisdom books; (2) the question of divine retribution; and (3) the place of creation.

1. The thin representation in the Wisdom books of the kind of divine action familiar from other strata of the Old Testament is very obvious when one thinks about it. Most readers, however, no doubt fail to notice it, because as they read they harmonize the text of Proverbs or Job with these other strata, thinking that these other images of divine action are somehow presupposed, or are present in the writer's mind even if nothing is said about them. Arguing in a similar direction but from a high scholarly vantage-point, von Rad maintained that Yahwism created the conditions for Israelite Wisdom. The 'fear of the Lord', characteristic of the special Israelite traditions, was the beginning of Wisdom. 'It was precisely because this knowledge of Yahweh was so strong, so unassailable, that Israel was able to speak of the orders of this world in quite secular terms' (von Rad 1972: 63).[2] And let us agree that something of this kind may be a scholarly possibility.

But against it there remains the heavy weight of the fact that the characteristics of Yahwism, as expressed in the Pentateuch, some of the historical literature, much of the prophets, and some of the Psalms, are *just not mentioned*, or not mentioned sufficiently. Why is there nothing, in the canonical Wisdom books, about the Exodus, Mount Sinai, the covenants, the prophets? Still more striking, in books full of moral advice, why is there practically nothing about the avoidance of idolatry?[3] Is it not more natural to admit that the older Wisdom literature is expressing a substantially different approach to God's relation with the world?

Not that a book like Proverbs sees God as inactive. He 'tears down the house of the proud, but maintains the widow's boundaries' (Prov. 15: 25). He weighs the spirit (16: 2), he directs the steps (16: 9), he tries the hearts (17: 3). He will repay the one who is generous to the poor (19: 17). If, rather than taking retributive action on one's own behalf, one waits for Yahweh, he will help (20: 22). All these are action of a kind. But they are not 'mighty acts' of a type comparable to the dividing of the Red Sea or the toppling of the walls of Jericho. They are more like an active presence of God in the order of the world, actions that are going on all the time but which may not be obvious or perceptible— which is precisely why Wisdom is there, in order to give assurance of their existence. Even some of the sayings that have been thought to come nearer to the 'mighty acts' pattern can probably be understood in the above way also. Thus

> The horse is prepared for the day of battle
> but victory belongs to the Lord
>
> (Prov. 21: 31)

is not really an evocation of the 'mighty acts' of Israel's other traditions, as Gese suggests (Gese 1958: 46); it is a true proverbial expression, which uses the horse and the victory as an analogy for what always happens: humans make the best preparations, but God decides what will come of them.

In all this we do not suggest that essential characteristics of Israelite faith are neglected in the Wisdom literature. In spite of its many relations with Egyptian Wisdom, it is notable that Proverbs dominantly uses the Hebrew name, Yahweh, when one might have expected more use of Elohim, which latter is dominant in Qoheleth. We are not suggesting that the essential characteristics are neglected, but the opposite: that the existence of this different mode of perceiving the world, in which special interventional, divine action is little invoked, is itself a part of that essential character. How the two aspects were held together is one of the difficult problems: but that they somehow coexisted seems to be beyond question.

If this is right, it has an important consequence. It helps to bring Qoheleth into the mainstream of biblical thinking. If it is true of Proverbs that it shows a different mode of perceiving the world, in which interventive action by Yahweh is muted or absent, then Qoheleth stands in better continuity with Proverbs than has often been perceived. Qoheleth searched diligently through everything that was *in our world* ('under the sun', as he put it) but could not find traces of God's activity or of meaning related to it. Clearly in part this bespeaks a crisis in the Wisdom tradition; but at the same time it follows on from something that was already there in the older Wisdom. Qoheleth is to be seen not merely as a 'sceptic', denying evidences of God, but also as a believer, following out tracks that had been prepared for him in his own tradition. Incidentally, it is interesting to note that it is the most Hellenistic of the Wisdom books, the Wisdom of Solomon, that does most to integrate Wisdom thinking with the traditional 'mighty acts of God': see his chapters 16–19, which rehearse the Exodus story with new refinements.

2. Secondly, we have the matter of *retribution*. According to familiar tradition, people do wrong, God perceives this, and he reacts by imposing a punishment. Something of this kind has been thought to be basic to the Wisdom tradition: indeed, it is often thought to be one of the reasons for the crisis in Wisdom evoked in Job. If someone was suffering, it was because they had done evil, and God had punished them: Job defied this belief. But Klaus Koch questioned the idea of retribution altogether, and for the entire Old Testament (see Koch 1972 for the best collection of essays). The belief there, he argued, was that the sin in itself began a unitary process which immanently included the consequences of destruction or disaster. The Hebrew vocabulary characteristically includes in the same terms the evil deed and the consequences. The consequences, therefore, were not an interventionary act of God, but an integral part of the sin itself.

This proposal, like almost all others, has been contradicted, and we cannot argue the case here. But even the possibility that it could be seriously suggested, with substantial detailed evidence, makes a difference to our discussion. It shows that the instances of God's reaction against sin, which at first sight form evidence of an interventionist type of divine action, may at least possibly be otherwise understood.

3. Thirdly, creation. The centrality of creation for our theme can scarcely be overstated. As is well known, the biblical theology of the mid-century accorded much greater importance to redemption or salvation, and tended to regard creation as a supplementary theme: the true beginning of the Bible was not Genesis, but Exodus. There was a certain air of suspicion about any theology that started from creation: it sounded like natural theology, it smelt somewhat heretical. But here again opinion has shifted. A scholar like H. H. Schmid, who has done distinguished work on Wisdom, has also moved creation into the governing position in Old Testament theology (see Schmid 1966, 1974). And even those who might not go so far, as a matter of their own theological convictions, agree on the centrality of creation for all Wisdom theology. 'The Wisdom of the Old Testament stays quite determinedly within the horizon of creation. Its theology is creation theology' (Walther Zimmerli as quoted in Hermisson 1978: 43). And the theme of creation has a prominent place in Professor Wiles's study of divine action (cf. especially Wiles 1986:

26–38). But in what respects does the prominence of creation in Wisdom theology affect our discussion?

Creation is of course a divine action, but as perceived in the Wisdom literature it is an action of a particular kind. First, the emphasis seems not to lie on the description of the act of creation, but on further relations. In Proverbs 8: 22–31, one of the major passages, though God's establishment of the ordered world is poetically described, the emphasis is that *Wisdom was there*, present with God himself, sharing in the work. In the speeches of God in Job 38–41, the emphasis is, by contrast, on Job's *absence* from the processes of creation and life-giving, and on his inability to enter into them. Both passages seem to *assume* creation rather than to announce it.

Moreover, the same is the case throughout the Wisdom literature. Scholars seem to be agreed that Wisdom depends on a creation theology even where there is no explicit mention of the theme. Study of the Egyptian and Mesopotamian parallels has only strengthened this conviction. As in other great creation passages, notably Genesis 1, the emphasis is on an *ordered world*, a basic theme being the separation of the land from the waters and the establishment of the earth as habitable territory. It is the sense of an ordered world that underlies the moral advice of the proverbs and their comments on experience. The idea of creation melts into the maintenance and sustenance of the world and its inhabitants: thus much of God's speeches in Job is not strictly about creation, but about entry into the current living processes of the living things. Similarly Psalm 104 is more about establishment and sustenance than strictly about creation.

But the sense of an ordered world offers us a foundation on which we can turn back to our original question, about the paucity of reference to God's mighty acts. The ordered world does not necessarily, in the long run, leave no room for these mighty acts, but it does offer a different perspective in which to see the world. That different perspective, it seems, was a very substantial part of Israel's understanding, and hence its presence in several entire books of the Bible is not surprising.

Moreover, we should be conscious of the important part played by the later Wisdom books in mediating the thought of the Hebrew Bible to later Judaism and especially to the New Testament. The Wisdom of Solomon has a key role in this respect. The understanding of Genesis under which Adam was created immortal, or for immortality, and death came into the world as a consequence of his disobedience—an idea heavily used by St Paul—has its first evidence in this book, and it also mediated the sort of 'natural theology' deployed by Paul in Acts 17 and Romans 1–2. It is this book that brings into the Wisdom tradition the emphasis of the attack on idolatry and through this the polemic against Gentile immorality as a result of idolatry, again so essential in Romans. Its understanding of creation, of modes of divine relation to the world, of ethics, and of death and immortality is likely to be equally important. Canonical or not canonical, the Wisdom tradition was a living link, highly significant.

Now I do not suggest that these brief thoughts about the Wisdom books can decide much about divine action, seen on the plane on which Professor Wiles is discussing it. But they can certainly have a significant side-effect. For some of those who disagree with him in these matters will very probably appeal to scripture. The Bible, they will think, is clear and powerful in its assertion of divine action. On the contrary, it seems, the Bible, taken as a whole, contains different perceptions of such action. Some will feel that the Wisdom literature of Israel is not sufficiently important as a factor. But on the other hand many may think it important that *all* the testimony of scripture should be taken into account. But, as I hope to have shown, if indeed all scripture is to be taken into account, the foundation for Wiles's argument must be substantially strengthened.

NOTES

1. For an excellent example of what can be done in this way, and one that touches on many of the same problems as are discussed here, see Heywood Thomas 1979: 290–4.
2. Von Rad was one of those who thought that 'secular' was a proper expression for the thought of Wisdom in the Solomonic age. In any case our point here is not affected by the rightness or wrongness of this term: either way, von Rad thought that it derived from an antecedent Yahwism.
3. Von Rad surely made a mistake here. His *Wisdom in Israel* included a whole chapter on 'The Polemic against Idols' (von Rad 1972: 177–85), but he failed to give value to the fact that the old wisdom books say

nothing about the matter. It was the Wisdom of Solomon that brought this theme into central emphasis within Wisdom.

REFERENCES

Barr, James (1966), *Old and New in Interpretation*, London.
Brueggemann, W. (1972), *In Man We Trust: The Neglected Side of Biblical Faith*, Richmond.
Crenshaw, James (1969), 'Method in Determining Wisdom Influence upon "Historical" Literature', *Journal of Biblical Literature*, 88: 129–42.
—— (1970), 'Popular Questioning of the Justice of God in Ancient Israel; *Zeitschrift für die alttestamentliche Wissenschaft,* 82: 380–95.
—— (ed.) (1976), *Studies in Ancient Israelite Wisdom*, New York.
Emerton, John (1979), 'Wisdom', in G. W. Anderson (ed.), *Tradition and Interpretation*, Oxford: 214–37.
Gese, H. (1958), *Lehre und Wirklichkeit in der alten Weisheit*, Tübingen.
Hermisson, H.-J. (1978), 'Observations on the Creation Theology in Wisdom', in John G. Gammie *et al.*, *Israelite Wisdom*, Missoula.
Heywood Thomas, John (1979), 'Philosophy and the Critical Study of Wisdom Literature', *Heythrop Journal*, 20: 290–4.
Koch, K. (ed.) (1972), *Um das Prinzip der Vergeltung in Religion und Recht des Alten Testaments*, Darmstadt.
Preuss, H.-D. (1970), 'Erwägungen zum theologischen Ort alttestamentlicher Weisheitsliteratur', *Evangelische Theologie*, 30: 393–417.
—— (1974), 'Alttestamentliche Weisheit in christlicher Theologie?', *Bibliotheca ephemeridum theologicarum Lovaniensium*, 33: 165–81.
Rad, G. von (1972), *Wisdom in Israel*, London.
Schmid, H. H. (1966), *Wesen und Geschichte der Weisheit*, Berlin.
—— (1974), *Altorientalische Welt in der alttestamentlichen Theologie*, Zurich.
Wiles, Maurice (1986), *God's Action in the World*, London.
Wright, George Ernest (1952), *God Who Acts*, London.

2

Making and Remaking in the Ministry of the Church

HENRY CHADWICK

Recent discussions of the ordination of women to the priesthood and/or the episcopate in some provinces of the Anglican communion have raised in particularly sharp form much wider issues of authority. In a body which understands itself to be part of the orthodox catholic tradition, and not to embody any breach of continuity with the Church built upon the foundation of the apostles and prophets, is it possible for unilateral decisions to be taken in indifference to other communions which, in Anglican eyes, unambiguously represent the same continuity of visible communion? Unilateral action has consequences not only for the internal coherence and interchangeability of ministry within the provinces of the Anglican communion but also for the progress of ecumenical dialogue and *rapprochement* between Canterbury and Rome or Constantinople and Moscow. The problem has a bearing, though in a different way, on conversations between Canterbury and Wittenberg.

In the present paper the intention is to try to disentangle some of the complexities by looking at the contemporary situation in the light of some pieces of the past record. Such a retrospect need not and does not imply that the Church is and needs to be imprisoned in the past. For some theologians, among whom Maurice Wiles has been prominent, an expert knowledge of Christian antiquity is the ground for a liberation from its legacies. Here let it suffice to say that an imprisonment in the past must be for the Church a betrayal of what is given in trust.

Nevertheless, all theology which is plausibly to claim the name of Christian is necessarily going to keep an eye on the past, since it must presuppose that in Jesus of Nazareth humanity is granted a self-disclosure of the Creator and the revelation of what God

intends humankind to be. The apostle was unsympathetic to those
who thought they had another gospel to offer. At the same time
he was sharp to a local Church where some believed themselves to
have so privileged an access to the word of God that they were
under no obligation to consider fraternal relations with other
Churches (Gal. 1: 8; 1 Cor. 14: 36). In so crucial a matter as the
memorial of our redemption, the apostle thought the Corinthians
would be wise to adhere to the *paradosis* (1 Cor. 11: 23). Relations
with other Churches could be affected if they did not do so.

It is today non-controversial among theologians that 'tradition'
is not some second source beside the deposit in scripture, out of
which truths of a quite different nature and kind can be produced.
To speak of Tradition (the typographical compliment of a capital
letter implying that it is regarded with a measure of considerable
respect) is to recognize that the prophetic and apostolic witness
of the past record can become revelation now because of the
experience of grace in the community of the Spirit through the
Church living out its life in history. In the life of the Church we
are anchored to the past as members, by faith and baptism, of a
community of discipleship which has a continuing history. We join
a community linked to Peter and Paul, to Mary mother of Jesus,
to Bethlehem and Golgotha, to the mission to the Gentile world
(which Paul at least did not understand to be shutting the door on
Jews), to the community's accepted norms and title-deeds in
scripture, in the baptismal confession of faith, in the ministry with
apostolic commission which so soon became a visible and concrete
manifestation of continuity.

Thereby the community is aware of possessing both a sacred
trust or deposit to be faithfully handed on, and also a living
authority in the universal fellowship of the Church guided by
ministerial organs of decision-making and by the 'reception' or
critical appropriation of these decisions by the whole people of
God. Even though the process may take time (as in the fourth
century with the creed of Nicaea), what is felt to be rightly defined
under the protection of the Holy Spirit is also received under the
same guidance and protection. In Church history a century is never
very long.

The ordained ministry, with apostolic commission to be pastoral
in relation to the community, does not exist merely to mediate and
transmit faithfully what has been received from a sacrosanct past.

It is also called to proclaim, to utter prophecy in the Spirit addressed to the contemporary situation, to teach (a term which must imply far more than a repetition of the formulas of long ago, shaped in utterly different circumstances and with metaphysical presuppositions no longer shared), and to serve the needs of the community in circumstances that are changing fast. To say so much is obvious enough. But perhaps it needs to be stated, platitudinous as it may seem, because it is the parameter which sets the context for our problem. The polarity of prophecy and tradition is inherent in the very being of the Church. We owe to Irenaeus, in reaction to the crisis precipitated by the Montanists, the contention that the spectacular immediacy of prophetic inspiration is not more supernatural than the transmitted catechesis and sacramental life of the community, assured by a succession of ministry continuous through time and space. The anchor to the past, to the incarnate Lord and to the apostles, to the deposit of faith providentially preserved in written form in scripture, might suggest that we have a duty to be ultratraditionalists, resistant to all changes. But the experience of the Holy Spirit here and now constantly calls us to confront changing situations requiring fresh approaches. What is it to be *semper eadem*? What is open to development, which is after all but a four-syllable word for change?

Reflection on the doctrine of the Paraclete in St John's gospel would suggest that the Spirit leads the Church into richer and deeper understanding of the will and mind of the Lord, but never into any break or discontinuity with that will and mind.

Coherent with this principle, we seek to interpret scripture by the closest attention to scholarly historical exegesis; but those who believe that the Bible is the book of the living God, interpreted in each successive generation, will think twice before committing themselves to the opinion that an exclusive application of critical historical method is all we need. Hence the concept of tradition combines both transmission and development, both the testing by the deposit of apostolic faith and order and the readiness to follow the Spirit guiding the Church in the confrontation of new problems. Tradition and prophecy are two antithetical poles which Christians have to learn to see as complementary, if only because it is being rooted in the past, in scripture and authentic interpretation of Scripture, that offers a rock on which to stand for the facing of the present and future. A doctrine of the Church has to be grounded both in Christology (or the historical continuity with the apostolic commission from Jesus) and in the freedom of the Spirit bestowed at Pentecost and ever granting renewal and correction and adaptation.

I must turn from tradition and prophecy to another issue. What must we share in common to be able to worship together at the Lord's table? Obviously diversity has at all times been a phenomenon in the life of the Church. In the generation following the death of the last of the twelve apostles, that diversity may have looked uncommonly like anarchy, whether in faith or in ministerial order or in moral practice. At a very early stage as the apostles passed from the scene, the Church found it necessary to lay down certain markers or frontiers. In the order of their appearing they are a familiar trio: a ministry in continuity with the apostolic community and with apostolic commission; a baptismal confession of faith structured round the affirmation of belief in God the Father, maker of heaven and earth; in Jesus the Christ his unique Son, who was so truly human that he was born and crucified, yet experienced both in such a way that the birth and crucifixion were divine wonders; and in the Holy Spirit in the Church; lastly in chronological order, but in no way inferior in weight, the biblical canon.

It seems a truism to say that there is sharp friction in Church history when someone wants to dig up and modify or even discard any one of these three elements. Perhaps in some superlunary realm the Church could get along happily without such bonds. But in this sublunary sphere the Church needs to affirm its faith, needs to acknowledge the witness of the prophetic and apostolic writings, needs to admit to its body by baptism and, in obedience to the Lord, to renew itself continually by the eucharistic memorial. Moreover, it needs for its own coherence a ministry generally accepted as possessing a commission, given by Christ in his Church, to serve and safeguard the Word and sacraments. In these areas of Bible, creed, sacraments, and ministry, the Church has believed it has divine gifts (cf. Ephesians 4), *dona data*, touching the deepest roots of Christian existence and therefore to be handled with the utmost sensitivity.

If these items fall in the category of basic and foundational things, that does not mean, or at any rate did not mean for the ancient Church of the patristic age, that there may not be considerable diversity, notably in liturgical custom. The notion that precise liturgical uniformity is essentially desirable has pastoral roots; but its actual imposition has owed more to Charlemagne than to medieval popes, or in England much more to successive Acts of Parliament wishing to restrain Anabaptist sedition and non-vernacular rites in Latin, using the engine of Acts of Uniformity, than to any ecclesiastical body. In fact, liturgical diversities have rarely been a cause of schism, though frequently a cause of mutual vituperation. On 27 July 1628 Canon Peter Smart preached in Durham cathedral to denounce his fellow canon John Cosin for 'ducking to the altar', standing at the altar in a cope, singing instead of saying the Nicene Creed, 'wearing strange Babylonish garments, with trippings and turnings and crossings and crouchings'. In Cranmer's first English prayer book of 1549, kneeling, crossing, and other gestures 'may be used or left, as every man's devotion serveth, without blame'. In St Augustine's time there were different customs in Africa, Rome, and Milan. His mother Monica arrived at Milan and began to observe customs not at home in Milan. When in Rome, advised Ambrose, do as Rome does. He meant, you are not in Rome now, and therefore should not be doing it here. And in one letter Augustine complains of the bewilderment caused to congregations when the clergy introduce liturgical usages they have seen abroad.

There are some liturgical differences which express a difference in theology, a deliberate difference, which may be the expression of separation and schism.

We have become accustomed today to a greater degree of plurality: Roman Catholics have four prayers of consecration from which to choose, the second of them sharing perhaps with Rite B in the American Anglican book (1978) the distinction of being among the finest canons in our English language. The Church of England's Alternative Service Book of 1980 is a bit more inhibited and bottled up, but certainly remains sure that in the eucharistic action there is a powerful work of the Holy Spirit through which believers are joined with the entire people of God and all the company of heaven, the spirits of righteous souls who have been made perfect, until we are granted to stand before the Father and Jesus the mediator of the new covenant as we make the memorial of his blood shed for our redemption. It is instructive that a recent pamphlet by an Evangelical writer has pleaded for an urgent revision of the eucharistic rites of the Alternative Service Book to eliminate not only the evident presupposition that consecration signifies a change but also the specifically Christian theme of redemption. Would not a simple thanksgiving suffice, as in the Jewish Passover ceremonies?

Unilateral declarations of independence are not something that the inheritors of Henry VIII's Act of Supremacy can easily deny ever to be appropriate in any circumstances. Admittedly his Act was not thunder out of a clear sky: English kings had long been agitated by the weight of papal taxation on English churches and by the invasion of rights of patronage and appointment. But we need not doubt that the unilateral act would not have occurred when it did, and in the form it took, had Henry not wished to divorce Catherine of Aragon. As Martin Luther tartly remarked, Henry had not so much abolished papal jurisdiction as transferred all its powers to himself. And if thereby, asked Bishop Stephen Gardiner of Winchester in 1555, he had taken his Church out of the *ecclesia catholica*, had he a Church to be head of? Henry's answer was given in the King's Book of 1543 (for which Gardiner disowned all responsibility): the Greek East refused to acknowledge papal universal jurisdiction after the union at the Council of Florence in 1439; therefore such jurisdiction lacked catholic consent, and there was no departure from the catholic tradition if organization were to return to being territorial.

The element of nationalism undeniable in the German and English Reformations had been asserting itself long before 1517 or 1534. The famous declaration of Bishop Aylmer of London in the 1570s that 'God is English' echoes the jingoism of the Hundred Years War. The battle of Agincourt in 1415 provoked vehement expressions of mutual hostility and national pride among the English and French delegations to the Council of Constance, gravely hindering Sigismond's work of reconciliation, peace, and reform. No one can read the enormously influential Protestant history of John Foxe, the *Acts and Monuments*, without discerning a powerful streak of English nationalism, a pleasure at the thought that Catholicism in England is happily discredited by Mary's loss of Calais and defeat in France, while Protestantism is divinely vindicated by the political successes of Elizabeth, 'our new Deborah'.

Perhaps there is still a residual element of nationalism latent in the English wish to make their own independent and sovereign decisions, whether about a common European currency or about the polity of the Church. Anglicans today, however, may find it hard to think as unilaterally as the men of the sixteenth century did, and the gradually strengthening consciousness of shared interests with other partners in the European community may have side-effects in ecclesiastical matters.

Henry VIII looked across to Byzantium and the Eastern Churches for precedent and justification of his assertions of independence. Himself a remarkably learned man, he was glad to see in Justinian's ecclesiastical supremacy an anticipation of his own claims. Was not this realm of England shown by sundry ancient chronicles to be an empire? And to be an empire was to have an emperor sovereign over matters both secular and ecclesiastical.

It has been the dilemma of the Roman see that, against national Churches, it has embodied the ideal of a universal community transcending nationalisms, and yet has to make claims for itself which make it particular and less than universal.

Conciliar writers such as Gerson had been anxious to set the authority of the Roman see in service to, and so in subordination to, a universal Church which was extended far beyond those churches and bishops in full communion with the Roman see. At a succession of fifteenth-century councils—Pisa, Constance, Basle, culminating in Florence—the agenda included reconciliation with the Orthodox churches, though only at Florence was there real conversation directed to that specific end. And at Florence Pope Eugenius IV badly needed restored communion with the Orthodox of Constantinople and Kiev to bolster his own weak position in the West. He adopted a wide programme of reconciliation with other separated bodies—Armenians, Copts, and others—and provided the Armenians (as he had not done for the Greeks) with a detailed Thomist catechism of instruction in the theology of the sacraments. For Eugenius IV the supreme authority of the Roman see was the prime and indispensable element in the re-establishing of unity. Gerson could hardly have denied that communion with the *cathedra Petri* was a sign of universal communion, but did not think of communion with the pope as an absolute *sine qua non* of catholicity, as if everything flowed from this one source. At a time when there were three popes to choose from, it was hard to think that way.

The Acts of the Council of Constance provide rich illustration of the difficulty experienced by those present in thinking of the papacy as the sign and instrument of something transcending national frontiers. After the Council had obtained the resignation of two out of the three rival popes and the withdrawal of obedience from the Spanish pope, Benedict XIII, who intransigently avoided resignation, the Italians wanted an Italian pope, the French a Frenchman who would live at Avignon, the Germans desired a German, and the little English delegation blew their trumpet with ear-splitting tones in the hope that someone would take them seriously. Each nation at Constance had its own ambitions, and got its own independent concordat from Martin V.

The national character of the Eastern churches is still strongly felt, e.g. in Romania or Russia, and is particularly in evidence in the case of the pre-Chalcedonian churches: Armenians, Copts, Ethiopians, Syrian Orthodox or 'Jacobites'. The Persian Nestorians survived in their old home until the terrible massacres in South-East Turkey in 1917 (and now have to make do in San Francisco where the American Presbyterians transported them in 1934). The Orthodox (Chalcedonian) churches are also a family of ethnic churches: Greek, Russian, Finnish, Bulgarian, Romanian, Serbian, Polish, and so on. Bonded in fraternal togetherness, each has its own patriarch, giving honour but little jurisdiction to the ecumenical patriarch at the Phanar. Independent of one another, they are not so independent of civil government, which may legislate for their constitution, control episcopal elections, veto synodical decisions, confiscate church property, and occasionally stand back to watch the Church fall apart in faction and strife because it lacks any central authority apart from the State. Moreover, ethnic churches (with a few exceptions) tend not to be strongly missionary. In England the fortuitous coincidence of the emergence of the trading corporation called the British Empire and the Evangelical Revival, followed by the Oxford Movement with its ideal of heroic priestly self-sacrifice, had the result of commerce and Christianity marching together up the Niger and the Zambezi with the Bible, *Hymns Ancient & Modern*, and perhaps (on the Zambezi) an English Missal. The Anglican communion has resulted from the extraordinary discovery that the way of worship expressed in the old English Prayer Book in Tudor prose possessed amazing powers of being found deeply evocative for peoples whose native tongue was not English, or at least not English English.

Nevertheless, the claim of Henry VIII to govern a territorially independent part of the Church has bequeathed a legacy of 'provincial autonomy', which turns the Anglican communion into a fairly loose federation of kindred spirits, often grateful for mutual fellowship but with each province reserving the right to make its own decisions. This concept of provincial autonomy does not prevent one province from putting pressure on other provinces to follow its example. Tension can arise when that pressure becomes imperative and demanding. A province which has vigorously asserted the right to make its own independent decisions may then press other provinces not only to acknowledge the 'catholicity' of what has been decided but also to take the same decisions.

Provincial autonomy may encourage regional diversities. Yet the pressure which one progressive province may place upon others is a reflection of an instinct to reduce diversity, to give expression to the universality of the Church by diminishing differences.

Differences in liturgical usage have always existed, and between East and West have occasionally been sources of friction. Cardinal Humbert deduced the invalidity of the Eastern celebration of the eucharist from the fact that Orthodox custom was to bury in the ground the consecrated remains, at a time when Western custom was either reverently to consume the remains or to commit them to the flames. The presence of the Filioque in the Creed was defended by Anselm at the Council of Bari (1098). Argument that it was a liturgical difference between East and West which was paralleled in other similar diversities is among those deployed in his later work 'On the Procession of the Holy Spirit', where (ch. 13 end) he even claimed that it is the kind of variation which the Church in one kingdom is entitled to make without departing from orthodoxy, and which is therefore the more justified when all the Latin-speaking kingdoms follow this usage. In the ninth century Ratramnus of Corbey had implicitly defended the Western Filioque by listing the variations of usage and custom in the Churches from the earliest times (*Contra Graecorum opposita* IV, *PL* 121. 303–11). Any Greek criticism of Western customs, such as sacerdotal celibacy, was in any event met by Ratramnus' assertions of the supremacy of the Roman see (IV. 8), a jurisdiction which made all argument superfluous.

But the arguments about the Filioque were a source of difficulty and embarrassment because there were always some in the West who thought the Greek Churches at fault in not having adopted it; a solid and overwhelming majority in the Greek Churches thought the Western addition, about which they had never been consulted, an act of gross irreverence to a creed agreed by an ecumenical council. On both sides there were those who wanted to put pressure on the other half of the Church, and found it hard to consent to the view that, in a matter so central, dogma could be regional and not of universal obligation. The sharp antagonism of Humbert has been more characteristic of the Latin West than the quiet plea of Anselm of Canterbury that both traditions be as freely tolerated as other liturgical differences. Admittedly even Anselm thought the Greek usage of leavened bread in the eucharist was a departure from that of Jesus and the apostles, and a mistake; but it remained the case that the Greeks used bread. Therefore, he said, there was agreement *substantialiter*. Anselm is, I believe, the earliest person to think of 'substantial agreement' as a way of asserting a common faith in essentials while allowing for diversity in inessentials.

Nevertheless, in matters of religious faith and practice, to be in agreement on 98 per cent has the consequence that the remaining 2 per cent comes to be of intense importance. Between Anglicans and Lutherans the differences seem remarkably small. The Lutheran confessional documents allow no doubt on the proposition that Melanchthon would have wished the Reformation churches to have been able to retain the episcopal order. But today there are Lutheran divines for whom a fatal obstacle to full *communio in sacris* consists in the Anglican conviction that a person ordained to the episcopate is ordained for life to that order of ministry. By contrast, there are Lutheran theologians who regard the ordained ministry as a function rather than an order, and deduce that a retired bishop has ceased to be a bishop. An Anglican will observe that Melanchthon himself affirms the classic distinction between the power of order and the power of jurisdiction: that is, a retired bishop may act episcopally subject to the jurisdiction of the diocesan in post, but not otherwise. So the power of order is retained, and the retired bishop may do what a bishop does if he has the permission of the diocesan, with whom lies the power of jurisdiction.

These reflections come close to the old distinction, found in Augustine and much exploited by Anglican theologians of the seventeenth century, between fundamental and non-fundamental doctrines. The distinction has some affinity with, but also some differences from, the more commonly Catholic concept of a hierarchy of truths which allows for the evident fact that, while the doctrine of the Trinity and the dogma of the Assumption of the Virgin may appear of equal importance to a canonist, inasmuch as for him both rest for their truth on the defining authority, they are not of equal significance or even value for a theologian. Any Mariological statement is sure to be dependent on and secondary to a prior Christological affirmation.

In this area of theological discourse, there is an obvious danger of blandly assuming disagreement to be a sign of unimportance. One cannot satisfy the sceptical or the questioning with the contention that what Christians disagree about must, for that reason, be deemed secondary, or even a matter of indifference. The impassioned debates of sixteenth-century Lutherans may suffice to demonstrate that people can take radically opposed views concerning the definition and identification of what is to be deemed 'indifferent'. For Acontius the area covered by the term *adiaphora* was the greater part of traditional theological understanding. So radical a reductionism solves the problem of remaking Christian doctrine by making most of it optional, with any actual assertion positively discouraged.

It is unnecessary to observe that behind the debate about the rightness and the consequences of unilateral action by part of the Church there lies a question about the concept of divine authority and revelation. What is non-negotiable because it is given *iure divino*?

For conservative minds, whether Catholic or Protestant, revelation is doctrine formulated as far as possible in clear-cut propositional statement grounded either in an inerrantly inspired Bible, inerrantly interpreted by men of the Spirit who show themselves to be so by their assertion of biblical inerrancy, or in an unfailing organ of teaching authority, a magisterium (as in modern times it has come to be called—the term is not ancient in this sense) whose rulings through the centuries can be conveniently gathered in a canonist's handbook, and whose verdicts are really all one needs to know.

A less hard concept of revelation would speak of scripture and the consensus of the faithful, expressed through the formative councils such as Nicaea and Chalcedon, the definitions of which 'witness' to a divine self-disclosure in Christ for the redemption of humanity. In the Church of England the current form of the Declaration of Assent speaks this language of 'witness'. It remains a presupposition that a criterion of truth in the Church is consonance with scripture and ancient tradition or at least an absence of evident dissonance.

An altogether softer evaluation of revelation would see it as a divinely inspired, immanent enhancement of the natural consciousness of the Christian community, enabling it to cut free from the shackles of the past and from the habits of religious convention. Thereby the Church is an agency of creative independence, whether by charismatic renewal or by jettisoning the ways of the past. The criterion of fidelity to the historical foundations of the faith, and to the formative decisions of the age when Christianity was, so to speak, deciding to be Christianity in the ordinarily recognizable form, becomes hardly more than marginal. For the basic criterion is that what Christians are now doing and believing should not appear locked into obsolete linguistic habits, such as 'exclusive language', or social presuppositions no longer shared. The crucial test is that Christians should not be ludicrously at loggerheads with the self-evident assumptions of their secular contemporaries who, after all, are also God's creation living in God's world and are likely to have things to teach those who allow their faith to shut them into a cultural ghetto.

This last, soft view of revelation may be accompanied by a fairly drastic rationalism towards the community of the Church, with the idea that if one is to understand the Church *qua* institution or the role of the sacraments, one will do best to study magic or textbooks on primitive Melanesian tribesmen rather than Küng, Rahner, or their Protestant counterparts like Pannenberg. To the historian it is familiar that the Protestant affirmation of *scriptura sola* may be so stated as to desacralize the dominical sacraments and the ordained ministers who have to serve and dispense them. There is always the latent suspicion that appeals to externally given and guaranteed revelation are forms of hidden coercion used to suppress dissent. The wish to repress dissent, however, is apparent as much in the 'liberal' camp as in the 'conservative'.

No Christian has a link with Jesus the Christ which does not in some degree depend on the medium of tradition, or a lifeline transmitted horizontally through the space-time continuum, a sacred tradition which, for all the earthiness of its transmitting vessels, mediates the gospel of God's love and judgement. Of the continuity of the present community with its roots and title-deeds, the scriptures, sacraments, and historic ministry constitute the primary and visible signs, and there is no escape from the disturbing consequences of changes in the way these are understood. A feeling of detachment from the legacy of the past, however beneficent that legacy is taken to be, encourages a relativizing of the degree of authority to be associated with scripture and with inherited custom. This relativizing process can make unilateral decisions by part of the Church easier, because the divisions of Christendom may come to seem less evil too.

The Latin patriarchate in Rome has in the past made unilateral decisions which have caused unsolved difficulties in relation to the Orthodox Churches. The Orthodox were complaining in the time of Anselm of Canterbury that they had not been consulted about the addition of the Filioque to the Creed in the eucharist. The Orthodox have no difficulty in agreeing with Rome that our Lord's mother was prepared by divine grace for the role which she had to fulfil in the mystery of our redemption, but have considerable qualms about the correctness of the definition of the Immaculate Conception in 1854, affirming Mary to be untouched by original sin. But then the Orthodox do not have in their bloodstream the Augustinian doctrine of original sin as an inherited psychotic cancer of the soul, common to humanity apart from Christ. The assertion of the pope's universal ordinary and immediate jurisdiction at the first Vatican Council in 1870 looks unilateral to the Orthodox, who have no difficulty about Roman primacy defined in terms of dignity, honour, and leadership. Pius IX's wish to defy the rationalism and liberalism of the secular world was expressed in an assertion of papal authority apart from the universal mind of the Church in the Catholic episcopate, and this was not the way in which the Orthodox have thought about conciliar authority.

The historian can do nothing to make unilateral actions appear constructive in their consequences for the *ecclesia catholica*. They are both a cause and a symptom of division. At the same time the difficulties they cause are also a reflection of the perennial tendency to merge unity and uniformity, and to demand that the 'others' should organize themselves and talk in the same way. That there is mutual confidence of shared faith and common possession of Bible, sacraments, and ministry seems a prerequisite condition for coherence and *koinonia*. But how far diversity can go without threatening separation is, like 'validity', a less objective matter than is often supposed.

A factor that has no doubt operated in unilateral decisions, whether in the Roman Catholic communion or among the Anglicans, is a latent feeling that the separated communions are not serious about the dismantling of barriers between them, and therefore that they do not need to take account of each other or of the judgement of other ecclesial bodies. While there are some fundamental dogmas which have to be universal, there is a legitimate diversity which is regional in origin. The argument for the ordination of women to the priesthood and/or episcopate seems, at least in some statements, to presuppose that in an American or European cultural context it is socially necessary because refusal is felt to be an injustice; such statements can allow for such ordinations not to be required in parts of Africa or Asia where the customs of society would be against them. To think along this line is to suggest perhaps that doctrines and practices binding upon Roman Catholics are not of universal authority, and that there are Anglican usages which Anglicans do not and should not expect others to appropriate, however splendid (like Anglican Chant for the Psalms) the others may think them to be. Within their own community the usages and doctrinal expressions are valid, but that validity is assumed not to be of general extension. We do not expect the customs of Birmingham to obtain in Bokhara.

The problem confronting the remaking of ministry to meet feminist criticism of the tradition is that there is no unanimity on the degree of relativism with which the matter can properly be handled. Unhappily the observation commonly met with that all will be reasonably well as long as diversity is not allowed within a given ecclesial body necessarily presupposes a total indifference to the dismantling of existing barriers between separated ecclesial communions.

In a Western liberal democracy we are acclimatized and conditioned to think that our values should be and are liberal by intuition, and that they are inherent in the culture which is our particularity. A secular liberal democracy does not naturally look for some external source to impart validity and authority to its values and judgements. Moreover, the various versions of liberal democracy in different Western countries are in some degree distinctive, perhaps even 'local'. We do what 'we' do. And the 'we' is coterminous with the society where we find ourselves. Nevertheless, most thoughtful people in the Western democracies would be hesitant before the propositions that the validity of certain customs and values is wholly dependent on what our particular and local society finds congenial or important, and that we do not need to bother our heads whether what we do and believe might need to be related to something universal, or even transcendental.

Unilateral decisions in the Church presuppose that the local and regional should be prior to the universal. That proposition is one to which we citizens of modern liberal democracies in the West are naturally inclined to warm. Nevertheless, there remains a question-mark as soon as the society which is 'we' extends beyond our local and regional frontiers to embrace an ideal universally extended in time and space. What is particular is often entirely compatible with what is 'catholic', both in the sense of universal extension and in the sense of unquestioned sacramental authenticity. But the Church in history has had and still has insoluble or at least hitherto unsolved problems arising from particularities which are felt to conflict with the universal and the unquestionable.

3

Why Three? Some Further Reflections on the Origins of the Doctrine of the Trinity

SARAH COAKLEY

In a justly famous article, 'Some Reflections on the Origins of the Doctrine of the Trinity',[1] Maurice Wiles sets out to foil attempts to give a rational defence to the doctrine of the Trinity based on religious (Christian) experience. His conclusion is that once the triadic baptismal formula became fixed, quite early in the church's life,[2] it exercised a strongly authoritative—but ultimately 'arbitrary'—clamp on more properly critical reflection. Attempts in the modern period, then, to provide *ex post facto* justifications for the doctrine of the Trinity out of the church's early experience are in Wiles's view fatally flawed: we find in the ante-Nicene Fathers, he shows, neither any consistent allocation of different *activities* to the three 'persons', nor (the epistemological correlate of this) any distinctive set of *experiences* associated with each of the three. And indeed—for here Wiles produces his Cappadocian *coup de grâce*—to look for such would, from the perspective of achieved fourth-century 'orthodoxy', be intrinsically suspect. The *homoousion* principle should debar any such possibility, since only 'internal relations' distinguish the divine hypostases;[3] in their experiential effects all are found to work together co-operatively.

The logic of Wiles's argument reveals the inherently circular nature of this problem, as is more starkly spelled out in *The Making of Christian Doctrine* (Wiles 1967: ch. 6). Looking back, argues Wiles, we see in the third century, in reaction to Sabellianism, an emphasis on the *distinctness* of Father and Son (and it seems that, in Wiles's view, the distinctness of the Spirit was here merely unthinkingly duplicated); whereas in contrast, in the fourth century, and in reaction to Arianism, the *unity* of Father and Son became the obsessive concern of the 'orthodox'. Developed trinitarianism thus unfolded in two distinct, but problematically

related, phases, which Wiles seeks now to expose: 'there is a
danger', he writes, 'that the arguments used in the second stage of
the inquiry may be logically incompatible with those in the first,
and that that inconsistency may remain wholly undetected' (Wiles
1967: 124).

This point does not only score against the divinity of the Son;
indeed, as this essay will seek to highlight further, it is the
question of the 'hypostatic' status of the *Spirit* which is structurally
more pressing for the maintenance of a credible trinitarianism in a
sceptical milieu. According to Wiles, this question of the Spirit's
personal distinctness (as opposed to his/her divinity) was never
adequately or rationally faced at all in the early centuries.
Binitarianism would have been more logical (accounting for divine
transcendence on the one hand and immanence or 'incarnation' on
the other); or, if one wanted to 'hypostatize' other divine attributes,
why stop at the 'Spirit' of God, he asks?[4] Wiles's argument about
the mesmeric hold of the triadic baptismal formula is here under-
girded by a more general thesis about the operation of the *lex orandi*
on the development of early doctrine (Wiles 1967: ch. 4).[5] He sees
the 'law of prayer' as primarily 'conservative' and soporific, a sort
of dogmatic slumbering of the patristic period, inviting both
gnostic-tending traits in christology, and a profound lack of critical
thinking in pneumatology, a failure to grasp that the Spirit's
'hypostatic' existence was demanded neither by experience nor by
reason.[6] In other words, the church was duped by its own
authority and tradition. From the perspective of post-Enlightenment
'autonomy', however, fatal illogicalities emerge; the deconstruction
of trinitarianism can begin.

There is something deeply refreshing about the critical clarity of
Wiles's approach here. It releases us from the characteristically
dogmatic tilt of most of the textbooks, the judging of the moves
of the earlier centuries as either 'false starts' or unclarified approxi-
mations to later orthodoxy.[7] And indeed, surely much of Wiles's
thesis is correct: the tug of liturgical tradition, the force of clerical
authority, and the impact of Scripture *as a given unity* all shielded
doctrinal debate from certain critical questions which we now take
for granted; it enabled, for instance, that strange swing between
third and fourth centuries which Wiles so perceptively highlights.
But there are elements in Wiles's thesis, even so, with which I wish
here to take issue; and they focus on the question which he himself

shows is critical for the maintenance of any trinitarianism: that is, 'But why three?' Why indeed 'hypostatize' the Spirit at all?

To answer this I have to make a number of distinct moves. First (section 1), I shall outline a rough typology of different sorts of contemporary trinitarianism, and claim that only one type—within which I count myself—is capable of meeting Wiles's distinctly modern challenge to found trinitarianism in 'religious experience'. Next (section 2), I shall move back to the New Testament and patristic period, and argue that there is material here that Wiles has either ignored or obscured, and which simultaneously provides some experiential reasons for a 'hypostatic' distinguishing of the Spirit, and also some political and ecclesiastical reasons for the church's nervousness about it. (A subthesis here will be that the *lex orandi*, far from being invariably soporific in effect, is capable of innovative and even subversive manifestations; moreover, if we search what the Fathers have to say 'on prayer', we may find the arguments of their more consciously polemical writings significantly augmented or illuminated.) Finally (Conclusions), I shall reflect briefly on the philosophical niceties of appeals to 'religious experience' in such ramified doctrinal contexts as these, ask what kind of status they may hope to achieve, and how certain sorts of epistemological naïvety can be avoided. Is Wiles's demand, for instance, that the 'activity of God [be] . . . of such *unquestionably* threefold character that we are forced . . . to postulate a threefold character in God himself'[8] too hard-nosed a stricture to be capable of satisfaction? And if so, what sort of 'evidential force' might appeals to the *lex orandi* justifiably have in this trinitarian context? Here, I shall argue that whereas Wiles's way of posing the question is misleadingly stringent (especially if addressed to a sceptical outsider), we are none the less justified in granting some veracity to the idea of the Spirit's distinct existence on the basis of experiential claims, and can successfully meet the charge of vicious circularity that is also implicit in Wiles's position.

1. *A typology of modern trinitarianism*

For my purposes here, I propose a rough characterization of five 'types' of influential modern trinitarianism. The usefulness of this typology lies in showing that only one type (the last to be

delineated) can adequately meet the deconstructive challenge of the
first (represented by Wiles and those of similar views). The
typology is however a rough one, admitting, as many typologies
do, of an element of caricature; and it should be noted that with
the exception of the first type, the categories are not mutually
exclusive: they may indeed be theologically complementary. Some
theologians therefore cut across the types, evidencing more than
one approach to the Trinity.

1. *Dismantling the Trinity: why 'hypostatize' the Spirit at all?* We
have already examined Wiles's distinctive version of this 'type'. In
his case the apparent 'arbitrariness' of the attribution of personal
existence to the Spirit is explained as an unwitting transfer to the
third person from the second under the influence of the baptismal
liturgy. Logically speaking, however, 'Spirit' could just as well be
seen as a metaphor (one amongst many) for God's action in the
world.[9] In the case of Geoffrey Lampe's *God as Spirit* (Lampe 1977),
however, the tables are turned against the Trinity in a slightly
different way, but with the same effect of de-hypostatizing
the Spirit. Here 'Spirit' just comes to mean 'God-in-God's-
communication-to-the-world', and need not be hypostatized as
personally distinct from the Father; and this 'Spirit' is precisely
what permeates *Jesus*: there is thus no need to hypostatize a pre-
existent Christ (Logos) either. Not dissimilar arguments are found
in James Mackey's *The Christian Experience of God as Trinity*
(Mackey 1983), though curiously Mackey expresses ultimate indifference about whether trinitarian, binitarian, or even unitarian
conclusions should result from his critical questioning.[10]

Well before these modern British critiques of trinitarianism, of
course, there were the somewhat similar systematic moves of
Schleiermacher, in whose *Glaubenslehre* the 'Spirit' becomes the
way of talking about what animates and unifies the Church (see for
example Schleiermacher 1963: ii. 535: 'the expression "Holy Spirit"
must be understood to mean the vital unity of the Christian
fellowship . . . its common spirit'). Again, no personal hypostatization is required: this is just the 'being of God' in the Church,
which, since it no longer proceeds 'directly' from Christ, can be
called something else, in traditional language 'the Holy Spirit'. It
was Schleiermacher, too, who first threw down the gauntlet about
the experiential verifiability (or supposed lack of it) of the doctrine
of the Trinity: the Trinity, he declared, was 'not an immediate

utterance concerning the Christian self-consciousness' (ibid. 738). It is precisely this issue that has to be examined; but if I am right, none of the next three 'types' of modern trinitarianism can fully, or adequately, address it.

2. *The 'economic' Trinity is the 'immanent' Trinity: the Spirit as completer and communicator of revelation.* This model is central both for the early Barth (Barth 1936) and for Rahner (Rahner 1970), set as they are on seeing the traditional trinitarian doctrine as precisely an implication of the (one) revelatory activity of God, and not as an optional piece of celestial geometry. However, neither author in my view convincingly faces the question we have just posed: both *assume* the hypostatization of the Spirit.[11] And in both one senses a slightly desperate search for something distinctive for the Spirit to do. This is perhaps primarily because the controlling vision is of the 'linear' revelation of the economy (first the Father, then the Son, then the Spirit) in which it remains for the Spirit only to recapitulate, unfold, or at best enable the recognition of what has already been achieved in the Son. Thus in the early Barth the Spirit becomes the means of God's 'meeting Himself from man's end', the 'subjective' side of revelation (Barth 1936: 516); and in Rahner there is an outright admission that the difference between the 'two moments' of God's self-communication in Son and Spirit is 'not clear' (Rahner 1970: 85), but—rather curiously—that the Son's contribution is somehow 'historical' (ibid. 98, 99) in a way the Spirit's is not.

For all that these authors retrieve the 'immanent' trinity from obscurantism, then, it is somewhat at the expense of a convincing doctrine of the Spirit. No less is this true, I find, of the complex pneumatology of Paul Tillich (Tillich 1963: part iv), for here too the Spirit is both chronologically and logically third, presupposing and fulfilling the 'aspects' of God found in creation and salvation, and characterized as 'ecstatic transformation', driving the 'dimension of life' called 'the *human* spirit' into 'a successful self-transcendence'.[12] David Brown's work, in contrast (Brown 1985), shows awareness of the Wilesian problem of the logical and experiential distinctness of the Spirit; but like others in this category his solution remains parasitic on the order of the 'economy'. Thus he is forced into some strange exegetical contortions in the attempt to demonstrate that the original 'experience' of the Spirit was really different from that of the risen

Christ (as Acts would have it, in its tidy demarcation of Easter from Pentecost). Paul, claims Brown, must therefore have been deluded in thinking he had had an 'experience' of Christ at all: it was really the Spirit all along, coming as it did so much later after Easter (ibid. 192, and ch. 4, *passim*). But, on the tight definition here of what qualifies as a New Testament 'experience of Christ', it is unclear whether anyone but the original Jerusalem disciples would ever have hoped to enjoy one (see ibid. 184), and even more unclear what a *simultaneous* 'experience' of the divine hypostases would now feel like.[13] In short, Brown's bold attempt to face Wiles's challenge only goes to show how ill such a response fits into this 'linear' or 'church-year' model on which this type of trinitarianism is based.

3. *The Trinity construed from reflection on the death of Christ: the Spirit as the uniting bond between Father and Son.* Nor is Wiles's question likely to find satisfaction in another influential approach characteristic variously of the later Barth, Moltmann, and von Balthasar, for here the trinitarian nature of God is even more obviously assumed rather than argued. In these authors we have an approach peculiar to the modern Western tradition, combining as it does Western (substitutionary) soteriological themes, the Lutheran emphasis on an underlying *theologia crucis*, the Augustinian representation of the Spirit as the 'bond of love' between Father and Son, and more than a whiff of Hegelian dialectics. In the complex position of the later Barth, first (Barth 1956), there is the daring (near-Hegelian) move to allow God to be 'in discontinuity with Himself, to be against Himself' in the events of the cross (ibid. 184).[14] Building on this, von Balthasar's interpretation of the cross stresses the 'mutual surrender' of the Father and the Son in love which in no way moderates the state of 'abandonment' that the Son undergoes; and on Holy Saturday in his descent into hell the Son, totally powerless, experiences for himself the terrible 'loneliness of the sinner who has rejected God' (von Balthasar 1982: 153). In all this it is the Spirit's task to hold Father and Son together in their extreme separation: 'the Spirit unites Father and Son while stretching their mutual love to the point of unbearability' (ibid. 149).

If this is paradoxical, still more is Moltmann's representation of the same theme. For according to him, the Father both deliberately 'abandons' the Son on the cross (importing a much more vengeful note than in von Balthasar), and simultaneously suffers with the

Son in his rejection (though without actual 'patripassianism').[15] Again, it is the Spirit who holds the relationship together: 'The common sacrifice of the Father and the Son comes about through the Holy Spirit, who joins and unites the Son in his forsakenness with the Father' (Moltmann 1981: 83).[16] Moltmann's trinitarianism is complex, and has become more ramified since *The Crucified God* (Moltmann 1974), adding for instance an eschatological note to speak of the Spirit's continuing 'doxological work' up to the end in drawing men and women into the 'circulatory movement' of the 'divine relationships' (Moltmann 1981: 178, for example); but the abiding motif is a reorientation of the Trinity to the events of the cross. That God *is* Trinity is never seriously questioned, only how to reconceive that truth 'post-Auschwitz'.

4. *The Trinity as prototype of persons-in-relation.* A more recent trend in British trinitarianism has been influenced by a reworking of Cappadocian thought by the Orthodox theologian John Zizioulas (Zizioulas 1985), and fired by a vehement rejection of Cartesian 'individualism'. The point is made (for example by Gunton 1991) that Enlightenment individualism and a non-trinitarian God are simply mirror images; if we could get our (relational) view of God right, the argument goes, then a right reworking of the concept of the self would follow.

Zizioulas's central claim is that 'There is no true being without communion. Nothing exists as an "individual" conceivable in itself' (Zizioulas 1985: 18). Yet, true to his Eastern heritage, Zizioulas insists that the starting-point for trinitarian reflection must be some kind of distinct ('hypostatic') concreteness for the 'persons': 'The person cannot exist without communion; but every form of communion which denies or suppresses the person, is inadmissible' (ibid.). If we ask why *three* are required for such 'communion', we receive only a partial answer: that the 'specific work' of the Holy Spirit is the forward drive to the *eschaton*, exemplified in the eucharistic *epiclesis* (ibid. 22). The question is not addressed (*à la* Wiles) whether this 'Spirit' might not just be a metaphorical expression for an aspect of the Father's (or Son's) action in the world.

Colin Gunton's recent work (Gunton 1991), much influenced by Zizioulas, argues that an appropriately 'relational' view of 'personhood' was compromised even by Augustine (in whom he sees, paradoxically, the remote sources of the derided Cartesian

individualism).[17] He finds only isolated and random detractors
from this individualizing tendency in the West—specifically,
Richard of St Victor, in his *De Trinitate*, and the neglected John
Macmurray (1961). The mention of Richard's *De Trinitate* book 3
(see Gunton 1991: 92) is revealing, for herein does indeed lie a
logical argument for a necessary 'third' which Gunton does not
develop in detail, but which could well constitute a form of
response to Wiles's challenge. (Admittedly this is a logical rather
than an experiential argument, and so only partially meets Wiles's
requirements. But perhaps it is a start.) Richard of St Victor argues
not only that perfect love must occur in a *relationship* of perfect
equality (requiring two persons) but also that such a relationship
(*if* perfect) must necessarily be outgoing, overflowing to at least
one other as a shared communitarian benefit (and so the 'third' is
needed).[18] It is ironic, however, that Richard Swinburne's recent, and
sophisticated, repristination of this Victorine argument (Swinburne
1988) is characterized precisely by a failure to revise the Cartesian
'individualism' which Swinburne takes as normative; hence, perhaps,
its revealing title: 'Could there be *more than one God*?', that is, more
than one further version of the *one* quasi-'individual' God described
in Swinburne's earlier work. Whilst Gunton and Swinburne con-
verge on Richard of St Victor, then, the former is motivated by an
abhorrence of 'individualism', the other by a desire to see its logical
extension (or multiplication) at the divine level. None the less, the
potential of Richard of St Victor's approach as a response to the
question 'Why three?' is to my mind considerable; as a meditation
on the trinitarian *logic* of divine love with its mutuality, non-
exclusivity, and non-possessiveness, it might well provide some
answer to our systematic question, and be a formal complement to
the 'experiential' response to Wiles to which I now turn. Only this
latter approach, however, or so I argue, can fully answer Wiles's
challenge in the way he poses it.

5. *The Holy Spirit as a means of incorporation into the trinitarian life
of God*. This is to be contrasted with the straightforward 'linear'
revelatory model of the Trinity (type 3, above), for here the Holy
Spirit is construed not simply as extending the revelation of Christ,
nor even as enabling his recognition, but as actually catching up
and incorporating the created realm into the life of God (or rather
the 'redeemed life of sonship', to use Pauline terminology). Thus,
whereas model 3 draws implicitly on Acts' distinction between

Ascension and Pentecost, and also on John's prediction of the 'other comforter' *replacing* Christ (John 14: 16), this one owes its first allegiance to Paul, and supremely to Romans 8: 9–30, with its description of the co-operative action of the praying Christian with the energizing promptings of the 'indwelling' Holy Spirit. On this view, what the 'Trinity' *is* is the graced ways of God with the creation, alluring and conforming that creation into the life of the 'Son'. But note that the priority here, experientially speaking, is given to the Spirit: the 'Spirit' is that which, whilst being nothing less than 'God', cannot quite be reduced to a metaphorical naming of the Father's outreach. To say this is admittedly to build on Paul, to go beyond what he explicitly spells out about the logic of prayer; we cannot therefore say that his insights lead inexorably towards an 'orthodox' trinitarianism. And yet there are seminal insights here. For instance, it is the perception of many Christians who pray either contemplatively or charismatically (in both cases there is a willed suspension of one's own agenda, a deliberate waiting on the divine), that the dialogue of prayer is strictly speaking not a simple communication between an individual and a distant and undifferentiated divine entity, but rather a movement of divine reflexivity, a sort of answering of God to God in and through the one who prays (see Rom. 8: 26–7). Here, if I am right, is the only valid *experiential* pressure towards hypostatizing the Spirit. It is the sense (admittedly obscure) of an irreducibly bipolar divine activity into which the pray-er is drawn and incorporated.

The 'Son', we note, in this model is released from a narrow extrinsicism. The term connotes not just the past earthly Jesus, nor even yet the risen person of 'Christ' (if that is individualistically conceived), but rather the transformed divine life to which the whole creation, animate and inanimate, is tending, and into which it is being progressively transformed (Rom. 8: 19–25). Moreover, it is important to underscore that the 'experience' claimed of the Spirit here is not that of some different quality, or emotional tonality, from the (simultaneously experienced) 'Father' and 'Son'; it is not that different *sorts* of discrete 'experience' attend the three persons. (Perhaps, indeed, this is why Paul notoriously slides between 'God', 'Christ', and 'Spirit' in straining to express the almost inexpressible in Romans 8: 9–11.) Rather, what I am claiming here is that the pray-er's total 'experience' of *God* is here found to be ineluctably tri-faceted. The 'Father' is both source and ultimate object of divine desire; the 'Spirit' is that (irreducibly distinct) enabler and incorporater of that desire in creation—that which *makes* the creation divine; the 'Son' *is* that divine and perfected creation.

I have written elsewhere of this 'incorporative' or contemplative trinitarianism,[19] and my more recent fieldwork researches found it also expressed amongst contemporary Anglican charismatics (though scarcely in conscious response to critiques such as Wiles's).[20] But few contemporary theologians, if any, have wielded this evidence explicitly against the deconstructive charges of the post-Enlightenment critique of trinitarianism. Michael Ramsey's *Holy Spirit* fleetingly mentions this approach, and even in direct response to Wiles (Ramsey 1977: 118–21); but, curiously, the argument is not made central to a book which might, on other grounds, seem closer to a form of binitarianism. There are, however, a few other modern theologians who occasionally take this approach to the Trinity. We have already discussed von Balthasar under our category 4 above. But his book *Prayer* (von Balthasar 1961) starts with a meditation on Luke 1: 35, where the Holy Spirit (again, here, the primary agent experientially) 'overshadows' Mary in order to enable in her the production of the Word, a logic that also attends contemplative activity, as von Balthasar goes on to explicate in trinitarian terms. Von Balthasar is therefore a case of a modern theologian who straddles more than one of our 'types' of trinitarianism.

To this 'incorporative' trinitarian category we must also allocate Vladimir Lossky's work (Lossky 1968, for example), though with some reservations, for here there is an important difference arising largely from Lossky's almost fanatical objection to Western *filioquism*. Thus, although the fundamental logic of trinitarian incorporation is the same as I have sketched, for Lossky it is essential that the Holy Spirit remains 'independent' from the Son 'as to His hypostatic origin', and so also able to do something entirely distinctive in the work of salvation. In this way a wedge is driven between the Son, who is 'manifest', and who restores our *human nature*, but with whom (curiously) we are not strictly speaking 'united' (ibid. 170), and the Spirit on the other hand, who *in se* remains fundamentally 'secret', but deifies the *whole person* and so is variously 'incarnated' in the saints.

Finally, the constructive conclusions of Congar's *I Believe in the*

Holy Spirit (Congar 1983) should also perhaps be placed in this broad trinitarian category. Despite, or perhaps partly because of, Congar's profoundly felt ecumenical concerns, his trinitarian theology is closer to a Cappadocian than an Augustinian model, and ends with the remaining strain of Neoplatonic subordinationism that often, it must be admitted, attends the commitment to this 'incorporative' pneumatology. The Spirit is 'an opening to communion between God and man', and thus 'wants to lead eveything back to the Father through the Son' (ibid. iii. 148, 272). As we shall see in the next section, however, the Cappadocian version of this incorporative trinitarian 'type' (which Congar emulates) is a variant with distinctly 'linear' tinges. The Spirit is indeed the experiential point of entry into the life of the Godhead (the hallmark of this model); but from there one proceeds so to speak back 'up' the divine hierarchy, via the Son to the Father.[21] The result is a conceptualizing of the Trinity's relation to the world rather less subtle and *reflexive* than that envisaged by Paul, in which, as we have shown, 'Sonship' is progressively expanded within the creative space of the Spirit's unimpeded answering to the Father. How often do we find *this* model explicated by the writers of the patristic period? And how does it relate to the emergent Cappadocian solution? To that question we now turn.

2. *The Trinity and the 'lex orandi' in the Fathers*

So far I have attempted to show that only one brand of modern trinitarianism could hope to answer Wiles's deconstructive challenge fully, and also that most even of those who espouse it (I exclude myself) are unaware of the potential of this approach for such a line of defence. We now confront, however, a more interesting question yet. Why was this prayer-based argument for the Spirit's 'hypostatic' (or distinct) existence never wielded by the early Fathers, especially granted the suggestive basis for this in Romans 8? Wiles would seem to imply a silence here, but is it really so? Of course, the early Fathers certainly did not face the critical question of the Spirit's distinctness in precisely the sceptical fashion of the modern theologian, and it would be anachronistic to expect them to do so. None the less, could it be that the textbooks' characteristic forced march from Nicaea to Constantinople has failed to

engage the Fathers at the moments when they do comment on such
an 'alternative' trinitarian approach, one not dominated by the
'linear' economy, but giving experiential priority to the Spirit in
prayer?

There are several gaps in Wiles's argument here, despite his
laudable attempt to take some account of the *lex orandi*. First, and
interestingly, Wiles does not seek to probe back into the New
Testament era, to argue why the triadic baptismal formula gained
the hold it did in the first place. This is a question at least worth
asking. Thereafter, according to him, the 'Second century writers
show comparatively little interest in the Spirit'; these were, he says,
'dormant years' for pneumatology (Wiles 1967: 79, 80). In what
follows, I shall question this viewpoint and suggest a rather
different story.[22] I shall argue that the earliest Christian period (up
to and including the second and early third centuries) was characterized by a normative association of the 'Spirit' with charismatic
gifts, and especially prophecy. To say this is to accept that the full
potential of Romans 8, the subtleties of a *simultaneous* experience
of 'Father', 'Son', and 'Spirit' was not immediately grasped. But
the emphasis we find in this period on the ecstatic quality of
experience of the Spirit is none the less in line with what I have
called the 'prayer-based' approach. Far from leading to a dormant
pneumatology in the second century, an idle and unthinking
repetition of the baptismal formula, this emphasis produced a
phenomenon, Montanism, deemed unacceptably dangerous to
ecclesiastical stability. In other words, the charismatic connotations
of a doctrine of the Spirit with *experiential* priority and authority
could, if not carefully checked and contained, lead to sectarian
aberration. Hence—or so I shall speculate—we find a nervousness,
subsequently, about making explicit any view of the Trinity not
firmly reined into the rationality of the Logos.

The potential of the Romans 8 approach did continue to emerge,
however, albeit more commonly in tracts 'on prayer' than in
dogmatic treatises (the interesting exception being Athanasius's late
dogmatic work on the Spirit, discussed below). The *implicit* logic
of eucharistic worship from the third century might also be said to
point to the model I am adumbrating; but the Cappadocians'
account of the Trinity, as I have indicated, seems to present a
variant more affected by a 'linear' and hierarchical perception of
the divine persons, despite occasional appeals by them to Romans

8 (and the cognate Galatians 4: 6), and despite Gregory of Nyssa's profoundly contemplative and apophatic account of the approach to God. My thesis, then, is not the rather hackneyed one that the East produced a 'mystical' and incorporative form of trinitarianism that the West never really appreciated;[23] for there are, as I shall show, Western writers who evidence a tendency towards this type of approach, even if rather implicitly. Instead, I wish to argue that giving *priority* to the Spirit (in contemplation, prophecy, charismatic ecstasy) leads, if not to outright sectarian rejection of the Trinity, to a form of trinitarian reflection that has tended to sit somewhat uneasily within the (sociological) 'church type'. We may call it, perhaps (wielding admittedly contentious Troeltschian terminology), a 'mystic' form within the 'church type'.[24] If this is broadly right, so to line up different forms of pneumatology with different forms of social organization, we should not be surprised to find the *earliest* church often manifesting a classically 'sectarian' pneumatology, that is, one allowing the workings of the Spirit not just an ecstatic effect but 'experiences' actually distinctive to it.[25] Let us briefly now survey the evidence for this thesis.

What, first, lay behind the initial construction of the triadic baptismal formula (Matt. 28: 19)? Wiles does not explain this. The obvious answer is the example of Jesus' own baptism (Mark 1: 9–11 and parallels), with its conjunction of the Father's voice, the Son's baptismal calling, and the Spirit's descent. But this is perhaps not the whole story. It is worth also recalling the testimony of Acts, which refers in its early chapters to a baptism simply 'in the name of Jesus Christ', but promises as a specific mark of that baptism the 'gift of the Holy Spirit' (Acts 2: 38). The confusing story in Acts 8 which suggests some delay between baptism and reception of the Holy Spirit probably does, as is often argued, reflect some untidiness in the earliest church which Luke is attempting to paper over: to record legitimation by the Jerusalem authorities of apparently free-lance evangelism (Acts 8: 14–17) is doubtless part of Luke's theological schema of smooth ecclesiastical expansion.[26] But this is not to say that there are no germs of historical truth here about the origins of the baptismal formula. Speculatively, we might suggest that Acts 19: 1–6 (the story of Paul at Ephesus) contains some insight into why the more primitive baptismal formula became expanded into the triadic one. Rivalry with John's baptism (see also Acts 1: 5) may have caused the early community to draw attention to the *special* gifts of the 'Holy Spirit' (tongues and prophecy) which marked out baptism in Jesus' name as superior (Acts 19: 1–6).[27] If, then, despite all the theological overlay, there is a germ of historical truth here in Acts, it was dramatic charismatic gifts—involving the ecstatic capacity—which were the hallmark of some of the earliest Christian baptisms. Acts associates the Spirit with manifest 'signs and wonders' (Acts 2: 43), whereas Paul's association of the Spirit with baptism is, as we have seen, more concerned with the incorporation into the effects of Christ's death and resurrection (Rom. 8: 9–11). None the less, we have here, albeit speculatively, a possible reason why the 'Holy Spirit' quickly became part of the baptismal formula (Matt. 28: 19), and one based precisely in distinctive 'experience', the ecstatic quality of the transformative reception of the divine.

To say this, of course, is to meet Wiles's charge of 'arbitrariness' only part way, for an 'experience of the Spirit', however distinct-ive, would not necessarily lead to 'hypostatization', any more than dramatic promptings of the Spirit in the Hebrew Scriptures did.[28] The further move required to answer Wiles, as we have seen, is a more conscious explication of the tri-faceted logic of Romans 8, and that is not immediately forthcoming. There is indeed, as Wiles shows, confusion in the early years about the allocation of attributes to Son and Holy Spirit. But what is also distinctive of the Apostolic Fathers is a continuing association of the Holy Spirit with ecstatic, visionary, and prophetic activity; and this Wiles passes over. The highly popular *Pastor of Hermas*, for instance, is rife with these prophetic and visionary claims, and also contains an extended and profound reflection on the transformative potential of the indwelling Spirit.[29] The *Epistle of Barnabas*, too, gives examples of prophecies 'in the Spirit' (9); and the *Didache* provides guide-lines on how to distinguish good and bad wandering prophets (11–13). Even the apologist Justin, who notoriously obscures the function of the Holy Spirit, and even subordinates the Spirit to the angels at one point (*First Apology*, 6. 1–2), continues to term the Spirit 'prophetic'.[30] Perhaps in retrospect, then, we may see Justin's *First Apology* (written not long before the outbreak of Montanism) as a revealing example of an implicitly trinitarian decision. Was the church to follow Justin's rationality-based theology, centred on the Word and *rapprochement* with Greek theology, and explicitly sub-ordinate the Spirit? Or was it to be true to the older heritage of the primacy of the Spirit's prophetic function?

The sectarian climax to which this older tradition was moving is revealingly described in Eusebius's *Ecclesiastical History* (*HE* 5. 17). The Montanist prophet, it was said, 'spoke in ecstasy', moving from 'voluntary ignorance' to 'involuntary madness of soul'.[31] Granting experiential priority to the Spirit in this abandoned way is now seen to have both political and sexual implications: political, because it could lead to challenging ecclesiastical authority with a higher revelation ('more than Christ');[32] and sexual, because (scandalously) this ecstacy released 'wretched women' into positions of power and authority, women who claimed to find the notion of 'Christ' so expanded and transformed that they even had visions of him *as* a woman.[33] This is good evidence, then, of the unmanageable sectarian *potential* of Paul's 'incorporative' vision: the transformative view of the Spirit might expand the reference of the redeemed life of 'Sonship' even beyond what the church could predict or control.

What happened to our 'alternative' view of the Trinity hereafter? Was it merely discredited, or could it be assimilated into a 'church-type' trinitarianism? The twin cases of Irenaeus and Tertullian, often treated side by side in accounts of developing trinitarianism, are here I believe illuminatingly different when examined in the light of this thesis. Although both appear to be 'economic' trinitarianisms of what we have styled the 'linear' type, it would be a mistake, in my view, to assimilate them too quickly into one category. Irenaeus's soteriological theory of 'recapitulation' is often discussed in isolation from his trinitarianism, which is misleading.[34] The theory of salvation is of course deeply Pauline, based on the mystical incorporation thesis of the 'first Adam' and the 'last' (see Rom. 5: 15–19, 1 Cor. 15: 22). It should not surprise us, therefore, to find Irenaeus's treatment in book 5 of the *Against Heresies* focusing on the incorporative outreach of the Spirit as that which *enables* the transformative process of 'recapitulation':

These things, therefore, He recapitulated in Himself: by uniting man to the Spirit and causing the Spirit to dwell in man, He is Himself made the head of the Spirit, and given the Spirit to be the head of man: for through him [sc. the Spirit] we see, and hear, and speak. (*Adv. haer.* 5. 20. 2)

In short, here we have our 'alternative' approach to the Trinity manifested in, and assimilated by, a 'church-type' author who otherwise might be quickly characterized as solely 'linear' and 'economic' in his approach. This seems, then, like a 'mixed type', perhaps befitting (if our sociological theory has any value) a bishop in an era of continuing persecution.

Tertullian is often seen as simply extending and refining Irenaeus's 'economic' trinitarianism. This is doubtless correct, but again there is another side to Tertullian, arising out of his Montanism, and so pointing back to the earlier tradition of associating the Spirit with particular, prophetic activities. (In his Montanist phase Tertullian is even willing to give credence to female prophets, a considerable achievement granted the vehement misogynism which is otherwise characteristic of his writings.[35]) Where Irenaeus has a 'mystical' Pauline streak, then, Tertullian's chiding of Praxeas for 'putting the Paraclete to flight' (*Adv. Prax.* 1. 1) is, I believe, a sign that specific prophetic manifestations must be defended. The Spirit is a *distinct* 'third stage' (ibid. 9). Tertullian's treatise *On Baptism* is written before his Montanist conversion, but even here the careful treatment of the theology of the Holy Spirit (*De baptismo*, 6–8) is not easily dismissed as an unthinking duplication of the distinct status granted to the Son; 'will God not be allowed', writes Tertullian, 'in the case of His own instrument [sc. the Holy Spirit] to strike the note of *spiritual elevation* by means of holy hands?' (ibid. 8, my emphasis).[36]

If my thesis is correct, that Montanism gave the Spirit a bad name, and that this discouraged explicit or apologetic use of a trinitarianism giving experiential priority to the Spirit, then Origen, too, represents a most interesting test case for the theory. If we turn first to the treatise *On Prayer*, we find a profound meditation on Romans 8 at the outset (*De oratione*, 1. 3–6), signalling commitment to the 'incorporative' trinitarian model: 'For neither can our understanding pray, unless previously the Spirit prays . . . nor likewise can it sing and hymn the Father in Christ with rhythm, melody, measure and harmony, unless the Spirit . . . first prays and hymns him' (ibid. 1. 4). The *Exhortation to Martyrdom*, too, contains such an incorporative logic; for readiness for martyrdom is also a 'yielding place to the Spirit' (ibid. 39), so that one may 'gladly accept the sufferings of Christ so that they overflow in us' (ibid. 42) and thus become one with the very life of the Trinity (ibid. 39). The more formal systematic work *On First Principles*, however, is seemingly guarded about the ecstatic dimensions of the Spirit. The significance of the divine 'reason' in

Christians is carefully stressed in the first discussion of the Spirit (*De princ.* 1. 3. 4–6); and later, in book 3 (7. 2–4), Origen argues that all 'rational creatures receive a share in Him [sc. the Spirit]' (ibid. 7. 2), but that there is a danger of confusion with 'common spirits' which 'excite dissensions of no small extent among brethren' (ibid. 7. 3).

We might speculate, then, that the mixed feelings evidenced here in Origen are a classic case of the ambivalence of a 'mystic' type operating within the boundaries of the 'church' (in the sociological sense). A purer 'sectarian' would, as we have seen, allow distinctive experiences to attend the reception of the Holy Spirit, and encourage them; a purer 'church' type might have less vibrant a sense of the contemplative model of incorporation. And yet, as has been pointed out in my earlier writing,[37] one could argue that the eucharistic worship of the early church *in toto*, at least from the time that Hippolytus witnesses to an *epiclesis* of the Spirit,[38] implicitly suggests an incorporative trinitarianism of the sort I have been outlining. The Holy Spirit is invoked as a transformative factor either on the people of God as Christ's body, or later, as in Cyril of Jerusalem, on the eucharistic *elements* as Christ's body. In an unofficial or implicit fashion, then, or so one could argue, the 'mystic' incorporative vision of the Trinity haunted the celebration of the eucharistic mysteries.

But this 'alternative' trinitarianism was yet to be brought to any clear dogmatic consciousness; and, more significantly, yet to be tidied into *homoousian* 'orthodoxy', since those authors we have so far detected employing it have clear subordinationist elements. Athanasius's use of Romans 8 in his mature work on the Spirit's divinity thus marks a watershed. Whereas his *On the Incarnation* interestingly mentions the Spirit not at all in its exposition of an incorporative *christology* (the comparison with Irenaeus is revealing), the later *Letters to Serapion*, in contrast, insist that 'The Father does all things through the Word *in the Holy Spirit*' (1. 28, my emphasis). We find this work almost obsessively appealing to Romans 8 (and its parallel passage Galatians 4: 6).[39] Commenting on Romans 8: 29, for instance, Athanasius writes: 'It is through the Spirit that we are partakers of God . . . the fact of our being called partakers of God shows that the unction and seal that is in us belongs, not to the nature of things originate, but to the nature of the Son who, through the Spirit who is in him, joins us to the

Father' (ibid. 1. 24). Elsewhere too, in one striking passage in *Against the Arians* (2. 59), Athanasius comments on Galatians 4: 6: 'Accordingly this passage . . . proves, that we are not sons by nature, but [by] the Son who is in us; . . . in receiving the grace of the Spirit, we are said thenceforth to be begotten also'.

It is hard to assess Athanasius on this theme. Wiles would object, doubtless, that Athanasius is not even here concentrating on establishing the distinctness of the Spirit; it is the Tropici, with their rejection of the Spirit's divinity, whom he is countering. He has still taken the 'hypostatic' distinctness for granted, even though he could have argued for it on the basis of his preferred Pauline passages. Moreover, the production of these arguments at a comparatively late stage in Athanasius's theological career, and for the purposes of seeing off a new heresy, leaves one wondering whether they are truly distinctive of his output: why was the Spirit ignored, indeed mentioned only fleetingly in the doxology of the *On the Incarnation*? None the less, as Shapland notes (1951: 36–7), there is a reflexive subtlety about Athanasius's late doctrine of the Spirit which even the Cappadocians do not quite emulate. He is true to the Pauline passages to which he constantly adverts; it is not that the Spirit simply 'enlightens' or 'sanctifies', but is transformatively present in all that we do. We pray therefore, he says, 'in the Triad . . . for inasmuch as we partake of the Spirit, we have the grace of the Word and, in the Word, the love of the Father' (*Ad Ser.* 3. 6).

In comparison with this, as I intimated above, the Cappadocian view of incorporation into the Trinity is more explicitly 'linear', and even at times distinctly 'hierarchical' (despite, of course, *homoousian* protestations to the contrary). For Basil, for instance (*On the Holy Spirit*, 9. 23), even 'drawing near' to the Paraclete is not possible unless one is already cleansed from sin; from there the Holy Spirit 'like the sun, will by the aid of thy purified eye show thee in Himself the image of the invisible, and in the blessed spectacle of the image, thou shalt behold the unspeakable beauty of the archetype' (ibid.). The metaphors are distinctly Neoplatonic: this is a step-by-step process of 'enlightenment', with the Spirit as point of entry into higher things.[40] Whereas Athanasius brought Son and Spirit together, then, Basil seems to redistinguish them, allocating 'enlightenment' and 'sanctification' to the third in the economy.

Gregory of Nazianzus and Gregory of Nyssa are subtly different, neither of them being happy with the allocation of 'sanctifying power' to the Spirit alone. (This point is discussed by Wiles himself (1976: 13).) For Nyssa, the invocation of the Holy Spirit is *for* the cleansing of sin (*The Lord's Prayer*, 3), rather than that cleansing being a prerequisite for engagement by the Spirit. But the 'order' of appropriation to the persons of the Trinity is again very clear: 'no notion of the Son is possible unless one is first enlightened by the Spirit'. So too, 'If you take hold of the end of a chain, you will pull the other end with it; in the same way if . . . you draw the Spirit, you will also draw through him the Son and the Father as well.'[41] What Gregory's *Life of Moses* makes memorably clear, however, is that spiritual advance towards intimacy with God ultimately leads to an unnerving 'darkness'—the 'darkness of incomprehensibility'—rather than the 'enlightenment' that characterized an earlier stage of the ascent. Gregory has the mystic's clarity that trinitarian doctrine does not strictly speaking *describe* God; but his incorporative vision of the Trinity is none the less still shot through with metaphors of a descending divine outreach and a human responsive 'ascent'.

What does the patristic evidence we have surveyed indicate? We have attempted to illuminate an 'alternative' approach to the Trinity which gives experiential priority to the Spirit and prayer, and which the textbooks have sometimes obscured by forcing false divisions between 'theology' and 'spirituality'. We have now seen, however, that this alternative tradition takes a number of forms: a type granting *specific* experiential effects to the Spirit, and manifesting a sectarian tendency; a type fumbling towards expression of the *simultaneous* experience of Father, Son, and Spirit in a reflexive divine 'incorporative' act which makes us participative of 'Sonship'; and a more hierarchical perception of 'incorporation', in which the Spirit is the point of entry in a movement of progressive 'ascent'.[42] Both the latter types I would dub 'mystic/church' in Troeltschian sociological terms; and though to place the Cappadocians solely in the third category would doubtless be to demean their subtlety, it is nevertheless not hard to see how that third variation would prove the most enduring of the incorporative understandings of the Trinity for a hierarchically ordered church. For here the linear vision of God presented to us serves to mirror the ordered arrangement of the church itself.

We have shown, therefore, that pneumatology was not 'dormant' in the early centuries, but rather a contentious and even embarrassing issue with political dimensions. Indeed, in subsequent generations, whenever leading authority was given to 'experiences of the Spirit', suspicions of heresy often followed (as in the Messalian-tinged *Macarian Homilies*, for instance).[43] It is perfectly true, as Wiles charged, that the Fathers here discussed nowhere seemed to make *explicit* the prayer-based logic of this need to keep the Spirit 'distinct' (and unthinking conservatism and respect for authority surely did play a large part). But our brief survey of the use of Romans 8 indicates that in some authors this argument was at least *implicit*. Finally, as our evidence has already shown, it would be misleading to say that only the East endorsed this prayer-based trinitarian logic; Augustine himself (contrary to the usual stereotypes) shows signs of it in his late work,[44] and Western mystics rediscovered it periodically, especially in a rich phase of 'indwelling Trinity' motifs in the later medieval mystics (such as Eckhart, Ruysbroeck, Julian of Norwich). John of the Cross's *Spiritual Canticle* provides a memorably beautiful instantiation of the type. Quoting Romans 8, John speaks of the Holy Spirit's action on the soul, which 'raises the soul most sublimely with that his divine breath, . . . that she may breathe in God the same breath of love that the Father breathes in the Son and the Son in the Father' (ibid. 39. 3. 4).

Conclusions: The Trinity and appeals to 'religious experience'

But how likely is it, finally, that this type of 'mystical' evidence would convince Wiles of some rational, and experientially based, grounds for 'hypostatizing' the Spirit? We recall that Wiles demands evidence here of a *demonstrative* force: that the activity of God be 'unquestionably threefold', such as to 'force' us to postulate a trinitarian nature (Wiles 1976: 3). But there seems to me here an unreasonable demand, and one possibly based on a kind of naïve realism. Demonstrating the trinitarian nature of God is emphatically not like examining G. E. Moore's outstretched hand; and even if it seemed to be so, there would doubtless still be hidden presuppositions lying behind the judgement.[45] To make this point is not to retreat into some kind of 'fideism'; but it is to admit that the rather subtle thesis expressed in this essay would be unlikely to convince someone not yet even seriously entertaining Christian theism. Arguments from 'religious experience' may be put to a number of uses: as part of a 'cumulative case' for theism *tout court* (which I am not attempting here),[46] or, more modestly, as is my task, in an attempt to *shift* conceptuality about a particular (intra-Christian) doctrine. A willingness to grant at least initial 'credulity' to one witnessing from experience still remains important, however, if we are to avoid what Swinburne has called the 'sceptical bog' (Swinburne 1979: 254 n. 1). If we dismiss all such evidence as 'viciously circular' in its intepretation, we foreclose all posibilities of expanding our own 'horizons' on the new.[47] Without such foreclosing, we must judiciously assess all our available evidence, its inherent quality, quantity, and testimonial value; the very fact that it presents an approach to the Trinity that is not the 'normal' one already eases the charge of *vicious* circularity.[48] It is, indeed, a characteristic of much 'mystical' experience that it both (psychologically) surprises the recipient and also links up with tradition in fresh and revivifying ways. It has been argued, to my mind convincingly, that this combination of factors is itself a good veridical sign, one reasonable test of the veracity of an experiential claim.[49] If so, the evidence presented here for an 'alternative' doctrine of the Trinity may yet prove worthy of further attention. It is, as we have shown, an argument in the church's mystic armoury which it has never adequately brought into doctrinal play;[50] but the time may now be ripe.

Maurice Wiles wrote in *The Making of Christian Doctrine*: 'Undoubtedly the practice of prayer has had its effect on doctrine, undoubtedly the practice of prayer *should* have its effect on doctrine. But that is not to say that the effect which prayer has actually had is at every point precisely the effect which it should have had' (Wiles 1967: 93). In this essay I have attempted to draw attention to some questionable assumptions which Wiles may have made about what the 'effect' of prayer actually was on the doctrine of the Trinity; I have speculated about sociological and political factors which may have been entangled in the different effects of such prayer; and I have highlighted an appeal to the Trinity that might thereby go some way to answering Wiles's sceptical challenge. If the results are 'idiosyncratic' (as Wiles wrote of an earlier form of my argument) I trust that they are still somewhat 'interesting'![51]

One thing is certain: they would not have been stimulated at all without the critical impetus of Maurice Wiles's decisive work; and they are offered to him with the deepest gratitude and affection.

NOTES

1. Wiles 1976: 1–17; originally in *Journal of Theological Studies*, NS 8 (1957), 92–106.
2. See Matthew 28: 19*b*.
3. Basil of Caesarea's attribution of 'sanctifying power' specifically to the Spirit as a distinguishing feature might be said slightly to flout this principle; the two Gregories avoid this danger by more abstract formulations for the Spirit (see Wiles 1976: 13, who is not, however, concerned here to make this distinction).
4. Ibid. 16–17.
5. See also Rebecca Lyman's contribution to this volume for remarks on Wiles's conception of the *lex orandi*.
6. To be fair, we should note that Wiles does allow that the *lex orandi* could sometimes play a 'more creative role' as well as a 'conservative' one (Wiles 1967: 65). This does not, however, seem to apply to Wiles's treatment of the *Spirit* in this chapter (ibid. 77–87).
7. Wiles can occasionally follow this sort of convention himself: see Wiles 1977: 31–2, where the two forms of early monarchianism are dubbed 'attempted short cuts'.
8. Wiles 1976: 3, my emphasis.
9. See again Wiles 1976: 16–17.
10. See e.g. Mackey's telling pessimism about securing a 'distinct "personhood" for the Holy Spirit' (Mackey 1983: 187), and his remarks about 'the saving presence of *God the Spirit as Jesus*' (ibid. 189, my emphasis). I discuss Mackey's book in detail in Coakley 1986.
11. Wiles criticizes Barth for precisely this: see Wiles 1976: 15–16.
12. See Tillich 1963: 112, my emphasis.
13. I have discussed Brown's book at greater length in Coakley 1986.
14. The difference between the earlier and later Barth on the Trinity is illuminatingly discussed in Williams 1979.
15. See e.g. Moltmann 1974: 243; and compare Moltmann 1981: 75–83.
16. The more recent association by Moltmann of the Spirit with 'femininity' in this model introduces some unfortunate gender stereotypes: it looks as if it is the 'feminine' Spirit's job to play peacemaker in a family of warring male giants. See esp. Moltmann 1991: 64–5.
17. See esp. Gunton 1991: ch. 3.

18. It has been pointed out that Richard was here reflecting a particular communitarian concern of the Regular Canons (see Bynum 1973).

19. As a member of the Church of England Doctrine Commission (1987: ch. 7); also see Coakley 1986.

20. See my contribution to the more recent Church of England Doctrine Commission report (1991: ch. 2), based on fieldwork with church groups in Lancaster.

21. I was not yet clear about this point when I wrote for the Church of England Doctrine Commission 1987. There I included the Cappadocians as straightforward exemplars of the 'incorporative' model, without making this rather subtle distinction between more 'reflexive' and more 'hierarchical' versions of it.

22. I am grateful in what follows for some references gleaned from an Oxford lecture series on patristic pneumatology by Anthony Meredith, SJ, given in the academic year 1991–2.

23. This may have been the impression given in the Church of England Doctrine Commission 1987: ch. 7. I have somewhat revised my views since then.

24. On the church/sect/mystic typology, see Troeltsch 1960, esp. 331–43, 730–2, and 993–4, for brief delineations of the 'types'.

25. This suggestion is in line with Troeltsch's (tantalizingly brief) parallel remarks about Christology and soteriology, and their different forms in different social settings (Troeltsch 1960: 994–7). I explored such a correlation between pneumatology and different sociological 'types' in a contemporary context in the Church of England Doctrine Commission 1991: ch. 2.

26. The historical reliability of the book of Acts is of course much disputed. My own view is that archaic strands of material are preserved *within* a Lukan theology of triumphant ecclesiastical expansion. On Acts 8: 15, e.g., Haenchen (1971: 304) comments of Luke's theology: 'in retrospect, Philip's success in the mission is minimized: the most important factor was beyond his powers'. Käsemann (1964: 145) remarks, 'The Church of a later day could not admit the existence in the sacred past of primitive Christian free-lances and communities resting on any other than apostolic authority.'

27. Käsemann's famous essay (1964) virtually discounts the historical reliability of Acts 19 and argues that it reflects Luke's unwillingness to acknowledge anything other than one sort of real Christian (in the '*Una sancta catholica*'). This may well be true; but again it does not, in my view, *rule out* the possibility that a dispute about authentic baptism, and its relation to manifest outpourings of the Spirit, could have occurred in some early Christian context (not necessarily at Ephesus).

28. Christopher Stead has surveyed the evidence, both in Jewish and Greek backgrounds to early Christianity, for tendencies towards multiple divine 'hypostatizations'; but these do not prove consistently triadic (see Stead 1974).

29. The *Pastor of Hermas* (1. 1. 1 and 1. 2. 1) speaks of the Spirit 'carrying me away'; and 2. 5. 1–2, 2. 10. 2, and 2. 11 all contain reflections on the experiential effects of the indwelling Spirit.

30. This is helpfully discussed in Barnard 1967: ch. 8. It is mentioned by Wiles 1976: 6.

31. To what extent we should interpret 'voluntary ignorance' as a deliberate *askesis* of banishing all thoughts in preparation for prayer is a moot point: this viewpoint is expressed by Chapman 1917: 91 col. *a*.

32. See Hippolytus, *Refutatio omnium haer.* 8. 19, in Bettenson 1967: 77.

33. Again, Hippolytus, *Refutatio omnium haer.* 8. 19, in Stevenson 1957: 114 (for 'wretched women'), and see Stevenson's 'Montanist Utterances' (ibid. 113) for the claim by Priscilla that 'Christ came to me in the likeness of a woman'.

34. So e.g. Kelly 1968 discusses Irenaeus's trinitarianism in ch. 4 (pp. 104–8), but his treatment of Irenaeus's theory of 'recapitulation' is left for ch. 7 (pp. 170–4).

35. See Tertullian, *De anima*, 9, in Bettenson 1967: 78.

36. The *On prayer*, it must be said, does not place distinct emphasis on the Spirit, and its opening remarks ('Jesus Christ our Lord, God's Spirit, God's Word and God's Reason, Word of Reason and Reason of Word and Spirit of both') suggest a confused trinitarianism compared with the later *Against Praxeas*.

37. See the Church of England Doctrine Commission 1987: 114–16. This section was written with Canon John Halliburton.

38. See Hippolytus, *Apostolic Tradition*, 8. 4, in Bettenson 1967: 76.

39. E.g. in *Ad Ser.* 1. 6, 1. 7, 1. 19, 1. 24, 1. 25, 4. 4.

40. In *On the Holy Spirit* Basil does cite Gal. 4: 6 (19. 49) and Rom. 8: 16 (26. 61), but only fleetingly.

41. See *Letter* 38, formerly attributed to Basil, now generally agreed to be by Gregory of Nyssa; in Wiles and Santer 1975: 34, 35.

42. To single out this passage is admittedly to focus on Basil at one of his most Neoplatonic moments; and, as we discussed at the beginning of this essay, the *intention* of the Cappadocians is to insist on the simultaneous activity (and thus also experiences) of all three persons in the Godhead. None the less, the hierarchical metaphors persist.

43. The 'incorporative' view of the Trinity based on Rom. 8 is present, e.g., in *Homily* 5. 7 (Macarius 1921: 52).

44. Augustine discourses on Rom. 8 in his Letter 130 to Proba on prayer (Augustine 1953: 398–9), and, as Louth (1981: 157–8) shows, the last

two books of *The Trinity* contain an 'incorporative' understanding of
the Spirit's function (see e.g. *De Trin.* 15. 17. 31).

45. This point is illuminatingly discussed by Jantzen (1987), drawing on
Wittgenstein's critique of Moore.
46. See Swinburne 1979: ch. 13.
47. See Jantzen 1987: 282–3, who appeals to Gadamer's notion of a 'fusion
of horizons'. She concludes (p. 283): 'Wittgenstein is right to
emphasize the *framework* within which . . . [a specific] experience
occurs; but the experience can in turn have a radical effect upon that
framework. . . . not only can experience falsify hypotheses; it can also
point the way forward to *new understanding*, positive learning' (my
emphasis).
48. Franks Davis (1989: ch. 6) has provided a sustained response to the
charge of 'vicious circularity' made against appeals to religious
experience, in particular by showing how 'beliefs, concepts and
experiences all *interact* in the development of our cognitive life' (p. 145,
my emphasis).
49. See Brown 1985: 80–1, 83. Despite my critical remarks about Brown's
trinitarianism earlier in this essay I find his discussion of the 'veridical
tests' for claims to 'revelation' subtle and illuminating.
50. As is well brought out by Nelson Pike's 'St. John of the Cross on
Mystic Apprehensions as Sources of Knowledge' (in Runzo and Ihara
1986: 75–98), there is a deep suspicion in some pre-Enlightenment
spiritual direction (esp. in John of the Cross) of taking mystic
apprehensions as a 'source of propositional knowledge'. Instead, 'the
assumption [is] that there is a [given] body of truth to which the
individual mystic has access by means other than mystic visions and
locutions' (p. 94). This helps to clarify the relative novelty of what is
being attempted in this essay: the subtle shifting of our conceptuality
of the Trinity by appeal to accounts of prayer-based 'religious
experience'.
51. See Wiles 1987: 462.

REFERENCES

Athanasius (1892), *Four Discourses against the Arians*, in *Select Writings and
Letters of Athanasius Bishop of Alexandria*, trans. A. Robertson,
Edinburgh.
Augustine (1953), 'Letter 130, To Proba', in *Saint Augustine: Letters*, vol.
ii, trans. W. Parsons, Washington, DC.
—— (1963), *The Trinity*, trans. S. McKenna, Washington, DC.
Balthasar, H. U. von (1961), *Prayer*, London.

—— (1982), *The Von Balthasar Reader*, ed. Medard Kehl and Werner Löser, New York.

Barnabas, the *Epistle of Barnabas* (1912), in *The Apostolic Fathers*, vol. i, trans. K. Lake, London.

Barnard, L. W. (1967), *Justin Martyr*, Cambridge.

Barth, Karl (1936), *Church Dogmatics* 1.1, Edinburgh.

—— (1956), *Church Dogmatics* 4.1, Edinburgh.

Basil of Caesarea (1895), *On the Holy Spirit*, in *Saint Basil: Letters and Select Works*, trans. B. Jackson, Oxford.

Bettenson, H. (ed.) (1967), *Documents of the Christian Church*, repr. of 2nd edn., Oxford.

Brown, David (1985), *The Divine Trinity*, London.

Bynum, C. W. (1973), 'The Spirituality of Regular Canons in the Twelfth Century: A New Approach', *Medievalia et humanistica*, 4: 3–24.

Chapman, J. (1917), 'Mysticism (Christian, Roman Catholic)', in J. Hastings (ed.), *Encyclopaedia of Religion and Ethics*, vol. ix, Edinburgh: 90–101.

Church of England Doctrine Commission (1987), *We Believe in God*, London.

—— (1991), *We Believe in the Holy Spirit*, London.

Coakley, Sarah (1986), 'Can God Be Experienced as Trinity?', *The Modern Churchman*, NS 28: 11–23.

Congar, Y. (1983), *I Believe in the Holy Spirit*, 3 vols., New York.

The Didache (1912), in *The Apostolic Fathers*, vol. i, trans. K. Lake, London.

Eusebius of Caesarea (1926), *The Ecclesiastical History*, vol. i, trans. K. Lake, London.

Franks Davis, C. (1989), *The Evidential Force of Religious Experience*, Oxford.

Gregory of Nyssa (1954), *The Lord's Prayer, the Beatitudes*, trans. H. C. Graef, London.

—— (1978), *The Life of Moses*, trans. A. J. Malherbe and E. Ferguson, London.

Gunton, C. E. (1991), *The Promise of Trinitarian Theology*, Edinburgh.

Haenchen, E. (1971), *The Acts of the Apostles*, Oxford.

Hermas, the *Pastor of Hermas* (1867), in *The Writings of the Apostolic Fathers*, trans. A. Roberts, J. Donaldson, and F. Crombie, Edinburgh.

Irenaeus (1868), *Against the Heresies*, in *The Writings of Irenaeus*, 2 vols., trans. A. Roberts and W. H. Rambaut, Edinburgh.

Jantzen, Grace (1987), 'Epistemology, Religious Experience, and Religious Belief', *Modern Theology*, 3: 277–91.

John of the Cross (1964), *The Complete Works of Saint John of the Cross*. 3 vols., trans. E. A. Peers, London.

Justin Martyr (1867), *The First Apology of Justin*, in *The Writings of*

Justin Martyr and Athenagoras, trans. M. Dods and B. P. Pratten, Edinburgh.

Käsemann, E. (1964), 'The Disciples of John the Baptist at Ephesus', in *Essays on New Testament Themes*, London: 136–48.

Kelly, J. N. D. (1968), *Early Christian Doctrines*, 4th edn., London.

Lampe, Geoffrey (1977), *God as Spirit*, Oxford.

Lossky, V. (1968), *The Mystical Theology of the Eastern Church*, Cambridge.

Louth, Andrew (1981), *The Origins of the Christian Mystical Tradition: From Plato to Denys*, Oxford.

Macarius the Egyptian (1921), *Fifty Spiritual Homilies*, trans. A. J. Mason, New York.

Mackey, James P. (1983), *The Christian Experience of God as Trinity*, London.

Macmurray, John (1961), *Persons in Relation*, London.

Moltmann, Jürgen (1974), *The Crucified God*, London.

—— (1981), *The Trinity and the Kingdom of God*, London.

—— (1991), *History and the Triune God*, London.

Origen (1849), *De principiis*, in *The Writings of Origen*, vol. i, trans. F. Crombie, Edinburgh.

—— (1954), *On Prayer* and *Exhortation to Martyrdom*, in *Alexandrian Christianity*, trans. J. E. L. Oulton and H. Chadwick, London.

Rahner, Karl (1970), *The Trinity*, London.

Ramsey, M. (1977), *Holy Spirit: A Biblical Study*, London.

Richard of St Victor (1979), *Richard of St. Victor: The Twelve Patriarchs etc.*, ed. Grover A. Zinn, London.

Runzo, Joseph, and Ihara, Craig K. (eds.) (1986), *Religious Experience and Religious Belief*, Lanham, Md.

Schleiermacher, F. D. E. (1963), *The Christian Faith*, ed. H. R. MacKintosh and J. S. Stewart, 2 vols., New York.

Shapland, C. R. B. (1951), *The Letters of Saint Athanasius Concerning the Holy Spirit*, London.

Stead, Christopher (1974), 'The Origins of the Doctrine of the Trinity', *Theology*, 77: 508–17; 582–9.

Stevenson, J. (ed.) (1957), *A New Eusebius*, London.

Swinburne, Richard (1979), *The Existence of God*, Oxford.

—— (1988), 'Could There be More Than One God?', *Faith and Philosophy*, 5: 225–41.

Tertullian (1919), *Treatises Concerning Prayer, Concerning Baptism*, trans. A. Souter, London.

—— (1919), *Against Praxeas*, trans. A. Souter, London.

Tillich, Paul (1963), *Systematic Theology*, vol. iii, Chicago.

Troeltsch, Ernst (1960), *The Social Teaching of the Christian Churches*, 2 vols., New York.

Wiles, Maurice (1967), *The Making of Christian Doctrine*, Cambridge.

—— (1976), *Working Papers in Doctrine*, London.

—— (1977), *The Christian Fathers*, reprint of 1st edn., 1966, London.

—— (1987), 'Review Article: Marching in Step?', *Theology*, 90: 460–4.

—— and Santer, M. (eds.) (1975), *Documents in Early Christian Thought*, Cambridge.

Williams, R. D. (1979), 'Barth on the Triune God', in S. W. Sykes (ed.), *Karl Barth: Studies of his Theological Method*, Oxford: 147–93.

Zizioulas, John D. (1985), *Being as Communion: Studies in Personhood and the Church*, Crestwood, New York.

4

Interpretation and Reinterpretation in Religion

JOHN HICK

Maurice Wiles has for a generation occupied both the Regius Chair of Divinity at Oxford and the position of Britain's leading 'liberal' or—according to one's relative vantage point—'radical' theologian. He has dealt with central issues, being in the forefront of the *Myth of God Incarnate* debate, and of the current discussions of divine action, as well as touching upon most other aspects of Christian doctrine. His treatments of these topics have been so challenging because he has never concealed his meaning in learned obscurity. The meaning has been evident and has called cumulatively for a development of Christian theological understanding. Thus his work has been a continuous exercise in the interpretation and reinterpretation of the Christian message.

It therefore seems appropriate to take as the theme of this essay the essentially interpretative, and hence ever revisable, character of theological doctrines. They are philosophical in character, in the sense that they are theories developed to interpret, and thus understand, our situation in the universe on the basis of a certain particular range of data. The data consist in both the primary moments of religious experience which have given rise to a tradition, as reflected at varying distances in its scriptures, and also in the continuing religious experience of the community, expressed in its life, liturgies, preaching, literature, and art.

As regards the scriptures, and restricting attention to the three Abrahamic traditions, there is an important distinction here between Judaism and Islam on the one hand and Christianity on the other. The Qur'ān is accepted as a divine utterance in the Arabic language, and Muslim theological work accordingly consists almost entirely of Qur'ānic exegesis. Theological discussion and debate consists either in agreeing upon the interpretation of a

Qur'ānic passage or in forming rival schools of interpretation. There has proved in practice to be endless scope for differing understandings of many of the Qur'ānic verses and their practical implications. But the fact that the revelation is already verbal in form greatly restricts the scope of speculative doctrines such as occur so abundantly in Christianity. There is of course a great tradition of Islamic philosophy, interacting for several centuries with Jewish and Christian philosophy; but this is largely distinct from theology in the sense of doctrinal formulation. In the case of Judaism the original revelation, as reflected in the Hebrew Bible, consists partly in divine utterances in the Hebrew language (particularly in the giving of the Law at Sinai) and partly in divine acts within human history (particularly the Exodus). The continuing interpretation of this revelatory material has taken place as much in life as in thought. Whilst there have been major Jewish philosophers—one need only mention Maimonides—there has been little interest in the creation of theological systems. The assimilation of revelation has taken place in the Talmudic interpretation of the Torah and in the development of religious observances, both within the ordinary fabric of daily life and on the sabbath and on the high holy days.

But in the case of Christianity the situation is more complex. This did not originate in a book but in a person, Jesus Christ. The scriptures of the New Testament began to be written, in the form of some of St Paul's letters, about twenty years after Jesus' death, and in the form of Gospels about twenty years later again, continuing until towards the end of the century, and were not collected and recognized by the church as sacred scripture until as late as the fourth century. Since then the New Testament has indeed often been regarded as divinely inspired in every word and thus as having an absolute revelatory authority. But this has not inhibited speculative theological construction, producing such elaborate doctrinal systems as those of Thomas Aquinas in the medieval period, John Calvin in the Reformation period, and innumerable lesser figures in the succeeding centuries. Such systems have always validated themselves from the scriptures; but they have never been simply exercises in biblical exegesis. In the present century, with the tremendous growth and influence of many forms of historical and literary criticism, the scriptural validation of theological speculation has become less straightforward and less generally convincing. But, more fundamentally, it is widely accepted that the basic Christian revelation occurred in the person of Christ and that the essential function of the New Testament is to witness to him. Such witnessing, however, has inevitably already involved interpretation; for as soon as the members of the early Christian community went beyond their original utterance of faith, 'Jesus is lord', they had to select categories in terms of which to express the significance of his remembered life. The range of options was, perforce, supplied from the conceptual and linguistic resources of their religious culture. Thus it would have been unthinkable for Jesus, in first-century Palestine, to be understood by his disciples as an avatar or as a bodhisattva; but entirely possible for them to see him as a prophet or as the messiah or as the Danielic son of man.

And so the New Testament documents, embodying a variety of early attempts to categorize Jesus, stand between the founding event and its later, developed theological interpretations. On the one hand, we only know of the Jesus Christ event through the New Testament; and on the other hand the New Testament documents already interpret that event in their own ways in order to speak about it. It is important to note the plurality of such ways. For in the New Testament period—roughly the second half of the first century CE—there was no single uniform understanding of the meaning of the Jesus Christ event but rather the beginnings of a variety of understandings, some of which were solidified in the Church's subsequent official theologies whilst others were later left aside.

In continuing now to study the role of interpretation in the making and remaking of religious doctrine I shall confine myself to the Christian tradition. For such study is inevitably controversial and whilst I feel entitled, and indeed obliged, to take part in the continuous theological development of my own tradition, I do not feel entitled to meddle in the internal deliberations of other traditions.

In considering the development of Christian theology we are immediately faced with the startling fact that it has come to hinge upon a cluster of sophisticated doctrines none of which were taught by Jesus himself. And yet, despite this, they are commonly held to express the authoritatively correct uderstanding of Jesus! By this central cluster I mean the doctrines of Incarnation, Trinity, and Atonement. In a loose sense of 'imply', the first of these implies

the other two. Incarnation, as the idea that the historical Jesus was
God incarnate, requires at least a binitarian concept of deity to
account for God's simultaneous activity 'in heaven' whilst being
for some thirty years on earth. When, for rather less obvious
reasons, we add God the Holy Spirit, we have the fully-fledged
trinitarian conception of God as One in Three and Three in One.
(I say 'for rather less obvious reasons' because in the early days the
experienced divine Spirit was sometimes regarded as the Spirit of
Jesus rather than as a third member of a Trinity—see e.g. 2 Cor.
3: 17; Gal. 4: 6; Phil. 1: 19.) And the further idea of atonement
arises from the question, *Cur Deus homo*? The accepted answer is
that God the Son became man in order to offer the atonement
demanded by divine justice if the fallen human race (or part of it)
was to receive forgiveness and be brought to eternal life in God's
presence.

In saying that this cluster of doctrines was not taught by Jesus,
and is thus a subsequent human construct, I have of course already
entered an area of controversy. As regards the idea of divine
incarnation, did not Jesus say, 'I and the Father are one' (John 10:
30), 'He who has seen me has seen the Father' (John 14: 9), 'No
one comes to the Father, but by me' (John 14: 6)? And do not such
sayings amount to a claim to be God, or the Son of God? It would
be hard to resist that inference. And until within approximately the
last hundred years it was entirely reasonable for Christians to
assume that these are words of the historical Jesus, who was
thereby clearly claiming a divine status. Today, however, it is no
longer reasonable for theologically educated Christians to assume
this. The large majority of New Testament scholars, including
conservative ones, have noted the significant differences between
the fourth gospel, in which these claims occur, and the earlier
synoptic tradition, and have concluded that these claims to divinity
were put into Jesus' mouth by a writer expressing the theology of
his part of the church in a period of some sixty or more years after
Jesus' death. There are also some passages in the synoptic gospels
that have been thought to imply a claim to divinity on Jesus' part;
but this view has not gained general scholarly acceptance. Thus the
moderately conservative New Testament scholar James Dunn, in
a major book-length study of the origins of the doctrine of the
Incarnation, says that 'there was no real evidence in the earliest
Jesus tradition of what could fairly be called a consciousness of

divinity' (Dunn 1980: 60); and the Anglican theologian Brian Hebblethwaite, in a book upholding the traditional Incarnation doctrine, says that 'It is no longer possible to defend the divinity of Jesus by reference to the claims of Jesus' (Hebblethwaite 1987: 74).

It seems likely that Jesus saw himself as a prophet, indeed probably as the final prophet, proclaiming the imminent coming of God's kingdom in power. He called himself 'son of man', perhaps (on some occasions at least) referring to the son of man in the Danielic prophecy, who was to come in glory on the clouds of heaven. Certainly the early church believed that when the kingdom came (which they expected within a few years at most) Jesus would appear in the heavens as the prophesied son of man. This 'son of man' would be a human, or perhaps superhuman, agent of God, but in no sense God in person. It would also be entirely natural if Jesus was thought of as a son of God—as in the case of the centurion in Mark's gospel who at Jesus' crucifixion says, 'Truly this man was a son of God', this being a common way in the ancient world of speaking about an outstandingly holy person, as well as about a number of royal figures, including the ancient Hebrew kings (see Ps. 2: 7; 2 Sam. 7: 14) and the expected messiah, who was to be of the royal line of David. But within Judaism this usage was metaphorical; no Jew thought that the ancient Hebrew kings or contemporary holy men were physically sons of God. Indeed a literal attribution of deity to Jesus would doubtless have seemed to him blasphemous. According to Mark, he even declined to be called 'good': 'Why do you call me good? No one is good but God alone' (Mark 10: 18). Nevertheless the closeness to God manifest in Jesus' charismatic personality, his teachings and healings, his way of life and his death, declared him to be a true 'son of God'. Such language was wholly appropriate for one in whose presence people became conscious in a new way of the reality and love of God and of God's total claim upon their lives, so that to encounter Jesus was for many a turning-point, a joyous entry into a new life of trust and of release from anxious self-concern.

In the very early church, then, Jesus was thought of as the deeply revered lord, leader, inspirer who mediated God's presence and power, and through whose dramatic life God had recently acted savingly on earth. In the words of Peter's speech at Pentecost in

Acts, he was 'Jesus of Nazareth, a man attested to you by God with mighty works and wonders and signs which God did through him in your midst . . .' (Acts 2: 22). However, the Gentile world into which the gospel was soon to be carried was one in which there were, in Paul's phrase, 'many gods and many lords' (1 Cor. 8: 5). Being divine had a more flexible meaning than that which it has acquired during centuries of Christian theology. Rulers and great men were often regarded as gods or sons of god in senses that ranged from the literal, through the quasi-literal, to the clearly metaphorical. And in such an environment a new religious movement would more or less inevitably come to think of its own founder as divine. Mithras was divine, the Emperor was divine, holy men and great philosophers were divine, and the world would expect the Christians' lord to be divine. And so as the gospel message was developed in relation to the Gentile world, particularly under the powerful impetus of St Paul's work, Jesus became established as a divine being, though still in a somewhat indeterminate sense. In addition to this pull of the environing Graeco-Roman culture there must also have been a pressure from within the church in a natural tendency for his followers to exalt the lord for whose sake they were being persecuted, and then later, when the church had become part of the imperial establishment, a political motive to exalt Christ as lord of the empire and indeed of the world. Thus the progressive divinization of Jesus was so natural as to be almost inevitable; and as the rather open-ended language of divinity solidified into a fixed theological dogma the original metaphorical 'son of God' was transformed into the metaphysical 'God the Son', Second Person of a divine Trinity.

What we see, then, in this classic instance is a theological interpretation of the historical Jesus that goes far beyond, and indeed contradicts, his own self-understanding, so far as we have evidence of it; and yet an interpretation that was more or less demanded by the circumstances of that time. The question that I therefore want to raise, under the heading of 'reinterpretation', is whether this classical theory is open to revision in a later age in which the circumstances that originally called for it have been replaced by different circumstances in which it has become something of an embarrassment.

The deification of Jesus could only be perceived as an embarrassment since it became evident, as a result of the historical-critical study of the New Testament, that Jesus did not teach his own deity. This realization has freed us to acknowledge that his deification has been used to validate and justify historical developments which cannot be defended. In particular, two such evils of enormous proportions, conflicting sharply with Jesus' own moral teaching, have been justified in the minds of Christian populations by arguments whose ultimate premiss is the deity of Christ.

One of these is anti-Semitism. This did not begin with Christianity; but when Christianity became the religion of the Roman empire the persecution of the Jews, instead of ending, soon escalated. As Rosemary Ruether says, 'we must recognize Christian anti-Semitism as a uniquely new factor in the picture of antique anti-Semitism. Its source lies in the theological dispute between Christianity and Judaism over the messiahship of Jesus, and so it strikes at the heart of the Christian gospel. It was this theological root and its growth into a distinctively Christian type of anti-Semitism that were responsible for reversing the tradition of tolerance for Jews in Roman law' (Ruether 1974: 28). This Christian anti-Semitism rose to appalling heights in the medieval period, then waned somewhat, but rose again in the nineteenth and twentieth centuries and reached a new extreme in the Nazi attempt to exterminate the Jewish population of Europe. Throughout this long period, anti-Semitism has justified itself as a morally appropriate treatment of those who had killed God incarnate. The fact that it was not Jews but their Roman overlords, who saw him as a potential political threat, who executed Jesus is discounted; for the gospels, written in a period of acute tension between church and synagogue, are concerned to place the blame firmly upon the Jews. This motif is at its strongest in the gospel of John, whose branding of the Jews as enemies of God has poisoned the Christian imagination for so many centuries. Thus the Johannine Jesus, amongst other attacks on 'the Jews', says 'you seek to kill me, because my words find no place in you' (8: 37); 'You are of your father the devil, and your will is to do your father's desires' (8: 44); and, concerning his own teaching, 'He who is of God hears the words of God; the reason why you do not hear them is that you are not of God' (8: 47). To quote Rosemary Ruether again, 'By mythologizing the theological division between "man-in-God" and "man-alienated-from-God" into a division between two postures of faith, John gives the ultimate theological form to that diabolizing of "the Jews" which is the root of anti-Semitism in the Christian tradition' (Ruether 1974: 116). The charge of deicide—which of course presupposes Jesus' divine status—continued to justify anti-Jewish attitudes, and recurrent phases of violent perse-cution, throughout the medieval period, and still lies in the background of the more secular anti-Semitism of the nineteenth century and its culmination in the twentiety-century Holocaust. Indeed the charge of deicide was only formally rescinded by the Roman Catholic Church in 1965 at its second Vatican Council. But neither at Vatican II nor elsewhere is there a full facing by the Church of the distinctively Christian character of anti-Semitism. One could wish for more public utterances like the inscription that was put up in 1955 at the Anglican cathedral at Lincoln in England. This replaced one set there in 1255 to record the supposed ritual murder of a Christian boy by Jews. The new, 1955 inscription says, 'Trumped-up stories of "ritual murders" of Christian boys by Jewish communities were common throughout Europe during the Middle Ages and even much later. These fictions cost many innocent Jews their lives. Lincoln had its own legend, and the alleged victim was buried in the Cathedral. A shrine was erected above and the boy was referred to as "little St. Hugh" . . . Such stories do not redound to the credit of Christendom and so we pray—"Remember not Lord our offences, nor the offences of our forefathers"' (quoted by Tamara Sonn in Wei-hsun and Spiegler 1989: 438).

The connection between the deification of Jesus and anti-Semitism is not a straight line of logical necessity leading from the former to the latter. It would have been possible for Christians to believe that the Jews had rejected Jesus, by failing to see him as God incarnate, and yet not to have needed to persecute and slaughter them. The connection lies in the historical fact that Jesus' deity was used to validate and intensify prejudice against a people who, because they adhered to their own distinctive faith and form of life, were forced into ghettoes and into unpopular occupations and then used as a scapegoat for society's ills. But the virulent intensity of the worst persecutions, and the religious rhetoric which enabled many otherwise good people to support them or to turn a blind eye, depended upon the faith that the Jesus whom Judaism failed to accept was none other than God in person living a human life—with the conscious or unconscious inference that the Jews must be rejected by the Christian world and may properly be ill treated in whatever way is currently in practice.

The fifteenth to nineteenth centuries' Western imperialist exploitation of what is today called the third world was a second major historical evil that has justified itself in the public conscience by its claim to serve the divine lordship of Christ. European colonization in Africa, India, South America, and the Far East was initially an outlet for the explorers' adventurousness and appetite for treasure. But the development of trade required military intervention to protect it, then political annexation to control the native people and keep out rival traders of other nations, and finally led to the massive and systematic exploitation of the subject populations. Their mineral wealth and other materials were exported to enrich Spain, Britain, Portugal, France and Germany, and later to feed the European industrial revolution; their people became a captive market buying back their own products, now processed into finished artefacts in the West; and in the case of Africa many of their people were subjected to the ultimate exploitation of being forcibly abducted to be slaves in the United States.

This massive exploitation of the peoples of the third world by the technologically more powerful nations of the first world was justified as a duty, a shouldering of 'the white man's burden', his vocation to take charge of backward continents so that they might benefit from the saving gospel of Christ and the blessings of Western civilization.

Many illustrations can be given of the way in which the universal claim of Christ to rule human life, and to offer the only escape from perdition, was used to provide a religious and moral validation of the imperialist enterprise. Two briefly indicated examples must suffice here. One is the sixteenth-century Spanish conquests in South America, whose motivation was, in the words of the historian Anne Peck, 'to win gold and glory for their King and themselves, and heathen people for the Catholic faith' (Peck 1941: 91). She adds that 'every conquistador of the sixteenth century was still a crusader, carrying the Cross into pagan lands'. Another standard history says:

The Spanish expeditions to America and the West Indies, as recorded by Spanish chroniclers, were marked by ferocious cruelty, unlimited bloodshed, unparalleled lust for treasure. A kindly reception by natives was recompensed by the wholesale enslavement of the people for enforced labour in the search for gold and other wealth. Nor was any vestige of humanity shown in the treatment of the various tribes thrown into bondage. . . . Yet these expeditions were conducted under the pretense of advancing civilisation and hallowed by the presence of priests. The hideous barbarities committed were cloaked by the fact that the Holy Cross was planted on Pagan shores and the heathen forced to accept the out-ward forms of Christianity. . . . An almost indiscriminate slaughter was countenanced as a necessary prelude to the foundation of Christianity. (Akers 1930: 6–7, 9)

Another example is the case of British India. As James Morris, historian of the British Empire, says,

The mission stations which, throughout the second half of the nineteenth century, sprang up throughout the tropical possessions, were manned by and large by militants with no doubts—this was a Christian Empire, and it was the imperial duty to spread the Christian word among its heathen subjects . . . The administrators of Empire, too, and very often its conquerors, were generally speaking practising Christians: the new public schools at which so many of them were educated were invariably Church of England foundations, with parson-headmasters. . . . Explorers like Speke or Grant saw themselves as God's scouts. . . . Generals like Havelock and Nicholson slaughtered their enemies in the absolute certainty of a biblical mandate . . . and most of the imperial heroes were identified in the public mind with the Christianness of Empire—not simply humanitarianism, not Burke's sense of trusteeship, but a Christian militancy, a ruling faith, whose Defender on earth was the Queen herself, and whose supreme commander needed no identification. Every aspect of Empire was an aspect of Christ. (Morris 1968: 318–19)

As in the case of Christian anti-Semitism, belief in the divine status of Christ did not logically require this human aberration. But given a 'fallen' human nature, apparently unredeemed by fifteen centuries of the church's influence, the Christian belief-system provided a sanction for the ruthless exploitation of the third world by the first. And again, as in the case of anti-Semitism, whilst this misuse does not show that the belief in the deity of Jesus is mistaken, it does cause us to ask whether an idea which has been so readily available to validate massive human evil must be an essential and permanent element of the Christian faith.

The third historical situation to which I want to point has a more direct connection with the dogma of Christ's status as the unique incarnation of the second person of a divine Trinity, namely the attitude of the Christian churches to the people of the other great world religions. This has for centuries consisted, and still today consists for large numbers of church members, in a religious superiority complex which readily manifests itself in arrogance, contempt, condemnation, and hostility. Such an attitude has affected, and still for many pervasively affects, the relationship between the Christian minority of the human race and the non-Christian majority. The missionary movement which was carried on the back of the imperial expansion of the West generally regarded Hinduism, Buddhism, Islam, Taoism, Sikhism, and African primal religion as areas of spiritual darkness from which souls were to be rescued by conversion. As late as 1960 the Chicago Congress of World Mission declared that 'In the years since [World War II], more than one billion souls have passed into eternity and more than half of these went to the torment of hell fire without even hearing of Jesus Christ, who He was, or why He died on the cross of Calvary' (Percy 1961: 9). And there continue to be large and powerful fundamentalist constituencies within which such ideas are still alive, still affect human attitudes, still determine the use of resources, and still influence political policies.

The logical connection between the Christian superiority complex and the traditional doctrine of the Incarnation is evident. If Jesus was God (i.e. God the Son) incarnate, the Christian religion is unique in having been founded by God in person. The Christian story is that in Christ God came down to earth and inaugurated a new and redeemed community, the church; and it seems self-evident that God must wish all human creatures to become part of this community, and that the church is called to convert the human race to the Christian faith. However, this implication has now long since come to seem unrealistic. The political independence of previously colonial territories has dismantled the imperial umbrella under which the missionaries worked. And with the continuing population explosion throughout much of the third world the (nominally) Christian proportion of the world's population has shrunk and is likely to continue to shrink. Indeed it is probable that early in the twenty-first century Islam will have become numerically the largest of the world religions. In this new situation, in which Christianity no longer expects to cover the earth, Christian thought is in a serious state of cognitive dissonance. One response is an intensification of absolutism within the large fundamentalist wing of the church. On the more liberal wing, various epicycles of theory have been developed to avoid the absolutist implication of the Incarnation dogma. Already in the nineteenth century the ideas of 'implicit faith' and 'baptism by desire' were in use, according to which individuals who have not had a proper opportunity to respond to the gospel of Christ, but whose spiritual state is nevertheless such that they *would* respond if it were properly presented to them, are unconsciously included within the sphere of salvation. In the twentieth century Karl Rahner has developed a concept of 'anonymous Christians' which was more or less adopted (though without using Rahner's term) at the second Vatican Council and reiterated by the present pope in his first Encyclical, *Redemptor hominis* (1979), in which he declared that 'every man without any exception whatever has been redeemed by Christ, and . . . with man—with every man without exception whatever—Christ is in a way united, even when man is unaware of it' (para. 14). (However, in his more recent Encyclical, *Redemptoris missio*, 1990, the pope says that 'Dialogue should be conducted and implemented with the conviction that the church is the ordinary means of salvation and that she alone possesses the fullness of the means of salvation' (para. 55), and urges renewed support for the missionary societies, quoting with approval the statement 'This must be our motto: All the churches united for the conversion of the whole world' (para. 84).)

This 'inclusivism', according to which non-Christians are included within the sphere of Christian salvation, probably represents the nearest approach to a consensus among Christian thinkers today. It is, however, being criticized by a minority, and I think a growing minority, as the continuation in a milder form of the older theological imperialism. For it still holds that salvation means, exclusively, Christian salvation, hinging upon the atoning death of Christ, although the benefits of that death are now generously extended, in principle, to all human beings.

The alternative being proposed both to the older exclusivism and the newer inclusivism is a pluralism which recognizes the validity of all the great world faiths as authentic contexts of salvation/liberation, not secretly dependent upon the cross of Christ. Those of us who advocate this pluralist option do so because it seems to us to be more religiously realistic than the alternatives. For we see taking place within each of the great traditions, and taking place apparently to more or less the same extent, the salvific transformation of human life, individually and corporately, from destructive self-centredness to a new orientation centred in the divine Reality. It cannot, alas, be claimed that any of the great traditions has been more than very partially successful in this; for each has also been burdened by immense historical evils which have partly cancelled the good that they have done. But viewed as complex, long-lived totalities, each a unique mixture of good and evil, none stands out—as it seems to me—as more salvifically effective than another. So far as human discernment can tell, the great traditions seem to be contexts of salvation/liberation to a more or less equal extent. This is of course a large-scale empirical judgement. I have elsewhere indicated the grounds for it (Hick 1987); but I recognize that it cannot be proved and that it is open to endless discussion. I would only insist here that the onus of proof lies upon one who claims that a particular tradition—doubtless one's own—is demonstrably salvifically superior to the others.

If the rough equality of the great traditions as contexts of salvation/liberation is accepted, it calls for a new direction in the ongoing stream of Christian interpretation and reinterpretation. As our theology develops it needs to encompass the understanding of Christianity as one of a plurality of histories of salvation/ liberation. It is already clear that this can be done in a variety of ways. The basic move is from the traditional Chalcedonian interpretation of Jesus as having two natures, one human and the other divine, to an understanding of him as having a single, wholly human nature, but as so open and responsive to God's transforming presence that we can say, in a natural metaphor, that he embodied or 'incarnated' the meaning of God's reality for human life. This type of interpretation has been variously described as a Spirit Christology (as for example in Geoffrey Lampe's *God as Spirit*, 1977), according to which Jesus was profoundly indwelt, as all human life is in varying degrees indwelt, by the Spirit of God; or again as a paradox-of-grace Christology (as in Donald Baillie's *God Was in Christ*, 1958), according to which Jesus exemplified to a remarkable degree the universal paradox that whilst our good deeds are our own they are also at the same time gifts of God's grace.[1] In more biblical terms, Jesus was the eschatological prophet, proclaiming the imminent coming of God's kingdom; and his disciples accordingly expected him soon to return in glory as God's messiah.[2] These expectations proved to be mistaken; but Jesus' teaching about the reality and love of God, and about how to live already within the sphere of God's rule, are permanently valid and challenging and continue to be at the heart of the Christian life.

This type of interpretation of Jesus does not require the philosophical speculation of an ontological Trinity consisting of three divine persons in the sense of three centres of consciousness and will. The idea of the Trinity can be seen instead as expressing the fact that there are, from our human point of view, a plurality of aspects of the divine nature—a fact that is symbolized in Judaism by the various biblical names of God as King, Shepherd, Father, etc., and in Islam by the ninety-nine Beautiful Names in the Qur'ān. And likewise the idea of God the Father accepting the death of God the Son as an atonement for human sin can be left behind and we can return to Jesus' own teaching in, for example, the parable of the prodigal son and in the words of the Lord's Prayer, of a free divine forgiveness that is available to all who truly and sincerely seek it, the only condition being that we extend the cleansing power of forgiveness to one another.

These are examples of the kind of reinterpretation that seems to me to be called for today within the continuous process of interpretation and reinterpretation in which the history of Christian thought consists.

Let me now return, finally, to the basic thesis that the language of faith is always interpretative or, for those who prefer the term, hermeneutical. Faith arises from experienced events occurring within the human spirit and in our envirioning world. But in being witnessed to, these events are interpreted, and as the original witness is woven into a more comprehensive message it is further interpreted and reinterpreted, with interpretations of interpretations developing in a cumulative process. This process is part of human history. It is an activity of human minds responding to all manner of pulls and pressures—intellectual, psychological, sociological, economic, and political. The outcome, expressed in credal statements, confessions of faith, formal dogmas, encyclical teachings, and so on, is usually regarded within the bodies that produced them as having divine authority. However, these pronouncements are manifestly related to the circumstances of the time and place in which they were created. To take examples from the Christian teaching concerning other religions, the Council of Florence (1438–45) declared that 'no one remaining outside the Catholic Church . . . can become partakers of eternal life . . . unless before the end of life they are joined to the Church' (Denzinger 714); on the other hand the second Vatican Council (1963–5) taught that people who remain outside the Catholic Church can also be saved; and the present pope, in an Encyclical from which I quoted earlier, spoke of all human beings without exception as having been redeemed by Christ, whether they know it or not. It therefore seems clear that either such pronouncements are human products, expressing changing human outlooks rather than eternal divine truths; or they are divinely inspired, and divine inspiration is an ongoing process that adapts itself to the changing needs of human life. If the former, we are free to go on seeking new and more appropriate interpretations of the tradition in our own time. If the latter, we may expect the divine guidance to continue to change; and on this issue, if it continues in the same general direction that led from the exclusivism of the Council of Florence to the inclusivism of Vatican II, we may expect it to proceed towards a pluralism which will thus in due course become officially validated. In other words, the kinds of development explored here should be considered on their own merit and not dismissed simply on the ground that they would represent a change in the church's outlook. For the church's outlook has been undergoing change throughout history; and the further developments now under consideration may prove to be those towards which God is gradually guiding the church today.

NOTES

1. Baillie and Lampe themselves, whilst offering a Christology which does not require a claim to unique maximality for Jesus, both in fact made that claim. The logic of their arguments gives an empirical rather than an a priori status to such a claim. However, they seem to have been unaware of this, and made no attempt to support their claim with historical evidence.
2. For the evidence for this widely accepted view see e.g. Sanders 1985.

REFERENCES

Akers, Charles Edmund (1930), *A History of South America*, 3rd edn., rev. L. E. Elliot, London.

Dunn, John (1980), *Christology in the Making*, London.

Hebblethwaite, Brian (1987), *The Incarnation*, Cambridge.

Hick, John (1987), 'The Non-Absoluteness of Christianity', in John Hick and Paul Knitter (eds.), *The Myth of Christian Uniqueness*, New York.

Morris, James (1968), *Heaven's Command: An Imperial Progress*, London.

Peck, Anne Merriman (1941), *The Pageant of South American History*, New York.

Percy, J. O. (ed.) (1961), *Facing the Unfinished Task*, Grand Rapids, Mich.

Ruether, Rosemary Radford (1974), *Faith and Fratricide*, New York.

Sanders, E. P. (1985), *Jesus and Judaism*, London.

Wei-suhn, Charles, and Spiegler, Gerhard E. (eds.) (1989), *Religious Issues and Interreligious Dialogues*, New York.

5

Chalcedon and the New Testament

MORNA D. HOOKER

When more than 500 bishops gathered together in the Church of
St Euphemia at Chalcedon in October AD 451, a copy of the
scriptures was placed in the centre of the Council as a symbol of
the fact that their deliberations began from scripture, and that they
believed themselves to be expounding scripture. The definition
they eventually produced was an interpretation of the Nicene
Creed, and that in turn was understood to be an exposition of
scripture.

It is, then, a little disconcerting to a New Testament scholar to
find the careful definition of Chalcedon couched in language which
is utterly foreign, not simply to the ideas and language with which
we are familiar today, but also to those we identify as belonging
to the writers of the New Testament: how very different is this
description of Christ's person from what the New Testament
writers have to say about him! We might perhaps have expected
the Fathers of the Church, being closer in time, to have been closer
in understanding. Yet the gap between the approaches of the first
and the fifth centuries appears to be as great as that between those
of the fifth and the twentieth. Nothing could be a clearer demonstration of the way in which scripture is always interpreted in the
language and thought-forms of the age—in this particular case an
age whose ideas are as far removed from those of our own time as
they are from those of our New Testament writers.

The problem in this particular instance, of course, lies in the fact
that the interpretation of the Christian story which was laid down
at Chalcedon became normative for later understanding of the
scriptures. Because of its crucial role in the formation of Christian
doctrine, this particular interpretation (albeit in less complex terms)
became the yardstick for future understanding of the person of
Christ. Whereas the interpretations which emerged in other periods
can be laid aside and abandoned, as belonging to the *Zeitgeist* which

helped to create them, the Chalcedonian definition became part of the given, with the result that generations of Christians have read the New Testament through Chalcedonian spectacles, unaware of the fact that they were imposing not simply the interpretations of their own age on to a first-century text, but those of the fifth century also.

Now whether the Chalcedonian definition was a proper interpretation of the New Testament for the fifth century is an interesting hermeneutical question which I must leave to others better qualified to answer; so, too, with the question as to whether or not it is a necessary starting-point for Christian understanding of the person of Christ today—a question which has been much debated recently, not least by Maurice Wiles, to whom this essay is offered in grateful acknowledgement of his work, support and friendship over many years. The question which concerns me here is the extent to which the influence of Chalcedon is still a positive hindrance to our understanding of what the New Testament authors were trying to say about Jesus in their own very different time and circumstances. The Fathers of the Church held that the Son, being 'of one substance with the Father . . . became incarnate'. This may have been a natural way for them to interpret the Fourth Gospel in their own time, but it was not, as we shall see, what the fourth evangelist himself said.

Students of the New Testament interpret its evidence in very different ways, as became evident during the debate which followed *The Myth of God Incarnate*. But while there is disagreement as to whether or not 'incarnation' is an appropriate word to use at any point in describing New Testament christology, there is widespread agreement that none of its authors speaks explicitly about Jesus as *God* incarnate. Indeed, many would go so far as to say that nowhere in the New Testament is Jesus actually referred to as 'God': the few passages which might be interpreted in this way are in fact all ambiguous. The idea of 'incarnation' is used explicitly only in John 1: 14, and even that refers to the Logos, rather than to God. Moreover, that passage has to be balanced by statements in some of our other New Testament books which sound suspiciously like what we today would term 'adoptionism'. As for the notion of pre-existence, one well-known New Testament scholar has attempted to explain away almost all the passages where this is generally assumed to be implied (Dunn 1980). Clearly we need to look at the evidence a little more closely.

Let us begin with our earliest writer, Paul. One of the obvious starting-points here is what may loosely be described as 'incarnational formulae': Galatians 4: 4, 'When the time had fully come, God sent forth his Son, born of woman, born under the law', and 2 Corinthians 8: 9, 'You know the grace of our Lord Jesus Christ, that though he was rich, yet for your sake he became poor.' The first passage explicitly refers to Jesus' birth (*contra* Dunn 1980: 40–2), and the second is also most reasonably understood in the same way. Attempts to explain it away by referring it to Jesus' decision to leave his home in Nazareth are frankly absurd: Jesus was no Francis of Assisi, giving up a life of luxury for an itinerant life, but a humble Galilean carpenter. It is true, of course, that the prophets were also thought of as having been 'sent' by God—but these two passages suggest that we are dealing here with the kind of idea which the creeds expressed in the phrase 'and became man'. But what is the point that Paul is wishing to emphasize? It is Christ's oneness with humanity, and in particular with the fact that he shared in the limitations and deprivations to which humanity itself has been subjected: he was born under the law; he became poor. We can find similar ideas elsewhere. Thus Romans 8: 3 tells us that God sent 'his own Son in the likeness of sinful flesh'; Philippians 2: 7–8 describes the way in which one who was in the form of God took 'the form of a slave, being born in the likeness of men; and being found in human form he humbled himself and became obedient unto death, even death on a cross'—the cross being the manner of death appropriate for a slave.

The fact that Christ became identified with humanity at his birth suggests first that he himself stands apart from fallen humanity, and secondly that he is also pre-existent. But we must not assume that the former statement necessarily implies that Paul is thinking of him as 'God'. As for the second, though Christ is clearly pre-existent, that does not, at this stage, lead to speculation or discussion by Paul about what the pre-existent Christ was or did; rather, it is a way of stressing that what the earthly Jesus did was part of God's eternal plan and purpose.

In order to understand more clearly what Paul is saying in these two passages in Galatians and 2 Corinthians, we need to remember that so far we have quoted only half of them. Thus Galatians 4: 4 continues, 'in order to redeem those under the law, in order that we might receive adoption as sons', while 2 Corinthians 8: 9

concludes, 'in order that by his poverty you might become rich'. For want of a better term, I have sometimes termed these passages 'formulae of interchange' (Hooker 1971; reprinted with other essays on the same theme in Hooker 1990), since what they say is reminiscent of Irenaeus' terse saying: 'he became what we are, in order that we might become what he is' (Irenaeus: *Adv. haer.* 5 *praef.*). We become rich—as he was rich; we become children of God—as he was Son of God; we are redeemed from the Law—as he was free from the Law. If we examine the context of Romans 8: 3 we discover that there, too, the result of God sending his Son in the likeness of sinful flesh is that we become children of God; and following on from Philippians 2 we discover in Philippians 3: 20–1 that we are to be conformed to the glorious body of the exalted Lord—the one who was, we have been told, in the form of God. If we now broaden the enquiry a little, we discover other texts—Galatians 3: 13 and 2 Corinthians 5: 21—which speak of Christ sharing in our human condition (becoming a curse, and being made sin) in order that we might share in his, though of course these two passages are generally held to refer to what we would label 'the atonement' rather than 'the incarnation'.

It is clear that what we become through Christ is what, in the purpose of God, we are meant to be—truly human; men and women are recreated in God's image, they are children of God, enjoying the liberty and privileges of God's children, and reflecting his glory. It is no accident that the language Paul uses when describing the redemptive activity of Christ refers to him in language which is appropriate to one who is truly what Man is meant to be: he is the Son of God—and as Son, obedient to God; he is the Man from heaven—standing in contrast to Adam, the man from earth; he is the image of God, and is in the form of God—as Adam was before the fall; and like Adam in the Garden of Eden, he reflects the glory of God; even the authority Christ exercises reminds us of Adam, for the first man was commanded to have dominion over the earth and its creatures. To use the language of Colossians, Christ is the first-born of creation, as well as the first-born from the dead, and therefore pre-eminent both in the universe and in the church.

Now I suspect that Paul took it for granted that Christ was pre-existent, though until we get to Colossians (which may or may not have been written by Paul himself) there is little sign of any interest in what he did in his pre-existence. Christ represents God's purpose for mankind, and he is certainly no afterthought or addition to the plan: he must therefore have been from the beginning. But pre-existence does not necessarily imply divinity. I believe that it was in fact in thinking out Christ's relationship with the Law that the idea of pre-existence became important (cf. Caird 1968). It is suggestive that the first indication of Christ's pre-existence (1 Cor. 8: 6) speaks of him as the one through whom creation exists—a role attributed in Jewish thought to the Law (*Midr. Rab. Gen.* 1. 1). It would take us too far afield to explore Paul's teaching on the Law in any detail: suffice it to say that in Paul's understanding of the relationship between God and his people there is a sense in which Christ replaces the Law; or rather, since Paul insists that his teaching *establishes* the Law, the Law is discovered to be a temporary dispensation which points forward to the finality which is revealed in Christ. Compared with Christ, the Law is a kind of rough first draft—an inadequate metaphor, since it suggests that God found it necessary to have several attempts before producing the perfect version. And this, of course, is precisely where the idea of pre-existence comes in, for in Jewish thinking the Law was pre-existent—inevitably, because it expressed God's will for his people. If Christ has taken over from the Law, and is found to represent God's will for his people even more profoundly than the Law, then of course he must be pre-existent also; the Law is not so much a first draft as a somewhat blurred xerox copy, whereas Christ is the perfect image. Christ is thus greater than the Law: he embodies God's will for his people more completely than the Law; moreover, what the Law could not do God has now done, working through Christ—namely, recreated mankind in the image and likeness of God.

In the various passages we have considered so far, Paul speaks sometimes of God sending his Son, and sometimes of Christ taking or becoming subject to human limitation. In the same way, when he writes of Christ's death, he refers sometimes to God giving up his Son for our sake, sometimes to Christ giving himself up. The essence of Sonship is that the Son is obedient to his Father's will, so that in speaking of God's purpose it makes little difference whether one refers to God sending or giving up his Son, or whether one attributes the action to Christ himself. Close examination of Paul's references to Christ as 'Son' suggests to me that he used this particular term (whether consciously or unconsciously) in speaking about God's saving activity in Christ in order to under-line the fact that God's purpose of salvation is brought about through one who (being Son) acts in accordance with and in obedience to that purpose (Hooker 1979: 55–68). The term 'Son' thus reminds us that, in all he does, Christ acts in obedience to God.

But this means, of course, that everything that happens through Christ is the activity of God himself. To use Paul's classic phrase: 'God was in Christ, reconciling the world to himself.' Thus when the disobedience of the one man Adam is weighed against the obedience of the one man Christ in Romans 5, the scales come down heavily on the side of Christ, who is a better man than Adam, precisely because the grace of God is at work through him. Because Christ is Son of God, truly obedient to God's will, the power of God is channelled through him. He stands over against the rest of humanity, even though he is one with them. Moreover, the same set of terms serves at one and the same time to identify him both as one with God and as one with mankind. We have already listed the language which Paul uses in speaking of Christ as the true Adam: he is Son of God; in the form of God; the image of God; Lord. This is language which *we* consider more appropriate for expressing what we would term Christ's 'divinity'. For Paul, these terms express the fact that Christ is one with God, precisely because they express his obedience as man. But because he speaks in terms of activity, rather than in terms of being, he thinks of Christ as one with God in purpose and will, rather than in nature.

The language which Paul used in speaking about Christ is thus language which is appropriate primarily to the proper relationship of men and women to God. Christ is the epitome of what humanity was meant to be: he is in the image of God (as was Adam), the Son of God who is obedient to God, and who, under God, by right enjoys the world's resources and exercises lordship over creation. This is what Christ was, before what we call his incarnation, and it is what he continues to be. But, equally important, it is what he enables men and women to become: for they, too, become 'sons of God' (Gal. 4: 5).[1] Christians share Christ's status before God—his righteousness (2 Cor. 5: 21), blessing (Gal. 3: 14), riches (2 Cor. 8: 9), and glory (Phil. 2: 9–10, 3: 21). They do not, of course, become his equals: the relationship is a dependent one, for what they receive is always due to the fact that they are in him. Christ continues to stand apart from men and women, even while enabling them to share in what he is. Nevertheless, the terms and statements which later theologians regarded as pointers to Christ's 'divinity' are for Paul the very terms and statements which describe the true humanity which becomes a possibility for those who are redeemed by Christ.

Thus it would seem that statements which appear at first sight to be 'incarnational formulae' are not, strictly speaking, 'incarnational' at all. Rather, for Paul, they refer to the conviction that by sharing our fallen humanity (i.e. life in Adam) Christ enabled men and women to become what he is: but Paul does not, as did Athanasius, understand that as meaning that they become divine (*De Inc.* 54). Paul's use of the pattern of 'interchange' suggests that he understands Christ's willing identification with our fallen humanity to be balanced by our resultant identification with his true humanity. If we use the term 'incarnation' of the statement that 'he became what we are', then what word are we to use of the balancing statement that we in turn become what he is? It is better to speak of 'Second Adam' christology: a new creation has taken place, and humanity has been redeemed through one who is (in Luther's phrase) 'proper Man'.

The closest any of our New Testament writers come to speaking of Jesus as the incarnate God is of course the famous statement in John 1: 14. In fact this passage speaks of the *Word* of God becoming flesh, not of God himself becoming flesh; it could of course be argued that since in 1: 1 we are told that the Word was God, there is little difference between the idea of 'God incarnate' and 'the Word of God incarnate', but that, I think, would be to misunderstand what John is attempting to say.

The Johannine Prologue is, I believe, wrongly interpreted if it is taken in isolation from the rest of the Gospel. It is a true 'prologue'—it serves to introduce the theme of the gospel and to explain it; without it, we will make little sense of the rest of the gospel, for it provides the clues which help us to make sense of everything which follows (Hooker 1974). Much of the gospel is made up of a series of signs, the meaning of which is spelt out in discourses: signs and discourses together demonstrate the extraordinary authority of Jesus in both actions and words, which amount, in effect, to a claim to be the fulfilment of Judaism.

Everything said in the past about the Law is now claimed by Jesus to be true of himself; everything achieved in the past in Jewish worship is now achieved by him. He is the total fulfilment of God's self-revelation in the past; and since the partial is no longer needed, he is also its replacement.

Interlaced with these signs and discourses we have a number of disputes between Jesus and the Jews, who are resisting the truth of the revelation. In these disputes we in fact overhear debates which were going on between Jews and Christians in the synagogues at the time when John was writing (5: 16–47; 6: 41–65; 7: 14–52; 8: 12–59; 9: 35–41; 10: 19–39). The Christian claims about Jesus are rejected by the Jews, who cling to the revelation of God in the past in the Law; the Christian retort is that if only the Jews understood Moses, they would realize that he pointed forward to Christ (5: 39–47; 9: 28–9). The issue in dispute is thus whether Jesus was an imposter or whether he came from God; again and again it is put in terms of Jesus' origin: where does he come from? The Christian claim is that he comes from above—i.e. from God.

The Prologue provides the justification for these claims about Jesus. The Word of God, active in the past in creation, in history, in the prophets, was believed by Jews to have been embodied in the Law given to Moses on Mount Sinai. Christians are now claiming that a fuller, more complete embodiment of God's Word, or Logos, has taken place in Jesus Christ. But it is the same God who speaks at creation, on Sinai, and through the prophets who now speaks in his Son: his Word is constant; his self-revelation is of a piece; he has not changed his mind. In speaking of this Word, the fourth evangelist naturally uses language which reminds us that in Hebrew thought a word once spoken had a dynamic life of its own. The Logos is referred to as though a separate being, over against God; but in a similar way, Jewish writers had already spoken of Wisdom as God's master-workman, helping in the work of creation, dwelling among God's people, speaking through the prophets (Prov. 8: 22–31; Wisd. 7: 22–10: 21; Sir. 24); Wisdom had been identified with the Law (Sir. 24: 23), which was described also as God's Word (Ps. 119; *De Migr.* 130). If Christ is to be slotted into this understanding of God's dealings with his people, it is hardly surprising if the evangelist speaks of him in these terms: God has spoken again; he has revealed himself once more. The Word which was with God at the beginning, through which all things came into being, by which light and life were created, has now come among us in the flesh. The glory of God, glimpsed on Sinai, but never seen by any human being, has now been fully disclosed in the person of God's Son, who is the full embodiment of all God's grace and truth.

Reading the rest of John's story, after reading the Prologue, we are able to appreciate the claims which the evangelist makes on Jesus' behalf. Since God speaks in him, his words are the words of God; his deeds, also, are the deeds of God (10: 37–8). He comes from above (8: 23). He is 'from God' (9: 33). He is one with the Father (10: 30).

Ought we, then, to speak of John's understanding of Jesus in terms of a doctrine of 'God incarnate'? After all, he declares in 1: 1 that 'the Word was God'; in 1: 18 he speaks of Jesus, according to what may well be the correct reading, as *monogenēs theos*. Moreover, at the end of the gospel he has Thomas confess Jesus as 'my Lord and my God'. Is this not what we understand as 'incarnation'?

I think not. I suspect that it is misleading to use that term because it disguises the very different frames of reference within which our evangelist, on the one hand, and the Fathers of the Church, on the other, were working. It is worth noting how, in each of these three instances, John also makes it quite clear that the Word, or Jesus, stands over against God. Thus in 1: 1 the declaration that the Word was God is sandwiched in between two statements that 'The Word was *with* God.' Whether or not 1: 18 does in fact describe Jesus as 'only God' (rather than as 'only Son'), this comment follows a declaration that 'No one has ever seen God.' And though in 20: 28 the risen Jesus is acknowledged by Thomas as 'my Lord and my God', Jesus himself, a few verses earlier, declares that he is ascending 'to my Father and your Father, to my God and your God'. Similarly, in the rest of the Gospel, though we find Jesus proclaiming 'Before Abraham was, I am' (8: 58), he also declares 'My Father is greater than I' (14: 28). The relationship between Father and Son is one of dependence on the Son's part: 'the Son can do nothing of his own accord, but only what he sees the Father doing' (5: 19); 'My teaching is not mine, but his who sent me' (7: 16). Though the term 'Son' is much more common in the Fourth Gospel than in Paul, its function is similar. This understanding of Jesus is greatly illuminated by study of the Jewish understanding of the agent who has been commissioned to work on behalf of someone else and as his representative: the claims made on behalf of Jesus can be explained, at least in part, when we see that he is presented as God's agent in the world, who acts in total accord with his will (see Borgen 1968; Bühner 1977: 181–267; Ashton 1991: 308–29).

The context in which a passage is read determines its meaning. To Christians of a later generation, it is natural to interpret John 20: 28 as a declaration of Jesus' 'divinity'. Yet commentators often point out that this passage is a confessional statement, not a dogmatic formula, and thus has to be treated with caution. It is also illuminating to consider alongside it a passage in John 10, where Jesus' claim in verse 30, 'I and the Father are one' (a claim to unity in will and activity, not in essence), is followed by Jewish protest at his 'blasphemy', which leads Jesus to respond by quoting and expounding Psalm 82: 6: 'I said, you are gods.' The argument here seems to depend on a tradition that the words were addressed to the Jewish people after the giving of the Law on Sinai.[2] If so, the reasoning is clear: if those to whom the Word of God comes are addressed as 'gods', how much more appropriate is it to think of the one who embodies the Word (and who thus does the works of his Father) in these terms. It is hardly surprising, then, if Thomas's acknowledgement of Jesus as his Lord and God forms the climax to the Gospel in 20: 28. But the evangelist's line of reasoning in chapter 10 reminds us that the debate underlying Thomas's confession was very different indeed from that about the divine and human natures of Christ which occupied the Fathers of the Church.

What John is trying to express is the notion of revelation. God has revealed himself in the past in various ways; now, supremely, he has revealed himself in the Son. No one has ever seen God, but the Son has 'exegeted him' (1: 18). He has revealed his glory: a statement which is equally true, however you explain the 'he' and the 'his'; above all, God has been glorified through the Cross—in other words, his true nature has been revealed there. The Revealer God is encountered in his revelation, and when one encounters the revelation, one encounters God. But it is surely more accurate to speak (as John himself does) of the incarnate Word, rather than of the incarnate God.

In many ways, the issues with which the fourth evangelist is concerned are those which occupy Paul: both are concerned to show how the self-revelation of God in Christ relates to his self-revelation in the past. Both are concerned to show how Jesus brings life and salvation to men and women. But Paul's notion of 'interchange' finds no echo in John: to be sure, through the coming of Christ, men and women are enabled to become 'children' of God (1: 12); but is the choice of the word *tekna* here perhaps a deliberate differentiation from the *huios* who is *monogenēs*? Certainly the giving and sending formulae in John 3 are expressed very differently from those in Paul: God gave his Son in order that believers might have eternal life, and sent him into the world in order to save the world. The end result is the same—salvation and life—but the way in which it is expressed is quite different. The Word may have 'become flesh', but the emphasis is on the Son's oneness with God rather than with men and women; as for those to whom he came, the Johannine vocabulary and imagery stress their dependence *on* him, rather than their unity *with* him: they see, believe, and live.[3]

John's portrait of Jesus is of course in many ways very different from those we find in the other gospels. Though we can certainly find interesting parallels in the Synoptics to some of the Johannine sayings, their significance for understanding the person of Jesus has not been explored by the other three evangelists. There is nothing in the Synoptics remotely parallel to the explicit Johannine presentation of 'the Word made flesh'. Whereas, in John, Jesus proclaims himself, in the other Gospels, he proclaims the Kingdom of God. In spite of recent attempts to rehabilitate John, on this point at least the Synoptics are more historically reliable. What is interesting about this, however, is that though in the Synoptics Jesus teaches about God and his Kingdom, and has very little to say about himself (and even that is in the form of enigmatic statements about the Son of man!), the way in which the evangelists tell their stories means that our attention is focused on Jesus throughout. The all-important question which arises is: who is this? We find Jesus forgiving sins, walking on water, stilling storms, providing bread, raising the dead. But only God is able to do these things! No wonder the common reaction of the crowds is one of fear. Men and women are confronted with the power of God in the person of Jesus; the synoptic evangelists explain this, not in terms of 'incarnation', but by speaking of the Spirit of God at work in Jesus. But all of them make it clear that this is a unique

experience. For though he calls men and women to follow him in
the way of discipleship, he himself stands over against them: in the
saying which is closer than any other to the Johannine teaching,
we are reminded that 'Everything is entrusted to me by my Father;
and no one knows the Son except the Father, and no one knows
the Father except the Son and those to whom the Son chooses to
reveal him' (Matt. 11: 27/Luke 10: 22). Jesus is acknowledged by
God himself as his only Son, and acts with an authority far greater
than that of Moses. Once again, all-important questions about how
Jesus fits into the divine purpose for Israel lie in the background:
he is God's last word to his people.

And what of Hebrews—frequently said to set out Christ's
'divinity' in the first two chapters, followed by his 'humanity'?
Hebrews begins with a remarkable passage which has interesting
parallels with the Johannine Prologue: God has spoken in past ages
to our fathers through the prophets (including Moses), but now he
has *spoken* through a Son. This Son reflects the glory of God and
bears the very stamp of his nature; through him he created the
world. The language once again echoes that which is used in the
wisdom literature both of Wisdom and of the Law; Jesus has
replaced the Law as the figure who embodies the plan of God. It
may well reflect also Jewish speculation about an angelic figure
who, though not God, is enthroned in heaven and shares God's
glory and even his name; interestingly, this speculation seems to
tie up with the kind of thing which is said about the figure like a
son of man in Daniel 7 and the Son of man in 1 Enoch—a figure
who represents mankind. We are somewhat surprised to find this
kind of speculation in Judaism, so passionately monotheistic, but
however exalted these various angelic figures may be, the power
and authority which they exercise are derived from God himself.
Perhaps, then, such speculation may help us to understand how
Jewish monotheists came to make this kind of exalted statement
about Christ (Segal 1977: 182–219; Rowland 1982: 94–113).

Hebrews continues by showing the superiority of Christ, first to
angels, then to Moses. We are inclined to be more impressed by
the former than the latter. Christ is superior to angels—an assertion
which is backed up by a catena of passages from the psalms: no
angel was ever addressed by God as Son; on the contrary, the
angels were commanded to worship him; the Son shares in the rule
of God and in the work of God in creation; he is eternal, and sits

at God's right hand. The final proof-text is introduced with the statement that the world was not subjected to angels; to whom, then, was it subjected? Psalm 8 says that it was to man, and to the son of man. So the climax of the author's argument is that Jesus is crowned with glory as man and as son of man! We are then told that through Jesus and his sufferings God has brought many sons to glory; Jesus is the pioneer of their salvation; he and they have one origin, and he therefore acknowledges them as brethren. This is why he shared their nature of flesh and blood and shared their death. Here is something remarkably close to Paul's notion of interchange. As in Paul, we have the idea of Christ as one who deliberately shares human nature and human suffering and who thereby is able to bring many sons to glory—that is, enables them to share in his glory and sonship. And as in Paul, we find that the exalted terms which suggest to us what we would call 'divinity' are linked by the author with Christ's humanity and with the conviction that God's eternal purpose is achieved through him: the one who reflects God's glory and bears the stamp of his nature is in fact the Son who is obedient to his Father's will, and the glory and sonship which he bestows on others are his by right because he is 'son of man'.

Next comes the comparison with Moses: both Moses and Jesus were faithful, but Moses was a servant, whereas Jesus is a son. This comparison is in fact just as important for our author as that with the angels, since Moses represents the Law, and we thus see how the revelation of the past stands in comparison with the revelation in Christ. Moreover, Moses set out the various sacrifices which were to be offered up in Israel—sacrifices which have now been rendered obsolete by the once-for-all self-offering of the heavenly high-priest. Like Paul and John (and to a lesser extent the synoptic evangelists), the author of Hebrews is concerned to relate Christ to God's self-revelation in the past, both in creation and in his dealings with Israel.

Paul, the fourth evangelist, and the author to the Hebrews all declare that God's self-revelation in Christ is final and complete: there is nothing to be known of God which is not known in him. In the language of Colossians, 'in him all the fullness of God was pleased to dwell'. All our writers are concerned to relate this self-revelation to what had gone before. All of them are faithful to their Jewish heritage: God has been active in creation, in the salvation of his people, in the giving of the Law, in prophecy, and now in Christ. Each of them uses the language of pre-existence, because it is inevitable in talking about Christ as the one who fully expresses God's will, and who represents God's purpose for mankind. And each of them sees Christ as the prototype of a new humanity: Jesus is the Son of God, but he brings many sons to glory; through him, men and women become children of God.

This brief survey of some of the more significant christological statements in the New Testament will perhaps explain why I feel that there is a great gulf between the thought-world in which they were fashioned and that which gave rise to the Chalcedonian definition. Though it is easy to see how the sayings of the Fourth Gospel came to be interpreted in terms of 'incarnation', none of our writers was in fact describing 'how God became man'. Moreover, those passages in the Pauline epistles and in Hebrews which seem to us like references to 'incarnation' are in fact concerned primarily to express the purpose of God for humanity, now fulfilled in Christ. Let me sum up by suggesting three reasons why the language of Chalcedon is so different from that of the New Testament.

First of all, Chalcedon was primarily intended as a bastion against heresy. Definition was necessary in order to make quite clear which heretical views were being excluded. In the days of the New Testament, on the other hand, Christianity was itself the heresy. This is something which is frequently forgotten by exegetes, who tend to read back later situations into the New Testament and suppose that our writers were defending the true Christian gospel against this or that heresy. But for most of the time they were not; they were propagating a message which was itself heretical, and were still in the process of working out its significance. The orthodoxy was Judaism; the Christian sect was trying to work out its position *vis-à-vis* the parent body and to reconcile faith in Jesus as God's Messiah with the conviction that God was indeed the God who had revealed himself to his people in the past. What our writers say about Christ has to be seen in this context.[4] By the time of the Chalcedonian Council, the statements which had once been heresy had become orthodoxy, and were therefore handled in a completely different way.

Secondly, our New Testament writers were primarily concerned to describe the activity of God: he had acted, he had redeemed his people. They used a great variety of imagery—anything and everything available to them—in order to describe this activity; it was natural to them to employ narrative and metaphor. Their concern was not to offer definitions of the being of God or the being of Christ. The nature of God is known by what he does: many of the most important New Testament christological passages are hymns extolling God for what he has done through Christ. This is what is meant by describing New Testament christology as 'functional' rather than as 'ontological'; it seems to me to be a valid distinction. Nor is this simply an aberration on the part of our New Testament writers: it is part of the biblical tradition. Nowhere in the Old Testament does one find God being spoken of in terms of pure being: even in Deutero-Isaiah, where the description of God is at its most majestic, God is still celebrated as the one who acts. He is the God who reveals himself to his people and acts on their behalf, 'the God of Abraham, Isaac and Jacob', the 'Lord your God, who brought you out of the land of Egypt' (Exod. 3: 6; 20: 2). But by the time of Chalcedon things had changed radically; after four centuries in which Christians had grown accustomed to the idea of a divine Father and a divine Son and were used to speaking of them as peers, the Fathers of the Church approached the questions of christology in a very different way (see Wiles 1960: 112–47; Wiles 1967: 73–93). What had been for our New Testament authors helpful images used to describe their experience of God have now become doctrines which themselves need to be defined and analysed.

Thirdly, leading on from there, our New Testament authors write from within a Jewish context and not a Greek philosophical one. One hesitates these days to make contrasts between Greek and Hebrew language, but in spite of the pitfalls involved in easy contrasts it is still true to say that there are differences in outlook. Paul, for example, could never have spoken of Christ as 'consisting of a reasonable soul and a body'. He speaks of man as *sōma psuchikon*, and the contrasts he uses are not between God and man, but between spirit and flesh. The debate at Chalcedon makes no sense to those accustomed to think in Jewish terms. Most important of all, the issues were quite different: our New Testament authors were wrestling with the question: 'How do our new beliefs about Christ relate to what we have always believed about God— about the creation of the universe, his election of Israel, and his promises to his people?' Their concern was to show that it was the same God who had been at work in the past who was now at work in Christ, and that his new work in Christ was the fulfilment of everything that had gone before: hence the importance of showing his superiority to Moses.

The idea of an incarnate God is, we suggest, foreign to Jewish thinking. Remember the prayer of Solomon: 'Will God indeed dwell on the earth? Behold, heaven and the highest heaven cannot contain thee' (1 Kgs. 8: 27). To be sure, the Shekinah dwelt on earth, but the Shekinah was a particular manifestation of God's universal presence, and like other manifestations (angels, wisdom, the Spirit, the Word) was a way of speaking of God's self-revelation (Rowland 1982: 80). Again, individuals were accorded divine honours: Moses, in particular, was said by Philo, elaborating Exodus 7: 1, to have been given the name of god and king (e.g. *Mos.* 1. 158; *De som.* 2. 189). Ezekiel the Tragedian relates a dream of Moses, in which he is enthroned by God on his own throne and given the emblems of rule—symbols of his future authority over men (68–89); the passage is reminiscent of that in 1 Enoch 45, where it is said that the Elect One (i.e. the Son of man) will sit on God's throne of glory. In these passages and others,[5] men share in divine honour because they are given divine authority, but this does not mean that they are themselves 'divine' beings: rather their authority and honour are manifestations of the fact that God is revealing his power and purpose through them.[6]

In his essay 'Does Christology Rest on a Mistake?' Maurice Wiles argued that the doctrine of incarnation arose within the Jewish framework of belief in creation–fall–redemption, and that it 'has been from its earliest origins . . . closely interwoven with the doctrines of creation and of the fall' (Wiles 1970: 70). The mistake, he suggests, was to tie each of these doctrines to a particular event, and since many Christians have long since recognized that there is no need to link creation to a specific creative action of God, or to take the story of the fall literally, they should be ready to accept that the redemptive act of Christ must be understood in a similar way: if creation and fall are no longer seen in temporal terms, what of redemption and restoration? Whether or not Professor Wiles is right in suggesting that if we demythologize what is said about Adam we must also demythologize what our New Testament writers say about Christ is an interesting question.

We should perhaps remember that the mythological ideas used by our writers were the appropriate ones for them to use, but that they were simply that—appropriate: while it was inevitable that the first Christians hammered out their new faith in these terms, this mythological language was not necessarily capable of conveying everything that had to be expressed, and it may be that at this point the Jewish eschatological framework is inadequate—as inadequate as the metaphysical language of Chalcedon! Perhaps it is significant also that Paul, at least, appears at times to 'demythologize' Adam (Hooker 1960) and in so far as restoration remains an eschatological expectation rather than an accomplished fact, there is a sense in which the work of Christ is not in fact tied to a specific point in history, but remains a possibility.

Be that as it may, it is significant that in discussing the early stages of Christian belief Professor Wiles finds it necessary to speak in terms of 'redemption' rather than of 'incarnation', for our brief survey of the evidence has indicated that 'redemption' is the more appropriate term within the Jewish complex of ideas. In keeping with traditional Jewish expectation, our New Testament writers thought in terms of the restoration not simply of humanity, but of the entire universe, and it was this that they claimed had been initiated in Christ. Equally significant was the fact that it was assumed that God's purpose for the universe would be achieved through his people Israel, and that redemption therefore centred on her: the first significant affirmation about Jesus was that he was the Messiah, and Moses is almost as important a figure in the schema as Adam. Though the belief that God acted in and through Christ belongs within this framework, and Professor Wiles is right to say that 'the doctrine of the incarnation arose in the closest conjunction with' the doctrines of the creation and the fall (Wiles 1970: 72), this doctrine was not yet, in New Testament times, what we would now recognize as one of 'incarnation', for the simple reason that our writers were not thinking in metaphysical terms. As he himself argues elsewhere, the idea of incarnation is anachronistic in the New Testament setting, and developed when New Testament writings were interpreted in a non-Jewish environment (Wiles 1974: ch. 3; see also Young 1977).[7] In other words, the earliest Christians used language which led others to speak of 'incarnation', rather than thinking in terms of incarnation themselves. The really significant development took place when the mythical was translated into the metaphysical, and what our New Testament writers spoke of in terms of 'redemption' was interpreted in terms of 'incarnation'. To impose precise metaphysical definitions on to a mythical framework may well be regarded as a mistake, for the focus is now on the pre-existence, incarnation, exaltation, and *parousia* of Christ, rather than on creation–fall–redemption, and concern is now with the salvation of individual souls, rather than with the redemption of the universe. But from the point of view of a student of the New Testament, the most serious mistake of all is the way in which this later resolution of the gospel story has been read back into our New Testament texts.

One of the false assumptions that has often confused the debate is the belief that the kind of interpretation of the New Testament evidence which we have been giving is of a 'low' christology, in contrast to the 'high' christology which focuses on incarnation. But it would be quite wrong to suppose that what we have discovered in the New Testament is a 'low' christology. Our New Testament writers are convinced that God acts through Christ, that he speaks through him, and that he reveals himself in him. They use terms which are dynamic rather than metaphysical, but in their own way they express the conviction that in Christ they have 'seen' God. To insist that the New Testament should be read in its own terms is in no sense to advocate a 'reductionist' christology. It is not a question of 'high' and 'low', but rather of *different* christologies, worked out in totally different thought-worlds in answer to different problems: to judge one in terms of the other and to find it wanting is to misunderstand what is taking place.

Whether or not Chalcedon was a proper development from what is said about Christ in the New Testament is, as I said earlier, another question. I suspect that—given the philosophical climate—it was an inevitable development. In that sense, the claim symbolized by placing the scriptures in the centre of the Council was justified: though there was disagreement at Chalcedon, the debate reflected the only kind of way in which the texts could be approached at that time. But the Chalcedonian definition is not a direct 'translation' of what is being said in the New Testament into another set of terms, for the questions its authors addressed were totally different from those which exercised the authors of the New Testament. When it comes to interpreting what the latter were trying to say, we must always remember to take off spectacles which have in any way been tinted with Chalcedonian beliefs. If we want to do justice to the ways in which the first Christians were trying to express their faith we must not suppose that when they speak of Jesus as 'Son of God' they meant the second person of the Trinity, or thought of him as being 'of one substance with the Father'; they were aware only that in Jesus of Nazareth God had spoken to them in a way which led them ever more confidently to identify the revealer with the revealed.

NOTES

1. The 'sexist' language jars on us, but it is necessary to retain it in order to stress the fact that Christians share Christ's relationship to God. For Paul, of course, the term 'sons' was not intended to be exclusive; indeed, he stresses the fact that it is inclusive—women are included on equal terms with men as heirs of the inheritance offered in Christ; see especially Gal. 3: 28.

2. *B. Abod. Z.* 5a; *Midr. Rab. Ex.* 32. 1, 7; *Lev.* 4. 1; 11. 3; *Num.* 7. 4; 16. 24; *Deut.* 7. 12; *Song* 1. 2. 5; *Eccl.* 3. 16. 1. See Ackerman 1966: 186–8. Another rabbinic tradition understood the words to have been addressed to the judges of Israel appointed by Moses (Deut. 1: 15–18). J. A. Emerton (1960) argues that the 'gods' in John 10: 34 are to be understood as evil angels, as in the Peshitta, an interpretation since reinforced by the discovery of 11Q Melch., where the first *'elohîm* in Ps. 82 is interpreted of Melchizedek (de Jonge and van der Woude 1966), and the second of evil angels. Though he is probably right in arguing that this interpretation is closer to the *original* meaning of the psalm, it seems less appropriate to the Johannine context. The reference to 'the Law' and the description of those who are addressed as those 'to whom the Word of God came' point us to Sinai.

3. e.g. the Johannine images of bread and water. Cf. John's use of the 'vine' whose branches are totally dependent on the tree in ch. 15 with Paul's image of the body, in which the limbs co-operate in the body's functioning. It is worth noting, too, that in the Synoptics Jesus and his disciples walk together 'on the way', but in John Jesus *is* the way.

4. In his recent book, John Ashton (1991) argues that it is possible in the Fourth Gospel to trace the way in which beliefs about the person of Christ were developed by one particular community as it thought out its faith in the context of Jewish opposition.

5. There is an interesting example at Isa. 9: 6, where the future king is addressed as *'el*.

6. It is sometimes suggested that these figures were in fact regarded as 'divine', but this goes far beyond the evidence; these figures were thought to exercise divine authority and to share divine honour because they had been appointed by God as his representatives.
7. G. N. Stanton (1979) speaks of 'incipiently incarnational christology' (p. 163), but admits that 'there may be more appropriate ways of expressing the convictions of the New Testament writers' than the statement 'Jesus is God incarnate' (p. 171).

REFERENCES

Ackerman, J. S. (1966), 'The Rabbinic Interpretation of Psalm 82 and the Gospel of John', *Harvard Theological Review*, 59: 186–91.

Ashton, J. (1991), *Understanding the Fourth Gospel*, Oxford.

Borgen, P. (1968), 'God's Agent in the Fourth Gospel', in J. Neusner (ed.), *Religions in Antiquity*, Leiden: 137–48, repr. in J. Ashton (ed.), *The Interpretation of John*, London, 1986: 67–78, and P. Borgen, *Logos was the True Light*, Trondheim, 1983: 121–32.

Bühner, J.-A. (1977), *Der Gesandte und sein Weg im vierten Evangelium*, Wissenschaftliche Untersuchungen zum Neuen Testament 2.2, Tübingen.

Caird, G. B. (1968), 'The Development of the Doctrine of Christ in the New Testament', in N. Pittenger (ed.), *Christ for Us Today*, London: 66–80.

De Jonge, M., and van der Woude, A. S. (1966), '11Q Melchizedek and the New Testament', *New Testament Studies*, 12: 301–26.

Dunn, J. D. G. (1980), *Christology in the Making*, London.

Emerton, J. A. (1960), 'The Interpretation of Psalm 82 in John 10', *Journal of Theological Studies*, NS 11: 329–32.

Hooker, M. D. (1960), 'Adam in Romans I', *New Testament Studies*, 6: 297–306: repr. Hooker 1990.

—— (1971), 'Interchange in Christ', *Journal of Theological Studies*, NS 22: 349–61: repr. Hooker 1990.

—— (1974), 'The Johannine Prologue and the Messianic Secret', *New Testament Studies*, 21: 40–58.

—— (1979), *Pauline Pieces*, London.

—— (1990), *From Adam to Christ*, Cambridge.

Rowland, C. C. (1982), *The Open Heaven*, London.

Segal, A. F. (1977), *Two Powers in Heaven*, Leiden.

Stanton, G. N. (1979), 'Incarnational Christology in the New Testament' and 'Mr Cupitt on Incarnational Christology in the New Testament', in M. Goulder (ed.), *Incarnation and Myth*, London: 151–65, 170–3.

Wiles, M. F. (1960), *The Spiritual Gospel*, Cambridge.

—— (1967), *The Divine Apostle*, Cambridge.
—— (1970), 'Does Christology Rest on a Mistake?', *Religious Studies*, 6: 69–76.
—— (1974), *The Remaking of Christian Doctrine*, London.
Young, F. (1977), 'A Cloud of Witnesses', in J. Hick (ed.), *The Myth of God Incarnate*, London: 13–47.

6

Reconstructing the Concept of God: De-reifying the Anthropomorphisms

GORDON D. KAUFMAN

Maurice Wiles is at once a historical theologian and a constructive theologian. He understands—and he shows effectively in his work—how important it is for theological reflection today to maintain significant continuity with the traditions from which it has grown; and he understands equally well, and shows in his work, how important it is for contemporary theologians to feel free, indeed obligated, to reconstruct (sometimes drastically) traditional theological understandings, concepts, and points of view in face of the enormous problems confronted by Christian faith today. He is right on both counts, and I salute him for his theological achievements. I am pleased to offer Professor Wiles this essay dealing with one small aspect of the reconstructive task to which theologians must address themselves today, as a contribution to this volume honouring him and his work.

I

In our culture 'God' is the name ordinarily used to designate that reality (whatever it may be) which grounds and undergirds all that exists, including us humans; that reality which provides us humans with such fulfilment or salvation as we may find; that reality towards which we must turn, therefore, if we would flourish. To what reality should we apply this name today? According to contemporary scientific and historical understandings, what actually creates and sustains human life are the physical, biological, and historical processes which provide its context; it is my contention, therefore, that it is with these processes that a theological perspective for today should connect what it calls 'God'. The name

'God' can take up and hold together these vast and complex processes in a distinct and powerful symbol that accents their meaning for our human existence. As we men and women seek to order our lives and our activities in terms of our understanding of human existence as situated among the many other realities of the vast ecosystem that is our world, the symbol 'God' can focus our consciousness, devotion, and work, thus providing orientation and direction for the concrete everyday decisions and actions of life.[1]

The symbol 'God' has always functioned in this way, as the focus for a world-view. In the world-picture in which this symbol originated, for example, however much God's radical independence and self-subsistence were emphasized, God was not portrayed as a being whom humans encountered directly in its solitary splendour, a being to be understood entirely in and by itself: on the contrary, a central biblical theme was that no one ever has direct or immediate contact with or experience of God. Even Moses, through whom God is said to have made Godself known decisively, was not allowed to see God's 'face', we are told, but only God's 'back' (Exod. 33: 23), for no one can see '[God's] face . . . and live' (33: 20). This inaccessibility of God is a theme that is frequently repeated; for example Job, in the midst of his tribulations, seeks God for an explanation, but God is nowhere to be found: 'Lo, he passes by me, and I see him not; he moves on, but I do not perceive him . . . Behold, I go forward, but he is not there; and backward, but I cannot perceive him; on the left hand I seek him, but I cannot behold him; I turn to the right hand, but I cannot see him' (9: 11; 23: 8–9). In the Fourth Gospel (1: 18) and again in 1 John (4: 12), we are told that 'No one has ever seen God.' For the biblical traditions in the main, God is simply not the sort of reality that is available to direct observation or experience.[2] For the most part subsequent theological reflection has taken this same line: it has held that all knowledge of God is analogical or symbolical; that is, it is never unmediated or direct but is based on likenesses drawn from ordinary objects of experience. The idea of God, thus, should not be regarded as epistemically similar to ideas of perceptual objects (for example, a table or a person or a mountain); it is not based on direct human perceptions of God. Rather, it is constructed imaginatively in the mind, built up on the basis of analogies, metaphors, and models thought to be appropriate.[3]

The most important defining (or constitutive) metaphors used in constructing the biblical conception of God appear to be creator, lord, and father; in this paper I shall be concerned particularly with these three metaphors and the image/concept of God constituted by them. In their theological use these metaphors function largely as models, each providing the idea of God with rather specific content. In this way they help to focus and interpret the picture of the world which is set out in the Bible: it is a picture which holds together in a meaningful and quite particular way the manifoldness of what humans take to be their direct and immediate experience. Each of these metaphors (creator, lord, father) functions in a *relational* way; that is, these metaphors identify and characterize God not primarily in terms of some meaning which God has in Godself, but rather in terms of God's relatedness to and significance for the world of human experience. For example, the Bible opens with God portrayed as the creator and ground of the entire finite order of reality ('the heavens and the earth'). Then, having made the universe and all its contents, God is portrayed as ruling over the creation, bringing it ever forward towards the realization of the righteous purposes that will constitute it as a perfect 'kingdom'. In due course expectations develop that this will be a community of peace, justice, and love, where wolves will dwell peacefully with lambs, and children will play with what are now experienced as poisonous snakes, but none 'shall . . . hurt or destroy in all [of God's] holy mountain; for the earth shall be full of the knowledge of the Lord' (Isa. 11: 6–9).

What we have here is a picture of the world—the context within which human life appears and flourishes—as coming from God, as pervaded by God's continuous activity, and as moving towards the fulfilment of God's benevolent purposes. But God in Godself is never directly available within this world as an object of experience and knowledge; what is available are *memories* of what (it is believed that) the creator/lord/father has done in the past, and *hopes* of what the creator/lord/father shall yet do (given the faith, the confidence, that God continues to work in the world). Human experience generally is grasped and interpreted in terms of images, categories, and concepts derived from the past and carried in language and memory, and so here also: the understanding of all reality as 'under God' acquired in Israel's history, provides the interpretative grid which gives present experience and future hopes their basic shape and deepest meaning. That is, God-talk (as we know it in the West) developed, not on the basis of direct perceptions or experiences of the divine being itself, but rather in connection with a *world-picture* (constructed by the human imagination over many generations) in which the creator/lord/father is taken to be the dominant active power. Within this world, human life is experienced as coming from some place (God's prior creative and governing actions) and going to some place (towards the realization of God's perfect kingdom). Hence, the meaning of life is sustained and nourished by (1) memories of what happened to the foreparents of presently living believers (in the conviction that God was actively working with them) and (2) hopes of what shall yet occur, as God overcomes the problems of present existence and brings the movements of history to their culmination.

For those living within this world-picture the joys and sorrows of present life are experienced and understood as expressions of the ever-present activity of the living God, the origin of life and its ultimate goal. The image/concept of the creator/lord/father is the great symbolic focus with the aid of which believers' imaginations bind everything together into a meaningful whole within which all life's vicissitudes have a proper place and significance. The meaning which the idea of God has, thus, should not be understood to derive from the encounters women and men have had from time to time with a particular *something*—a something which we also might encounter 'face to face' sometime; it derives, rather, from its employment as the principal symbolic centre for an entire world-picture. The creator/lord/father provides a focus for human devotion, meditation, and service, a focus to which women and men have believed they could give themselves without reservation.

This focus takes up into itself and pin-points in a dramatic image/ concept the whole structure of meaning that this world-picture provides for the understanding and interpretation of human life. It presents believers with an understanding of (1) what the world really is—namely God's creation; (2) what the movements of history mean—they are the working out of God's purposes; (3) what place human life has within the cosmic scheme of things—as the very 'image of God', women and men are made for communion and covenant with each other and with God, and human experience has its meaning as these covenants are fulfilled and that communion is realized; (4) what aspirations and hopes men and women may legitimately have—to participate in the kingdom God is creating;

and (5) what humans ought to do here and now—obediently follow God's will, as made known through the law and the prophets. Since the whole world-picture was brought into sharp focus and held together by the symbol 'God' ('Yahweh') it is not difficult to understand why devotion and service to God were seen to be the principal concerns of human life. And conversely, since the symbol 'God' acquired its meaning not in and through itself, as it were, but as the centre and focus for an all-encompassing world-picture, devotion to God and service to God were regarded as consisting in nothing else than living and acting in terms of the patterns and structures of meaning which this picture itself provided.

The world-picture in connection with which the image/concept of God developed was essentially *dualistic*: with the help of materials drawn from our human experience within this world it depicted an *other* world; and in so doing it presented to humans who are on this side of the great divide in reality, what it is important that they know about the *other* side.[4] Metaphysical dualisms of this sort are, however, fundamentally incoherent: they lead us to suppose we know something(s) that we cannot possibly know. This idea of an 'other world' or 'other side'—the idea of a Most Important Reality outside this world in which we find ourselves and have our experience—leads us to imagine and speak of things that, though totally inaccessible to us in principle, are spoken of with confidence, even certitude. In the biblical stories we are told much about God, and about what God does; but these stories—these myths created by the human imagination thousands of years ago—are, of course, the only basis we have for this information. Rudolf Bultmann's proposal that we demythologize stories of this sort, dropping their time-bound details in order to get at their profound existential significance, really does not address the fundamental issue which they pose; for he seems to retain the basic idea of the 'other side'—another reality outside this life, this world of our experience—which is more important than anything on 'this side', since it is the real foundation of life and its meaning. That is, he retains the fundamentally *dualistic* presupposition on which the traditional understanding of God and the world is founded (though he wishes to drop many of the more incredible details of particular stories). It is, however, precisely this dualism itself that is the most problematic feature of this product of the human imagination.

I propose that we go much further in our reconception of the biblical mythology than has Bultmann, and that we refrain from postulating an 'other side' or 'other world' at all. There seems no good reason for such a postulate—except that that is the way these ancient myths, regarded as authoritative in our religious traditions, spoke. I contend that since we now can see that such stories—and the dualistic way in which they present the context of human life— are all products of the human imagination, we should today undertake to do our own imagining; but we should do it in a critical fashion unavailable to the ancient prophets and poets, a fashion informed and disciplined by modern scientific and historical know-ledge and philosophical reflection. In particular we should, in our attempt to construct conceptions and pictures of humanity, the world, and God, attempt to speak only in terms of *this world*, of the realities of *this life*—making as clear as possible the respects in which what we say has a firm basis in our experience and knowledge, as well as the respects in which it is an imaginative elaboration and interpretation. In all of this, of course, it is important that we keep in view the fact that our 'knowledge' of this world in which we live, and all the realities within it, always shades off into ultimate mystery, into an ultimate unknowing.[5] (Through introducing the concept of mystery here, I am seeking to retain what is valid in dualistic ways of thinking, without falling into their fallacies.)

The dualistic world-picture which we find in the Bible and much of Christian tradition does not accurately describe or meaningfully interpret the actual world in which educated people today (at least in the West) take themselves to be living; nor is it directly relevant to much of their experience in this world. Moreover, it seductively intimates that it can unveil features of the Ultimate Mystery which otherwise must remain hidden from human view, that it can make known to us the ultimate reality with which we humans have to do. Although this world-picture may well continue to represent for us a beautiful poetic expression of the meaning of life, it remains, nevertheless, quite unclear how it bears on the world in which we now take ourselves to live, how it can directly inform our actual lives today. We need, therefore, to redraw our inherited religious picture of the world and the human so it describes the actual world in which we take ourselves to be living, as well as our understanding of ourselves. And we must also redraw our picture of God—if we are to continue to see God as the proper focus for our devotion, reflection, and service in this world daily experienced.

II

Let us turn first to the images of creator and lord, to see in what ways they can be related to our modern conceptions. Through a long evolutionary process the world-system of which we are a part has given birth to life; eventually humanity emerged, with its potential for cumulating historical development and its capacity to take responsibility for the future. What is of most direct importance to human beings in all of this, of course, has been the emergence of an evolutionary trajectory or movement giving rise to human existence. The picture of God creating the world and governing history, we could say, presents in a kind of poetic way the meaning of what has actually transpired here. From a theological point of view it is significant that directional movement appears to be an intrinsic expression of the creativity working through the evolutionary process,[6] and that the course which cosmic evolution and history have taken need not, therefore, be thought of as simply a metaphysical accident or surd. The metaphors 'creator' and 'lord' emphasize this point and go on further to suggest that this directionality is the expression of some sort of intentionality or purposiveness at work in the broader cosmic and historical movements—a consideration of great import when the question of the meaning of human existence is at stake. It is hardly surprising that, to the extent that the cosmic process as a whole seemed to the biblical people to be 'going somewhere', they symbolized and focused their understanding of it with the image of a cosmic maker and purposer who had set certain goals and was working to achieve them. The only *locus* of outright intentional or purposive activity known to us humans is, after all, us humans: we women and men regularly make decisions, set goals for ourselves, and work towards their realization. Purposive activity, thus, as we directly experience it, is always grounded in a self or community, in a *purposer*; and these images express and significantly interpret this sense that life and history are moving forward towards goals of importance to human beings. All the multifarious events, processes, and activities in the world of human experience are now seen to be held together, focused, and interpreted by purposes in the mind of the creator and lord of the world.

I want to suggest now that it is not necessary to reify this idea of the creator and lord (as has often occurred in the past) for it to be useful in symbolizing and focusing the vast cosmic movement of which we today are aware; that is, we do not need to think in terms of some 'cosmic person' out there somewhere, who at some point in time envisaged creating the world and working in it in certain specific ways, and then proceeded to do so. Reification is at the root of many of the problems in traditional God-talk, and I shall be presenting arguments against it shortly. What the symbols 'creator' and 'lord' signify is the conviction that the directional movement(s) which we discern in the cosmos are not to be thought of as simply accidental happenstance but rather as grounded in the ultimate nature of things; for they have been 'created by'—that is, produced or brought about by—the creativity underlying and at work in all things. To be devoted to God the *Creator* is to be devoted to that ultimate reality—that ultimate mystery—which expresses itself in and through all that exists, including the evolutionary and historical development of the ecosystem that has given birth to us and to many other creatures. And to seek 'to do the will' of God the *Lord* is to seek to order one's life in accord with this actual evolutionary-historical trajectory within which we humans find ourselves to be living. That is, devotion to the 'creator/lord' today should be understood as consisting in the attempt to live in rapport with the movements of life and history that provide the actual context of our human existence; it is to attempt to be in tune with what we discern as the nature of things, to live and to work 'with the grain' of the universe as apprehended in our part of it. These metaphors and images out of which the traditional notion of God was constructed need not, then, be given up completely to accommodate our modern world-view; but, if we continue to use them, they should be interpreted as essentially poetic metaphors not ontological models or concepts. If we are to understand what they can properly signify today (that is to say), it is important above all that we do not reify them.

What is 'reification'? It is taking the content of a symbol (or image or word) to be a proper description or adequate representation of a particular reality or being; in Kant's apt phrase, it is 'treating our thoughts as things' (Kant 1929: A395; cf. A384). We reify the symbols 'creator' and 'lord' and 'father' when we take them to mean that God *really is* a creator/lord/father. (The literal meaning of the word 'reify' is simply 'to make into a thing'.)

It is useful, I think, to distinguish between 'reifying' and 'referring'. From the point of view of faith such symbols as 'creator' and 'lord' *refer* to something 'real'—for us today this will be the evolutionary and historical processes which produced us. We take these processes to be real, and it is to these realities that we today can understand ourselves to be referring when we use these traditional theological symbols. This means, however, that our theological symbols by themselves do not enable us to grasp precisely *what* it is to which we are actually referring here; and that we dare not, therefore, attempt to answer this question simply through reification of these symbols, i.e. through taking them to refer to some particular being or person who could appropriately be characterized as a 'creator' and 'lord'. According to the theological reconception which we are working out here, that to which these terms actually refer must be understood in much vaguer and more abstract terms, perhaps something like 'those evolutionary and historical processes creating, sustaining, and enhancing our humanity'; our terms 'lord' and 'creator', thus, function as *metaphors* for us, not as concepts. To regard a metaphor as *referring* (without reifying it) is to take it as indicating something real, something in some way significantly related to the metaphor's imagery (so that it can justifiably be said to 'represent' or 'symbolize' the reality concerned), but it is not to regard this reality as a straightforward exemplification or instantiation of the content or imagery of the metaphor. The metaphor functions, thus, to help focus our attention on certain features of the reality in which we are interested, but it is not an adequate concept of that reality.[7] Understanding our theological language as largely metaphorical in this way allows what is *really there* to remain veiled in mystery: it is something only dimly intimated in the symbol, never fully grasped. To speak of this mystery as 'creative' or as 'governing' is to give it an interpretation that highlights certain aspects of our world and our experience in a way which can help orientate men and women in life today; but we really do not know precisely what it is in the world-process to which these metaphors refer. Faith believes *that* they refer, but to what they refer remains in many respects mystery.

Reification began early in religious history. It has never been easy for humans to distinguish clearly the mental images and concepts important to them from actual objects in the world; and it is not surprising, therefore, that from early on the creator/lord/father was taken to be an objectively existing powerful agent-self, a supernatural character. In the Bible God stands behind and governs all that exists. In this picture it was apparently the autonomous, free agent, the 'I' (ego) existing alone in its solitude, that was the core model on the basis of which the image/concept of God was constructed. When Moses, in a very early story, asks the voice from the burning bush, 'Who are you? What is your name?', the answer that comes back to him is, 'I AM; I AM WHO I AM' (Exod. 3: 13–14, paraphrased). God is identified here as the great 'I AM', the ego-agent *par excellence*, sheer unrestricted agential power. Given this model, it is not surprising that God has often been conceived as an all-powerful tyrant, a terrifying arbitrary force before whom women and men can only bow in awe and fear.

As long as it was not understood that this whole world-picture, with God as the centre and focus for all human devotion and activity, was a creation of the human imagination (like all other world-pictures), it was difficult to avoid objectifying and reifying these received images and concepts of God; even today one may feel disinclined to oppose theologically, or decisively to modify, this conception of God—so deeply rooted in the biblical stories and the mainstream religious traditions of the West—as an arbitrary, imperial potentate, a solitary eminence existing 'somewhere' in glorious transcendence of all else. It is a serious mistake, however, to take the symbol 'God' in this objectifying and reifying way: for (as we have seen) it actually is but one feature of a larger mythic map of reality. The function of all such world-pictures or maps is to provide orientation in life and the world for women and men; and the adequacy and effectiveness of such conceptual frames is to be assessed in terms of the respects in which and the degree to which they actually contribute to human flourishing (salvation). To the extent that our received traditions about God appear inadequate to or destructive of humankind and the environment within which it has emerged and by which it is sustained, it is theologically requisite that we transform or eliminate them; for our objective must be to formulate a conception of God which is appropriate to focus human devotion and orientation in today's world.

III

As we give up literalization and reification of the traditional imagery and concepts, some things dear to traditional pieties will be undermined. God will no longer be pictured or conceived as a personal being in the heavens above who 'before the foundation of the world' (Eph. 1: 4; 1 Pet. 1: 20; Rev. 13: 8; etc.) devised a detailed divine plan that included a special place and task for each of us; and we will no longer, therefore, be able to imagine ourselves as in direct personal interaction with this divine being, as we seek to learn and do 'his'(!) will. Much of the intensely personalistic flavour of the relationship of individuals to God, which traditional piety cultivated and enjoyed, we can now see, was the product of a rather literalistic reading of the metaphors which dominated the tradition. For the reconstruction I am suggesting here, it will no longer be appropriate to expect and to long for a relationship of this sort—or to despair when it is absent or has become incomprehensible (e.g. in experiences of tragedy or evil, including the massive evils of the twentieth century). Our experiences of personal warmth and meaning have their real grounding in our actual interpersonal relations on the human level, with other men and women; and (as we shall see) it is in and through these relationships (theologically interpreted) that we come to realize whatever personal relationship with God—with the reality which has actually created us as human—is possible for us and appropriate to us.[8]

It should not be thought that this radically de-reified and mediated conception of the love of God—both God's love for us, and our love for God—is a far-fetched new idea. A similar understanding is already present in early Christian sources, though it has not frequently been given as central and defining a place as I am proposing. In 1 John, for example, after pointing out that 'no man has ever seen God' (4: 12)—i.e. that humans do not have direct or unmediated personal relationships with God—the writer goes on to declare that it is in our 'love [for] one another, [that] God abides in us and his love is perfected in us'. Indeed, this love of humans for each other is presented here as the very criterion of the presence of God's spirit and God's love: 'By this', the writer says, 'we know that we abide in him and he in us' (4: 13). To underline further his claim that the love of God is indivisible from love of our fellow humans, he states emphatically: 'If any one says, "I love God", and hates his brother, he is a liar; for he who does not love his brother whom he has seen, cannot love God whom he has not seen' (4: 20). Thus, our personal relation with the ultimate reality with which we have to do—God—is to be found most fundamentally in and through our *interpersonal* relationships with our fellow humans.

To the extent that the traditional images of God have suggested otherwise—that what is really important for human beings is a direct personal relationship with God *rather than* with our fellow humans—they have been extremely misleading, indeed oftentimes destructive, as a great deal of human brutality, terror, murder, and war bears witness. All too often, among persons who considered themselves Christians, activities of this sort were undertaken in obedience to what was believed to be explicitly 'commanded' by God—with very little consideration of whether they were an expression of genuine love for those women and men directly affected. In recent years we have become aware of the way in which such reified imagery has promoted and helped to sustain racist and sexist oppression. 'God', thought of as white and male, has been the ultimate symbol legitimating and sanctifying white-dominated social institutions and customs and practices, as well as male domination over every area of life. God the creator/lord/father was seen as the ultimate authority figure to whom everything in the created order must be subordinated. This cosmic hierarchical pattern, then, provided the basis and the justification for similar hierarchical patterns of order in human affairs: those who are male/white/wealthy/powerful determine the order to which those who are female/black/poor/weak must submit.

This religious symbolism has had repressive and oppressive power of this sort not so much because of its particular content as because that content was reified: God was taken to be *in actual fact* a kind of creator/lord/father 'out there' who really established—consciously willed and deliberately created—the patterns of order governing life here on earth. Everything changes, however, once we de-reify this cosmic picture. We come to see that our religious symbolism is not valid in its own right, but only to the extent that it represents, and thus reinforces, those cosmic and historical tendencies and forces which actually move us towards further humanization, towards a more humane and ecologically sustainable order—that is, which promote what was called (in the tradition) human 'salvation'. The problems which the traditional metaphors pose arise primarily from their reification, and the excessive authority with which this reification invests them, not simply from their content. If God is conceived as that reality working through the actual humanizing and relativizing cosmic and historical powers which give us our humanity (as I am proposing here), we are provided with a means for criticizing and reinterpreting these symbols; and they may thus still be able to perform significant salvific functions.

IV

This view not only offers some protection against important symbolic abuses; it goes a long way towards addressing one of the most intractable issues with which theologians have had to deal, the problem of theodicy, the justification of God in view of the massive evil in the world. This problem arises because God, understood as the creator/lord/father of all that exists, has often been portrayed as in direct personal control of all that happens. God planned the course which historical events take, and if impossible difficulties arise for the faithful, it can be hoped (according to traditional piety) that God will perform a miracle which will lift them out of their misery. A literalistic understanding of the images in terms of which God was conceived obviously lay behind such views as these; and it is hardly surprising that the piety which accompanied this understanding often found itself in difficulties, since the expectations it generated were so frequently disappointed. The so-called problem of theodicy is actually rooted in the same literalism as this piety: if God is an all-powerful, all-knowing, absolutely righteous and merciful Person, why are there such horrible evils—enormous misery, injustice, suffering—in the world? Why would a good God ever have made such an evil order? Why has God not straightened it up long since? These questions were already posed in the Hebrew Bible—by Habakkuk, Job, Ecclesiastes, and some of the Psalms—and they have come up repeatedly since, in the conversations of Jesus, in the reflection of Paul and John, and in much subsequent theology and philosophy, as well as in the meditations and the jibes of many ordinary women and men. Traditional piety has often attempted to put these questions down by retreating into the inscrutable mystery of the divine will, even while desperately holding on to faith despite powerfully negative experiential evidence: 'Though he slay me, yet will I trust in him' (Job 13: 15 *KJV*). This is a wonderfully moving sentiment which has comforted many suffering individuals. But 'after Auschwitz', as Richard Rubenstein and many others have argued (see Rubenstein 1966), it seems bland and weak; the massive human suffering already witnessed in the twentieth century, and which may be outdone by what is still to come, renders highly problematic all such traditional pieties and arguments.

Reification of the traditional image/concept of God is the deepest root of this problem. Everyone agrees that a just and merciful *human* king or father would do everything in his power to protect his subjects or children from meaningless evils and sufferings: it seems appropriate, therefore, to assume that so must it also be (indeed, many times more so) with our creator/lord/father in heaven. If these traditional metaphors are taken literalistically, this conclusion surely follows; and the problems which it poses are insoluble. However, if we de-reify our understanding of God, all these problems fall away: the images of creator and lord and father are, then, not regarded as concepts from which we can deduce rather specific ideas of omnipotence, omniscience, goodness, and the like, and on the basis of which we can legitimately imagine God to be governing the earthly order in accord with detailed divine plans for history, including even highly particularized miraculous acts of intervention. Misleading pictures and expectations of this sort have often been generated by the reification of the highly metaphorical language of our religious traditions; but (as we have seen) this language does not adequately identify or describe the evolutionary-historical trajectory which has in fact brought humanity into the world and continues to ground and sustain it, and in relation to which, therefore, contemporary faith should define and understand itself. For the perspective we are working out here, the difficulties encountered in life are to be understood as arising largely out of the complexity of the patterns of nature and history in which we are living—with a good deal of human bungling and malevolence added to the mix; they are not a direct intentional expression of some 'will' thought to be divine.

According to this (more contemporary) picture of human-life-in-the-world, it is a mistake to suppose that everything which happens to men and women is somehow a direct expression of a specific intention of God. Rather, each event is but one small piece of the ongoing massive and complex movements in the nature/history ecosystem; and particular events and developments are to be understood and explained, therefore, largely in terms of the (more or less) local contexts in which they occur. This means that the various 'evils' of human existence must be analysed and understood with reference to their empirical causes, the particular historical developments or natural events which brought them about; they are not to be seen as the expression of some single universal evil condition—sin, estrangement from the divine creator/lord/father, rebellion against the divine will—which is regarded as the root of all misery and suffering. And our attack on the evils of life will consist in the attempt (1) to identify the major human problems found in the world today—poverty, disease, oppression, racism, sexism, war, injustice, inhumanity, destruction of the ecosystem, and so on—and (2) to ameliorate these as much as possible through modifying or radically transforming the institutions and ideologies and practices that are their proximate conditions and causes. There is still a proper place for talk about sin and alienation from God, but now these notions will have a more general and less highly personalized meaning: they symbolize our failing to live and act in harmony with the basic ecological and historical trajectories which have created human existence and which alone are capable of continuing to sustain and enhance it—rather than serving as explanations for some deep feelings of shame and guilt before a personal creator/lord/father whom we believe we have offended and whose forgiveness and justification we desperately need.

I have been suggesting in these remarks both some of the positive uses of the metaphors which have traditionally constituted the image/concept of God, and also some of the difficulties these metaphors pose when they are reified. It is clear (I hope) that it would be a serious mistake to continue defining the symbol 'God' largely in the terms they provide: these metaphors need to be complemented and supplemented by others which significantly qualify them and balance some of their misleading emphases. If we decide to continue using personalistic/anthropomorphic metaphors like creator and lord in our worship and reflection—despite their tendency to induce misleading or even false expectations about God's personal involvement in all the problems and difficulties which afflict each of us as individuals (as well as our society as a whole)—we will want to add other less traditional ones that bring out features of our interpersonal and social life which these neglect, for example, mother, friend, lover.[9] It is also important deliberately to use naturalistic metaphors in our thinking and worship—nature, world-process, life, ecosystem, evolution, and the like—which emphasize our embeddedness in the natural order and remind us of our interconnection with and dependence on the vast and complex ecological network which provides the context for our existence. And more abstract metaphysical concepts and metaphors, such as ultimate reality, being, eternity, transcendence, the One and the All, which bring out in a special way God's universality and ultimacy, have important functions to perform as well, in both theological reflection and personal meditation. Above all, a central place should be given to the concept of *mystery*, which reminds us how limited, incomplete, and inadequate are all our religious convictions and theological concepts, how much they need continual criticism and revision, how little justified we are in taking dogmatic positions on the ultimate questions of life and death. This symbol, when properly employed, is the best protection we have against our tendencies continually to reify our theological ideas.

V

Thus far in our analysis of the creator/lord/father symbolism, most of our attention has been devoted to the metaphors of creator and lord: we have not yet looked closely at the notion 'father', so central for Christian faith. In many ways this is the most difficult of the principal traditional metaphors to deal with today, because of its intensely personalistic overtones, on the one hand, and the sexism and paternalism which it implies, on the other. Is it appropriate to continue using this metaphor to symbolize the relatively impersonal cosmic evolutionary-historical process we have been discussing? If it is not, does that not imply that there is really very little significant contact left between the symbol 'God' (as we are reconstructing it here) and the central themes of Christian faith?

Here we must be very careful. In the traditional image/concept of God, which was initially constituted primarily by the metaphors of creator and lord, the metaphor 'father' (or 'parent') served as an important qualifier. The earlier images (as we have seen) together symbolized the creative and purposive power believed to be at the foundation of the world and working within the world; but the metaphor 'father' emphasizes a further distinctive note: the divine activity is moving history towards a *humane order*, God is working towards patterns of life which will make possible human fulfilment. The world and history are ordered, that is to say, not by an arbitrary divine will that works its way however it pleases: rather, the trajectory of evolution and history (as we are calling it) is moving towards human salvation, towards providing a context for human life and an ordering of human life which will fulfil the personal, moral, and spiritual values towards which we humans, in our best moments, aspire—much as loving parents seek fulfilment and happiness for their children, and attempt to arrange the period of their growth and development so this will come about.

According to widely accepted developmental and psychiatric theories, contexts of love, care, and trust (usually provided by the immediate family) are required if human infants are to develop into free and responsible and loving persons. Familial and communal contexts pervaded by hatred and malevolence, arbitrariness and instability, despair and guilt, tend to produce warped selves with paranoid self-understandings that inhibit free and responsible relationships to other persons; but contexts that are well ordered but open, in which there is peace and joy and love, promote the formation of free and responsible and loving women and men. If the creation of persons able to take full responsibility for themselves and the world in which they are living and acting depends on social contexts most clearly typified by families with genuinely caring and loving parenting figures, it should not surprise us that the ultimate symbol for that which grounds and creates our humanness has been drawn from parenting: God is thought of as a father and/or mother. But God is not just any father or mother: God is a loving parent, just yet merciful and forgiving, working towards the full maturity and freedom of us children. The symbol 'God' obviously must include certain highly personalistic dimensions, if it is to bring into unified focus all the major cosmic and historical forces or powers which ground our humanity, which bring us into being and draw us on towards realization: virtually the only concrete symbolism which can express some of the most important features of what is involved here is parental, the images of mothering and fathering.

To speak of God as 'father' or 'mother' is to acknowledge the importance of these familial interpersonal relationships in the creation of free selves and loving communities, and to affirm that this indispensable condition for our becoming fully human is itself grounded in the ultimate nature of things. These parenting metaphors, thus, symbolize forthrightly a central dimension of the meaning which the image/concept of God must convey: faith's conviction that the entire range of human moral and spiritual values and virtues—mercy and love and justice; trust and loyalty; beauty, goodness, and truth—is grounded in the overflowing creativity of the cosmic process. For faith in God our striving for humane values and a thoroughly humane order is not to be taken as a merely human enterprise; these struggles are, so to say, important to God, and they are to be understood as an expression of God's activity in the world. Our deepest human aspirations, then, are not alien to this ecological-historical order into which we have been born: the world in which we live is a humane-seeking order (in certain significant respects), and we can give ourselves wholeheartedly to responsible life and work within it.

The struggle for humane order in the world has not, of course, been easy. It has moved forward only very slowly through the millennia of human history; and perhaps only in the last two or three thousand years has the vision of a truly humane existence gradually emerged into view. Given this vision, however, and the conviction that our struggles and hopes to become fully human and humane are grounded in the creativity working in and through all things—in God—we can say of the cosmic evolutionary and historical process which has brought forth human life on earth (paraphrasing Job): 'Though it slay us—as individuals, even as whole communities—yet will we trust in it.' For we believe and hope that the trajectory which has brought us into being is drawing us onward towards a humane ordering of life—the coming 'kingdom of God', as our religious traditions envisioned it; and we, will, therefore, commit ourselves willingly to whatever is required to enable communities of genuine love and peace, truth and justice, to come into being. Since these indispensable interpersonal and social dimensions of the evolutionary-historical trajectory in which we humans 'live and move and have our being' (Acts 17: 28) are most effectively symbolized and evoked by such metaphors as 'father' and 'mother', these continue to be appropriate when thinking and speaking of God—if properly de-reified for a contemporary faith-stance. When such metaphors are used, however, it is important to make clear that it is only within our actual interpersonal relationships with women and men here on earth that God's 'fatherliness' and 'motherliness', God's 'sisterliness' and 'brotherliness' are experienceable[10]—as we receive our humanity from others and are able to offer the gift of humanity to them in return (cf. Matt. 25: 31–46).

VI

Anthropomorphic metaphors continue to be useful, even indispensable, to a contemporary image/concept of God which can provide a focus for human devotion and energies, and for the orientation of life. For faith today the symbol 'God', if not narrowly or one-sidedly construed, expresses—in a more effective way than any other symbol available to those of us heir to Western religious traditions—the profound meaning of the situatedness of human life in the world. Because of the unique power and significance which it has acquired in a long history of religious devotion and meditation, of religious experience and life, this symbol can focus in a powerful way our attention and devotion and lives on those dimensions of the ecological and historical order in which we live that facilitate our moving further towards responsive and responsible human-life-in-the-world—towards attaining our full humanity.

NOTES

1. This way of reconceiving the symbol 'God' (in the light of contemporary scientific and historical knowledge) is thoroughly worked out in my recent book, *In Face of Mystery: A Constructive*

Theology (Harvard University Press, 1993). This article is drawn largely from ch. 22 of that volume.

2. The Bible is not entirely consistent in this emphasis; many 'theophanies', for example, are reported in the Bible, but these seem to be more manifestations of God's *power* than of God in Godself. However, Enoch 'walked with God' (Gen. 5: 22, 24), we are told; God 'appeared' to Abraham (Gen. 17: 1; 18: 1) and spoke to him; Jacob wrestled with 'a man' all night long (Gen. 32: 34) and then later said he had 'seen God face to face' (Gen. 32: 30). But it is not evident that much should be made of these stories theologically, especially in view of the explicit statements that humans cannot 'see' God.

3. For a full discussion of this constructed character of the idea of God, see Kaufman 1975, Kaufman 1981, and also Kaufman 1993.

4. Cf. Rudolf Bultmann's definition of mythology: 'Mythology is the use of imagery to express the other world in terms of this world and the divine in terms of human life, the other side in terms of this side' (Bultmann 1953: 10 n. 2).

5. For further discussion of this point, see Kaufman 1993. I have found Maurice Wiles's use of the concept of mystery particularly illuminating as I have reflected on these matters; see especially Wiles 1982.

6. See especially Bronowski 1970. Obviously, the sweeping claims made in these brief sentences of my article need much fuller elaboration and justification. I cannot, however, present that here; it is provided in Kaufman 1993, Pt. 3.

7. In thinking about the distinction between metaphors and concepts, Sallie McFague's work has been especially helpful to me—see McFague 1987: ch. 2; McFague 1982.

8. It should be emphasized that this last is no small point: it is in and through interpersonal relationships (especially in the family) that we are (quite literally) first *created* as selves—brought into our full humanity; and it is precisely in such social contexts that the divine creativity continues to be present to us, effectively shaping and reshaping our lives and our world.

9. In *Models of God*, Sallie McFague (McFague 1987) shows how thoroughly these three metaphors, if taken seriously, can reorient our thinking about God.

10. For Jesus (and many of his followers in the past) the word 'father' was apparently employed in connection with a sense (or experience) of intense, intimate, personal relationship with God. Though for many such claims generated experiences that have been among the most precious features of the Christian life, for others the disappointed expectations to which they gave rise often led to deep inconsolable despair. Expectations and experiences of both these sorts appear,

from today's standpoint, to have been grounded largely on the widespread reification of the personal metaphors so prominent in traditional Christianity.

REFERENCES

Bronowski, J. (1970), 'New Concepts in the Evolution of Complexity: Stratified Stability and Unbounded Plans', *Zygon*, 5: 18–35.

Bultmann, Rudolf (1953), 'New Testament and Mythology', in H. W. Bartsch and R. H. Fuller (eds.), *Kerygma and Myth*, London.

Kant, Immanuel (1929), *Critique of Pure Reason*, trans. Norman Kemp Smith, London.

Kaufman, Gordon D. (1975), *Essay on Theological Method*, Atlanta, rev. edn. 1979.

—— (1981), *The Theological Imagination: Constructing the Concept of God*, Philadelphia.

—— (1985), *Theology for a Nuclear Age*, Manchester.

—— (1993), *In Face of Mystery: A Constructive Theology*, Cambridge, Massachusetts.

McFague, Sallie (1982), *Metaphorical Theology*, Philadelphia.

—— (1987), *Models of God*, Philadelphia.

Rubenstein, Richard (1966), *After Auschwitz*, Indianapolis.

Wiles, Maurice (1982), *Faith and the Mystery of God*, London.

7

St Gregory the Theologian and St Maximus the Confessor: The Shaping of Tradition

ANDREW LOUTH

One of St Maximus the Confessor's most important works is his *Liber ambiguorum*, as it is usually referred to in the title given it by its first, and for the most part only, translator, the ninth-century John Scotus Eriugena—his *Book of Difficulties* (for the Greek behind Eriugena's *ambiguum* is *aporia*, perplexity or difficulty). It is, in fact, as is generally known, not a single work, but consists of two parts: Ambigua 6–71 are a discussion of a string of difficult passages from the writings of St Gregory of Nazianzus that had been raised with Maximus by John, Archbishop of Cyzicus, to whom Maximus' replies are addressed. Polycarp Sherwood dates these to 628–30, during Maximus' earlier African sojourn; Sherwood's work on these 'Earlier Ambigua', as he calls them, is indispensable (it is, incidentally, only these earlier Ambigua that Eriugena translated). Ambigua 1–5 are addressed to a certain Thomas, described as 'the sanctified servant of God, spiritual father and teacher': the first four discuss difficult passages in Gregory, like the earlier Ambigua, the last a difficult passage in Denys the Areopagite's fourth letter (the letter that contains the famous phrase about Christ's 'divine-human energy'; Maximus' discussion in this difficulty includes a long analysis of this phrase). Sherwood dates these slightly later, to 634 or shortly after, just as the Monothelete controversy (at this stage I suppose 'monenergic' would be better) was getting under way. How and when these two parts were put together to form the *Book of Difficulties* is the subject of much controversy: it does not look as if there will be any definitive answer until we have a proper critical edition of all Maximus' works.

But the *Book of Difficulties* is one of the most important of Maximus' works. Some of the discussions of difficult passages are very extensive and constitute virtual treatises in their own right: Ambiguum 7 is a massive refutation of Origenism; according to Sherwood, 'it is here that one finds, perhaps alone in all Greek patristic literature, a refutation of Origenist error with a full understanding of the master' (Sherwood 1952: 32); Ambiguum 10 is even longer (fifty columns of Greek in the Migne edition) and is a sustained meditation on the Transfiguration of our Lord. For the most part, the Ambigua have been used as a quarry for the teaching of the Confessor, and it is certainly true that most of the central topics of Maximus' theology—his doctrine of deification, his doctrine of double creation, the importance for him of the ordered triad generation–change–rest, much of the detail of his anthropology —are discussed in the course of his responses to these 'difficulties'.

Much less has been done on a rather different question raised by these works, and that is the light they shed on the relationship between St Gregory the Theologian and St Maximus the Confessor. All the difficulties, save one, are raised by passages in the works of Gregory Nazianzen. This suggests to me that Maximus' relationship to Gregory is, in some respects, *ambiguous* (to use the word with its usual meaning) or double-edged. The *Book of Difficulties* is often cited as evidence for the influence of Cappadocian thought on Maximus the Confessor, but it is equally, and perhaps more obviously, evidence for the difficulties Maximus had with his Cappadocian heritage, and in particular with the heritage of St Gregory Nazianzen. As we look at the relationship between these two theologians, as evidenced in this collection of difficulties, what we are seeing is something about the nature of tradition or, perhaps more exactly, something about the *shaping* of tradition, something about how Gregory is received by Maximus as a part of tradition, indeed a mouthpiece of tradition. To use language that Professor Wiles has made familiar, we are looking at the *making* of doctrine, and a making which is also a *remaking*.

To begin with, one might ask: why Gregory? And this can be answered at two levels. First, what kind of evidence is there for discussion of Gregory that might lead to someone sending Maximus a collection of 'difficulties' to clear up? There is, in truth, not a lot of evidence, but there is one very valuable piece of evidence in the letters of Varsanuphios and John—the Great Old Man and the Other Old Man of the Gaza desert in the first half of the sixth century. One of the queries addressed to Varsanuphios speaks about those who believe in pre-existence as appealing to the authority of Gregory the Theologian on this matter. Varsanuphios' reply is not, perhaps, very helpful: he says that such speculative matters are beyond him, that all God requires is 'sanctification, purification, silence and humility', that the mysteries of God are even beyond the Fathers themselves, that consequently their works contain both true ideas and speculations that are not inspired, and that we should 'walk in the steps of our father, Poemen, and his disciples' and weep and grieve for our sins (Barsanuphe and Jean de Gaza 1972: 395–8 (Letter 604)).[1] But we have here evidence that Gregory was being used, a century earlier than Maximus, as an authority by Origenist monks for their ideas. And that is not at all surprising. As a young man, Gregory with his friend St Basil the Great had compiled a book of extracts from Origen, which they called the *Philokalia*; and Gregory himself had called Origen 'the whet-stone of us all'.[2] The *Book of Difficulties* is evidence that the problems caused by Origenist recourse to the authority of Gregory were continuing to exercise monastic minds in the seventh century.

That is one level: Gregory was discussed because Origenist monks sought to make capital out of him. But there is another level. According to Gregory the Presbyter, the author of a life of Gregory Nazianzen, Gregory was 'the only one to be called theologian after the evangelist John'.[3] Gregory the Presbyter was writing in the sixth or seventh century: either a little before Maximus, or contemporary with him. The presbyter's words suggest that by his time Gregory Nazianzen had acquired a kind of pre-eminent authority among the Greek Fathers: he was *the* theologian, to be ranked with the evangelist John, also the theologian. So in authority he seemed to stand alongside the scriptural writers themselves (in the writings of Denys the Areopagite, at the beginning of the sixth century, *theologos* meant exclusively a scriptural author). But the real evidence for this is to be found in Maximus himself. For Maximus, what Gregory says is unquestionable, virtually infallible. The twenty-first Difficulty is caused by the fact that in the Second Theological Oration Gregory refers to John the Evangelist as the 'forerunner'. It does not occur to Maximus that Gregory, in the midst of his flights of rhetoric, might have forgotten for a moment to whom he was referring and thus confused the two Johns. No, what Gregory has said must stand, and Maximus is obliged to develop a complex explanation

of how John the Evangelist, too, can be called 'the forerunner of
the Word, the great voice of the Truth' (though I think it is worth
noting in passing that the ingenuity demanded of Maximus here is
not unrewarded: as he tries to show how the Evangelist, too, can
be called 'the forerunner' he produces an understanding of the
gospel as having a spiritual interpretation that would delight the
heart of Cardinal de Lubac, who finds something similar among
the Latins:[4] that just as the law is a preparation for the Incarnation
and the proclamation of the Gospel at the First Coming, so the
Gospel is a preparation for those who are led through it to Christ,
the Word in spirit, and are gathered up in the world to come
according to his Second Coming, which leads into an elaborate
analysis of the *stoicheiosis*—both preparation and composition—of
the spiritual cosmos). Or again, the sixth difficulty is concerned
with what the distinction can possibly be between *kataspasthai* and
katechesthai—to pull down and to hold down—which Gregory
seems to use synonymously in his sermon on the love of the poor.
We would be tempted, I think, to say that they simply *are*
synonyms, that Gregory's rhetoric demanded a certain expansive-
ness here. But not Maximus: there must be a difference. Gregory
would not have wasted a word by using it to say something he had
said already.

For Maximus Gregory is *the* theologian, the 'great and wonder-
ful teacher'. Just as for Denys, the writings of the 'theologians'—
the Holy Scriptures—are to be understood within a tradition of
interpretation, or—earlier still—for Clement of Alexandria, the
utterances of the Teacher, the Word himself, are captured and laid
bare by the tissue of patient explanation he explores in his *Stromateis*,
so for Maximus the writings of Gregory are a source of truth,
handed down by tradition, and interpreted by repeated meditation
within that tradition. The *Book of Difficulties* is not just evidence
for Maximus' attempts to come to terms with an authority become
traditional, they also bear witness to a tradition of interpretation.
Eight times (seven times in the earlier, once in the later Ambigua)
Maximus appeals to the authority of a certain 'old man' (*geron*), a
'blessed old man', or 'the frequently mentioned great and wise old
man'. He is anonymous, his authority is not just the authority of
one who was Maximus' mentor, but the anonymous authority of
tradition. It is for that reason, I suspect, that he is *deliberately*
anonymous, for it certainly seems that Maximus is referring to an

identifiable individual (that is, I think, implied by the last phrase quoted above: someone 'frequently mentioned') and Polycarp Sherwood may well be right in guessing that it refers to Sophronius, whom Maximus had known in Africa and who became Patriarch of Jerusalem in 634 and led the early resistance to the Monothelete heresy (Sherwood 1955: 9). Whoever he was, this 'old man' is a living witness to tradition as Maximus has received it and, to judge from the tenor of his remarks, one who naturally expressed his understanding of tradition in language redolent of the Areopagite. Mention of the Areopagite reminds one of Denys' own relationship to his revered mentor Hierotheos, a relationship which seems to have combined something of both Maximus' relationship to his *geron* and his relationship to Gregory the Theologian. Apart from appearing in the *Difficulties*, this 'old man' appears in Maximus' book on the Ascetic Life and in his *Mystagogia*.

What did Maximus make of Gregory as he discussed the difficulties raised by his writings? Maximus' responses vary considerably. As we have seen, some are virtual treatises, while others are no more than *scholia*. So we find Maximus explaining what is meant by 'critical sweat', a medical term used metaphorically by Gregory in one of his sermons (Amb. 43); in another place he gives a definition of grammatical terms—*symbasa* and *parasymbasa*—that Gregory had used without explanation (Amb. 69); Ambiguum 70 deals with a real textual obscurity in Gregory's panegyric on Basil, which Maximus attempts to solve by putting the phrase in the context of the argument of the sermon. A whole series of difficulties supplement the allegorical explanations of people associated with the Passion of Christ that Gregory had already given in his second Easter Sermon (Amb. 52–9). In these responses, Maximus is simply helping the reader to understand Gregory more intelligently. In terms of the distinction George Steiner has made between the different kinds of difficulty encountered when reading (Steiner 1978: 18–47), Maximus is here dealing with 'contingent' difficulties in Gregory's sermons.

Other difficulties we might call—to continue with Steiner's taxonomy—'tactical' difficulties. What I mean by this (developing rather freely Steiner's own explanation of his taxonomy) is difficulties caused by the shift in interpretative framework between Gregory's time and Maximus'. The doctrinal issues of Gregory's day were largely concerned with trinitarian and christological

problems: in these contexts Gregory's language is careful. In
Maximus' day, the doctrinal issues were much more provoked by
the debate caused by Evagrianism (the Monothelete controversy
developed after Maximus had written his *Difficulties*): read in that
context, some of Gregory's language seemed somewhat careless.
It is sometimes careless because he uses an expression—for instance
moira theou, part of God—that Evagrians could pick on as support
for ideas regarded as heretical by the orthodox. In this case
(discussed in Amb. 7) the idea that we are 'part of God' was being
used to support the notion of the pre-existence of the human soul;
Maximus responds by developing his notion of God's *logoi* in
creation (an idea that would not have been foreign to Evagrius, but
which is developed by Maximus in a way that owes a lot more to
Denys). But Gregory's language sometimes seems careless to
Maximus (i.e. constitutes a difficulty) because it ignores what for
Maximus is an accepted pattern of thinking (often itself due to
Evagrius). An example of this is the difficulty dealt with in
Ambiguum 10. Here Maximus has to deal with a passage in
Gregory's panegyric on St Athanasius where he speaks of those
who ascend to kinship with God and are assimilated to the most
pure light through 'reason and contemplation'. Here the problem
is that Gregory has said nothing about *praktike*, the active struggle
against temptation that in the Evagrian scheme is the absolute
bedrock of monastic or Christian progress. Here Maximus is an
Evagrian, and Gregory must be interpreted as an Evagrian. It is
not difficult: Gregory has not denied the place of *praktike*, he has
simply concentrated on the role of contemplation, and he *has*
spoken of passing beyond 'cloud', which Maximus is able to
interpret as alluding to the stage of *praktike*. Maximus' difficulty
with Gregory here produces a profound discussion of the Christian
life that we are grateful to have for its own sake, however little it
seems to be needed for making Gregory's words acceptable. Here,
as often, the point is that Gregory's words—or thought—are not
systematic, whereas Maximus' thoughts, for all their episodic expression, have in the background a pretty clearly worked-out
system.

What this suggests to me is that an underlying difficulty, behind
all the difficulties, is what Steiner calls 'modal' difficulty. What
Steiner means by that is the difficulty we encounter in reading a
poem (say), when, even after we have done all our homework,

looked up all the unfamiliar words and worked out all the allusions and metaphors, we still find that the poem refuses to 'speak' to us. We are not looking for what the poem has to say, we are not responsive to its meaning. There is a difference of 'register'. I think this 'modal difficulty' is often there as Maximus seeks to respond to difficulties raised by Gregory. For he is *reading* Gregory, whereas Gregory wrote his sermons to be delivered, to be listened to.

Gregory was a rhetor by training, one of the most accomplished amongst the Fathers of the Church: one of his sermons would be an oratorical performance, particularly brilliant displays of rhetorical mastery would be applauded by his congregation. The aim of the rhetor was, by a display of verbal wizardry, to persuade, to induce a sense of achieved insight. A story told by Jerome, who met and was deeply impressed by Gregory in Constantinople, is worth relating here. He had asked Gregory about the meaning of a particularly obscure expression in St Luke's Gospel (6: 1: the expression 'on the "second-first" sabbath', perhaps the first sabbath but one: that is the current best guess). Gregory had been unable to come up with a satisfactory explanation, and had smilingly advised Jerome to come to church and hear him preaching about it: there, amid the wild applause of the congregation, he would understand, or at least imagine he understood, its meaning (*Ep.* 52: 8; discussed in Kelly 1975: 70). Gregory has sometimes been taken to task over this story, the German scholar Grützmacher, for instance, accusing him of 'gelehrte Charlatanerie'. But that is to take Gregory too seriously, and to miss his tone of voice: *eleganter lusit* are Jerome's words. Dr Kelly is nearer the mark when he says, 'the great orator was sufficiently human to be vain about his powers to move an audience, but also realistic enough to appreciate the worthlessness of the persuasion so induced' (Kelly 1975: 70). But is the persuasion thus induced really so worthless? Doubtless so, if one is concerned with a philological point like the meaning of an odd word. But Gregory's rhetorical persuasion always had a much higher purpose: in the Theological Orations he was trying to lift the mind and heart of his congregation to an apprehension of the coequal and coeternal Trinity of the Nicene faith. The unity of God, the equality of the persons—the apprehension of these is not a matter of logic alone, but a vehicle for praise and wonder. Denys the Areopagite used the verb 'to hymn', 'to celebrate', to describe what we are doing when we devise appropriate theological language. It is a terminology Maximus gratefully adopts: and it is, it seems to me, something Maximus makes explicit at one point in the course of the tenth Difficulty. 'When the saints are moved by visions of things as they are, it is not primarily to behold and know them as they appear to us, but in order to celebrate [Denys' word: *hymnēsosi*] God who is and manifests himself in many ways through all things and in all things and to gather together for themselves a great capacity for wonder and a reason for giving glory' (Amb. 10: 1113D–1116A). Being caught up in wonder is the goal rather than just knowing things.

Nevertheless, Maximus is interested in knowing things, in understanding: the influence of Aristotle is found not just in the dry analytical quality, on occasions, of his prose (which often draws on Aristotle, through the medium of his Neoplatonic commentators), but in Maximus' tireless patience as he seeks to understand. It is this, I think, that makes Maximus' difficulty with Gregory at root what I have called 'modal' difficulty. For Maximus, to use words and concepts to understand is not a matter of rhetorical persuasion but of philosophical understanding. But this does not mean, as it might with us, that Maximus simply finds that Gregory leaves him cold—offering him a mode of understanding that is not his. It means rather that if Maximus is to find his mode of understanding in Gregory, he has to work for it. Gregory's rhetorical flights have to be nailed down.

What I am trying to do by drawing out the different forms of difficulty that Maximus finds with Gregory is to suggest that there is no easy answer to the question of the nature of Gregory's influence on Maximus. Gregory speaks to Maximus over a gulf that can be indicated in various ways: the gulf between a learned lay culture and a monastic culture (that Maximus may have spanned in his own life, if the Greek life is right in suggesting that he had risen high in the imperial civil service before becoming a monk), the gulf separating the fourth from the seventh century, the gulf separating the rhetor from the philosopher. Gregory's voice crosses this gulf not least because it is a voice that has been conceded authority, which means, in part, that it is a voice that had shaped the culture of the hearer, the culture of Maximus and his monastic contemporaries.

But can we say anything to answer what may once have seemed a simple enough question: how Cappadocian is Maximus, how much does he owe to the Cappadocians? It is usually said that the Evagrian or the Dionysian heritage is much more important to Maximus than the Cappadocian, and that seems to me to be broadly true. It is easy to give an indication of how this manifests itself in the *Book of Difficulties*. All the difficulties but one are concerned with passages from Gregory's works: and in all these cases where the explanation advances beyond the merely 'contingent', what Maximus almost invariably does is to interpret Gregory in Evagrian or Dionysian categories or language. In the one difficulty drawn from the *Corpus Areopagiticum* (Amb. 5), Maximus' explanation seems to me to be nothing more than a Dionysian paraphrase. The Dionysian language is, as it were, Maximus' own language: Gregorian rhetoric is not.

There are, however, two areas where we might press this question somewhat harder, and these areas are Christology and Trinitarian theology. In both these areas the Cappadocian Fathers —and St Gregory Nazianzen in particular—shaped decisively the dogmatic language of the Church.

The principal Difficulties to raise Christological issues are to be found, not in the earlier Difficulties, but in the later ones: Difficulties 2–5 all raise Christological issues, though the fifth is occasioned by a passage from Denys, not Gregory.[5] What we have in these three difficulties raised by passages from Gregory is really a paraphrase of Gregory's condensed and oxymoronic language. At first sight it is difficult to see anything other than useful paraphrase. But these passages are meant to be *difficulties*, and Maximus' responses are meant to clear up problems raised by these passages. If we ask why they are difficult, it quickly becomes clear that it is because they make statements that, while relatively unproblematic in the categories of Gregory's thought, *are* problematic within another Christological tradition, that of Maximus. And that tradition is what Meyendorff has called 'Cyrilline Chalcedonianism' (what used to be dubbed 'Neo-Chalcedonianism'). Take Difficulty 2: the passage from Gregory that is causing difficulty is this: 'And, in a word, what is exalted is to be ascribed to the Godhead, to that nature which is superior to sufferings and the body, what is lowly is to be ascribed to the composite that for your sake emptied himself and took flesh and—it is no worse to say—became a man.' In Gregory's Third Theological Oration this is his response to the Arian argument that one who is God cannot be said to hunger, sleep, fear, and so Christ cannot be God: it ushers in Gregory's brilliant oxymoronic celebration of the Incarnate One as a coincidence of opposites. What makes it a difficulty for Maximus and other Cyrilline Chalcedonians is the way it suggests a separation between the divine and human attributes of Christ, that might imply something like two subjects in Christ (though I do not think that Gregory suggests that at all), and certainly seems to keep suffering away from the Godhead. Maximus' response is a paraphrase of Gregory that emphasizes the unity of subject in Christ and, in particular, expressly justifies theopaschite language by using, and repeating, an expression from Gregory's Fourth Theological Oration—'God passible'.[6] In the fourth Difficulty, Maximus is similarly concerned to justify theopaschite language: 'therefore he was also truly a suffering God, and the very same was truly a wonderworking man, because also there was a true hypostasis of true natures according to an ineffable union' (1045A). I would suggest then that Maximus is not happy with Cappadocian Christological language and 'corrects' it with a theopaschite emphasis more typical of the Cyrilline tradition.

In the case of Trinitarian theology there are two difficulties I want to look at, both of which discuss the same passage from Gregory's sermons. The Difficulties are no. 23, from the earlier set, and no. 1, from the later. Both are concerned with the passage from the Third Theological Oration which runs thus: 'Therefore, the monad, having moved from the beginning towards the dyad, rests in the triad.' The difficulty this poses for Maximus is the way Gregory seems to speak of movement in God. Difficulty 23—the earlier one—starts off by proving that God cannot be said to move. His conclusion is uncompromising: 'If therefore what is without cause is certainly without motion, then the divine is without motion, as having no cause of being at all, but being rather the cause of all beings.' Maximus then discusses the way in which something that causes movement (or change) might be said itself to be moved (or changed), even though in reality it is motionless (or changeless): for example, light makes it possible for eyes to see, it might be said to move sight to vision, and might be spoken of as being moved, though properly it occasions movement, rather than being moved itself. Maximus then invokes Denys and his discussion of how God can be called desire (*eros*) and love (*agape*), and summarizes the Areopagite's teaching in these terms: 'as desire and love the Divine is moved, as desired and loved the Divine moves towards itself everything that is capable of desire and love.' Maximus is now in a position to interpret Gregory's statement:

'The monad, moved from the beginning towards the dyad, rests in the triad': it is moved in the mind that is receptive of this, whether it be angelic or human, and through it and in it makes inquiries about it, and to speak more plainly, it teaches the mind, to begin with, the thought about the monad, lest separation be introduced into the first cause, and immediately leads it on to receive its divine and ineffable fecundity, saying secretly and hiddenly to it that it must not think that it is in any way barren, this good of reason and wisdom and sanctifying power, of consubstantial and enhypostatic beings, lest the Divine be taken to be composite of these, as of things accidental, and not believed to be these eternally. The Godhead is therefore said to be moved as the source of the inquiry as to the way it exists. (1260D)

For Maximus the movement spoken of by Gregory is really a movement in the mind—whether angelic or human—that seeks to understand God; such a mind passes from the thought of unity and rests in that of the triad. Difficulty 1 discusses this same passage, together with another similar passage from elsewhere in Gregory's work, in very similar terms. In this difficulty Maximus ventures further in explaining the language of monad and triad:

There is therefore no explanation of the transcendent cause of beings, but rather a setting out of pious thought concerning it, if it is said that the Godhead is monad but not dyad, triad but not multitude, as being without beginning, bodiless and free from rivalry. For the monad is truly monad; for it is not the beginning of beings alongside it, by expansion and contraction, so that it is naturally poured out leading to multitude, but it is the enhypostatic reality of the consubstantial Triad. And the triad is truly triad, not made up of perishable number (for it is not a composition of monads, so that it suffers division), but is the real existence of a tri-hypostatic monad. For the triad is truly the monad, for it is so, and the monad is truly the triad, for thus it exists. There is then one Godhead, in monadic being and triadic existence. (1036BC)

Such analysis of the language of monad and triad is not characteristic of Gregory, for whom the language of monad and triad is an occasionally used rhetorical antithesis;[7] it seems to me that it is suggested rather by some of Denys' trinitarian discussion.[8] Maximus then goes on to make the same point as in Ambiguum 23, that movement in God means movement in the mind contemplating God.

There seem to be two points about Maximus' engagement with the trinitarian thought of Gregory. First, he reaches for Denys as he tries to understand it; and secondly, his understanding of movement in God is really quite different from Gregory's. Gregory is clearly thinking of something within the divine being itself: a kind of eternal movement, and if eternal then beyond any experience we might have of movement.[9] Maximus' understanding is explicitly subjective: movement in this context really refers to something going on in the mind of one who seeks to understand the Trinity.

This discussion of the relationship between Gregory the Theologian and Maximus the Confessor shows that even the formation of Orthodox tradition is not an unproblematic matter. It would be difficult to find two such revered pillars of Orthodoxy as Gregory and Maximus. But if Gregory is to be seen as part of the making of classical patristic doctrine, then what Maximus is doing in refining what I suppose would be called the Byzantine theological tradition must be seen as some kind of remaking of doctrine. For interpretation is a necessary part of receiving tradition and understanding it: interpretation encounters difficulties such as we have explored, and difficulties cannot be resolved simply by repeating the deliverances of tradition. Maximus' remaking of doctrine involves some rethinking. Engagement with tradition is, however, more than a matter for the intellect. In concentrating on Maximus' *Book of Difficulties* it is intellectual difficulties of one sort or another that we have mainly encountered. In Steiner's taxonomy of difficulty there is one category not so far mentioned: that is what he calls 'ontological difficulty'. 'Ontological' difficulty is a difficulty in reading that calls in question what it is to read at all (Steiner's examples are the poems of Mallarmé or Celan).[10] This category is not perhaps particularly illuminating for trying to understand Maximus' reading of Gregory, but it might be relevant were we to look at the way in which phrases and expressions of Gregory's sermons have fertilized the liturgical tradition of the Orthodox Church. For transposed into that context they suggest a very different kind of reading, and it may be that it is there—in the liturgical poetry of the Church—that Gregory the rhetor most truly becomes St Gregory the Theologian.

NOTES

1. Cyril of Scythopolis records a similar appeal to Gregory Nazianzen: see his *Life of Cyriacus* cited in Norris 1991: 103.
2. So Suidas, *Lexicon*, s.v. 'Origines' (ed. A. Adler (Leipzig, 1928–38), iii. 619).
3. Cited in G. W. H. Lampe (ed.), *A Patristic Greek Lexicon* (Oxford: Clarendon Press, 1961–8), s.v. 'theologos'.
4. See his *Exégèse médiévale*, in *Théologie*, Études Publiées sons la Direction de la Faculté de Théologie S.J. de Lyon-Fourvière, 41–2, 59 (Paris, 1959–64).
5. Amb. 41, though on a christological passage from Gregory's sermons, is really much wider in scope.
6. That Maximus is consciously alluding to Gregory's use of the term *theos pathetos* seems to be clear, since the first time he uses it he quotes the whole phrase: 'God passible to overcome sin' (*Orat.* 30. 1).
7. In the *Orations* Gregory only seems to use monad and triad antithetically at 20. 2 and 23. 8 (the two passages discussed by Maximus in Amb. 1) and 25. 17. Such language occurs, too, in his *carmina*, but his usual way of referring to the Trinity is to use triad alone.
8. See, in particular, *Divine Names*, 13. 3. It seems to me very likely that Denys has taken the juxtaposition of monad and triad from the passages in Gregory cited above. But what was an occasional theme in Gregory becomes something more settled in Denys, if we can rely on his few discussions of the Trinity, and it is Denys' settled use of the antithesis that Maximus reflects.
9. The next sentence after the one commented on by Maximus reads: 'In a serene, non-temporal, incorporeal way, the Father is parent of the "offspring" and originator of the "emanation" . . .' (Wickham's translation in Norris 1991). This as a comment on the phrase about monad moving to triad must mean that there is some kind of 'serene, non-temporal, incorporeal' movement in the Godhead itself.
10. It is interesting in this context to note that Henri-Irenée Marrou's positive revaluation of Augustine in his *Retractatio* published in 1949 also draws on the example of Mallarmé: see Marrou 1958: 649 ('saint Augustin nous invite à retrouver dans l'Écriture une conception mallarméenne de la poésie').

REFERENCES

Barsanuphe and Jean de Gaza (1972), *Correspondance*, trans. L. Regnault *et al.*, Solesmes.

Kelly, J. N. D. (1975), *Jerome*, London.

Marrou, Henri-Irenée (1958), *Saint Augustin et la fin de la culture*, 4th edn., Paris.

Norris, F. W. (1991), *Faith Gives Fullness to Reasoning: The Five Theological Orations of Gregory Nazianzen*, Supplements to *Vigiliae Christianae* 13, Leiden.

Sherwood, P., OSB (1952), *An Annotated Date-List of the Works of Maximus the Confessor*, Studia Anselmiana 30, Rome.

—— (1955), *The Earliest Ambigua of St Maximus the Confessor*, Studia Anselmiana 36, Rome.

Steiner, George (1978), 'On Difficulty', in *On Difficulty and Other Essays*, Oxford.

8

Lex orandi:
Heresy, Orthodoxy, and Popular Religion

REBECCA LYMAN

Throughout his works on ancient and modern theology, Maurice Wiles has eloquently defended the unity between religious experience and critical theological enquiry. Thus, his studies of Arius, Asterius, and Eunomius include attempts to recover the possible spiritual concerns of those theologies traditionally understood as heretical (Wiles 1962, 1985, 1989). On the other hand this has also led him to ask critical questions about the necessary unity of certain spiritual and theological principles in orthodox soteriology or Christology (Wiles 1968, 1970). This less comfortable move is of course critical to any living theological enterprise: can there be essential or self-evident principles of Christian experience which anchor theological doctrines? As might be expected changes in religious experience and reasoned reflection go together, though exactly how remains a controversial and ambiguous question (Wiles 1986: 13). The affirmation of the unity of faith and doctrine is often expressed in the formula *lex orandi, lex credendi*. However, this formula is understood rather differently by theologians, historians, and liturgists. Ironically, if we take seriously the unity between prayer and belief, we may find less certainty than traditionally ascribed to the development of doctrine.

This point was well made by Wiles in his chapter 'Lex orandi' in *The Making of Christian Doctrine*. Using liturgy or styles of prayer as a source for ancient Christian devotion, he argued that popular religion exercised a conservative role in Christian thought, particularly in Christology. While Origen may attempt to nuance patterns of prayer to Christ to ensure the priority of the Father, such theological finesse is ineffective in the face of widespread popular prayer to Christ as God (Wiles 1967: 65–70). On the whole popular belief tended towards modalism so that theological positions such as dynamic monarchianism, Origenist subordinationism, and philosophical Arianism failed because they did not do justice to the Son as an object of worship (Wiles 1967: 87). Although public prayer continued to stress the mediation of Christ, so that the Arians might appeal to traditional liturgy to support their opinions, the Nicenes modified liturgy successfully in line with Trinitarian theology and popular devotion. Religious experience is therefore important to theological development, but rather unpredictable: 'But that is not to say that the effect which prayer has actually had is at every point precisely the effect which it should have had' (Wiles 1967: 93).

This contrast of 'conservative' popular religion and 'speculative' theology is a common one in the history of early Christianity. In his classic study of 1923–4, J. Lebreton outlined the tension between popular faith and philosophical theologians such as Hippolytus, Clement, and Origen in the third century. In contrast to their speculative interests, he cited the definitions of Irenaeus (*Adv. haer.* 1. 10. 2–3) and Tertullian (*De praescr.* 3) of theology, which avoided specious questions and focused on the economy of salvation (Lebreton 1923: 484–7). Although one cannot merely accept popular opinion as orthodoxy, this simple faith was a tide against which philosophical Arianism failed (Lebreton 1924: 34–6). H. J. Carpenter's study in 1963 of the second century followed a similar pattern. Ordinary people were interested primarily in ethics, institution, and scripture; with the influx of educated converts in the second century, these believers became 'alarmed at speculation' practised by the philosophical theologians (Carpenter 1963: 299).

Both studies reflect similar problems in their approach to this question in pre-Nicene Christianity. 'Popular religion' is largely undefined; depending heavily on literary sources, they have more evidence about the attitudes of 'speculative' theologians than about those of ordinary believers. Carpenter constructed his definition of popular belief from the 'less reflective' and more pastoral works such as the Apostolic Fathers (Carpenter 1963: 295). While these writings contrast in style to those of Origen or Tertullian, it is not clear that the theological interests or abilities of Ignatius, Clement of Rome, or Barnabas are equivalent or equal nor should we assume that their piety as educated leaders is equivalent to ordinary believers in Rome or Antioch. By his definition of popular religion

as focused on ethics or institution, Carpenter also narrows excessively the interests of the theologians; Tertullian and Hippolytus
separated from the community eventually over disciplinary issues
rather than theological ones, and Origen became more involved
with church life in Caesarea through regular preaching. It is not
self-evident therefore that their devotional or theological interests
were as distinct from those of ordinary believers as is often claimed.
Finally, these studies do not address the power of heresiological
rhetoric in ancient theological texts. Lebreton's definitions of
normative theology from Irenaeus and Tertullian were drawn from
polemical texts, and hardly have the neutral interest he claimed;
both works focus precisely on speculation and philosophy as
the source of Gnosticism in particular and heresy in general.
Carpenter's claim that ethical charges against the Montanists reflect
a popular preference for discipline over theology ignored the basic
doctrinal orthodoxy of the movement (Carpenter 1963: 298).

'Popular belief' itself therefore is a problematic term, but
particularly in ancient Christianity. First, it assumes a division
between the belief of the majority and the educated élites; is lay
piety only an inferior derivative from an ecclesiastical norm (Davis
1974)? Secondly, popular belief is characterized as not only passive,
but also uniform and unchanging (Brown 1981: 17–18). Several
recent studies would seem to require a substantial modification of
the assumed gulf between educated speculative theologians and a
mass of uneducated Christians, uninterested or threatened by
theological questions. W. Meeks and P. Brown (Brown 1987) have
described the urban Christians of the second and third centuries as
of middling social class with literate and spiritual interests. It is not
clear therefore that popular belief was as docile and unspeculative as
either theological apologists such as Tertullian or Graeco-Roman
polemicists such as Celsus might have wished. Taking the varied
literature of the second century as a whole from *The Martyrs of
Lyons* to Ptolemy's letter to Flora, it would appear that spiritual
and theological issues on a variety of levels were very lively in the
second and third centuries. Several ancient historians have in fact
denied the existence of popular religion in Christianity of the later
empire (MacMullen 1966; Momigliano 1972; Brown 1981). The
focus on teaching and belief led to a greater unity between the
educated and the uneducated, so that the usual language of
hierarchy in relation to religious practice is noticeably absent. This

however should not blind us to the continuing existence of social or educational hierarchies within the community (MacMullen 1989). To a large degree it remains difficult in antiquity, particularly in pre-Nicene Christianity, to reconstruct concretely the common or special interests of the ordinary from the accounts of the élite.

The flourishing of Christian teachers and movements in the second and third centuries was probably a response to a variety of interested believers: 'I listened gladly to Justin, but my Christianity I received from my parents,' commented an early martyr (*Acts of Justin*, 4). The variety of literature including Gnostic works, martyrdom accounts, pastoral writings, and apocryphal acts reflects a theological and literary liveliness characteristic of Late Antique religions (Harris 1989: 298). Theological writings therefore played different roles within different communities from edification to speculation (Wisse 1986). To see this varied literature as 'popular' in contrast to the philosophical works of an Origen creates an artificial opposition within Christian theology rather than a continuum of various works accessible to the literate Christian. Although inevitably cited as an example of the gulf between popular religion and philosophical theology, Origen's writings in fact reveal his continuing encounter with the variety of theological abilities and interests in the early community. On one hand his language often echoed the hierarchy of Platonism on the inadequacy of *pistis* as *alogos*, yet he did not dismiss the 'simple believers' as superstitious outsiders or unworthy of salvation (Hällström 1984). On the whole Origen's writings reveal impatience rather than hostility or strife with simple believers, who from his perspective included most Christians including many bishops. In his description these were unphilosophical rather than anti-philosophical people, who by laziness or fear did not push deeply enough into the Bible, but rather accepted the words of others. Rather than opposition one should therefore see a more complex continuum in varied styles of theological reflection and interest within the early Christian community.

To a large degree this complexity has been hidden because of the power of heresiological categories which emerged in the second century. As outlined by A. LeBoulluec, the construction of heresy by Justin and Irenaeus in the second century from philosophical polemics and Jewish notions of a false prophet effectively masked the religious motivations or shared community life of heretical movements (LeBoulluec 1985: 543). The conflicting theological positions were highlighted, attributed to philosophical speculation, and placed in abstract doctrinal classifications. Accepting the heresiological rhetoric of ancient texts, one may therefore more easily assume that popular belief, however inchoate or hidden historically, would have been against the lone and speculative theologian (Wilken 1988).

Until recently this characterization dominated historical and theological interpretations of the Arian controversy. The activities of Arius as a popular preacher in Alexandria or the large urban churches of the Arians were submerged beneath discussions of their philosophical backgrounds and motivations (Norris 1991: 56–8). Heretical movements, even if theologically coherent, eventually foundered therefore on their inadequate spirituality or their distance from popular belief: Athanasius and Cyril spoke the language of the people (Frend 1972) or offered a theology in tune with popular devotion (Kannengiesser 1982: 35, 39, 86; Williams 1987: 110–11). However, these studies are vague as to the definition of this popular belief except as a devotion to a high Christology which allowed the Athanasian critique of Arius to succeed: only a wholly divine saviour can save. This picture seems to be dominated by the assumption of a unity of popular piety and orthodoxy which may not be supported historically. For example, in contrast to usual readings of the later Nestorian controversy, T. Gregory has shown that both Nestorius and Cyril drew on and orchestrated crowds to strengthen their positions; one cannot predict a certain theology which would be 'popular'. This conclusion cuts against the usual portrayal of Cyril as continuing the populist legacy of Athanasius to a high Christology (Frend 1972).

What little liturgical and archaeological evidence we have about early devotion to Christ is less certain than often supposed. Whereas theologians or historians of doctrine often assume a clear continuity of *lex orandi* (Lienhard 1987), liturgists map the changes and ambiguities of early liturgical practices. For example, in the rite of baptism anointing was not clearly evident as an orthodox practice until the fourth century (Lampe 1967). This reveals not only the communication or borrowing between various religious communities at the time, but also points to the openness of meaning in liturgical acts; the same rite may have different meanings to distinct individuals or communities. Eusebius records the touching story of an Alexandrian Christian who was a faithful member of the mainstream community for many years before realizing his earlier baptism had been Gnostic (*HE* 7. 9). Such a story reminds one of the necessarily dynamic and loose connection between ritual and theology in spite of the appeals to definitive boundaries between orthodox and heretic beliefs and practices (Wainwright 1980: 227–50). Both 'heretical' and 'orthodox' communities modified liturgies and prayers in line with particular theological interests.

In the light of this how can one evaluate the common appeal to the conservative function of devotion to Christ as divine in pre-Nicene Christianity? In his classic study on prayer to Christ J. Jungmann outlines the ambiguity of practices of devotion in the pre-Nicene period. Rather than a division of popular or élite devotion, he makes a distinction between private and public prayer. Public prayer was not formalized until the third and fourth centuries; presiders improvised at particular points in the service. Jungmann therefore would see liturgy reflecting the continuity and diversity of the devotional practices of early communities. He is therefore less certain of the doctrinal effect of liturgy in the first few centuries, calling prayer directly to Christ a 'blunt weapon' in theological controversy; the prominence of Christ as high priest or lack of prayer directly to Christ was highly traditional (Jungmann 1925/1989: 218). Mediating prayers to the Father through the Son would not necessarily exclude devotion to Christ as *theos*, yet spontaneous and direct prayer would not necessarily convey the full sense of divinity later codified at Constantinople. Origen in spite of his attempt to distinguish prayer to the Father and to the Son prayed directly to Christ in his homilies (Jungmann 1925/1989: 160). Ironically, the most direct prayers to Christ were in the apocryphal acts of John and Thomas, and the earliest liturgical address to Christ appears to have been Gnostic (Jungmann 1925/1989: 165). The patterns of prayer in the first centuries, public or private, therefore do not convey the sort of certainty that one can use to explain the eventual triumph of a particular doctrine. This is most evident in the extensive revision of liturgies in the fourth century by both Arians and Nicenes to reflect their own theologies.

Archaeological evidence supports a similar ambiguity in terms of Christocentric devotion or definition. The earliest representative pictures portray Jesus as a youthful wonder-worker who conveys a sense of power and deliverance (Snyder 1985). The portraits of Jesus as teacher are also present, but less central. In the fourth century a shift occurs to show Jesus as a bearded and elderly figure surrounded by disciples—an image of a philosopher, but also of an emperor or a bishop. These images tend to exclude the suffering of Christ, yet the positive Christology portrayed here is also ambiguous. Christ represents deliverance and divine power, but how this can be translated theologically into a more than general definition of divinity is unclear. Eusebius tell us that some ancients kept images of Christ, with Peter and Paul, yet this transfer of Graeco-Roman practice of honouring 'saviours' again does not convey clearly how the divinity of Jesus was necessarily understood (*HE* 7. 18. 4). In the same way the image of the suffering Blandina as Christ in *The Martyrs of Lyons* or Perpetua's vision of the grey-haired shepherd or figure on the throne with white hair and a youthful face tell us about power, deliverance, and reassurance, but do not translate directly into the categories of *homoiousios* or *homoousios* divinity. The images of Christ as *theos* reflect the same ambiguities as literary arguments as to his status in a spiritual world crowded with intermediaries (Gallagher 1982).

These images and patterns of devotion therefore do not deny or confirm the claims of popular Christianity as generally modalistic (Origen, *Contra Cel.* 8. 14; Lebreton 1923–4: 488; Wiles 1967: 71). In devotion and art Christians celebrated the delivering power of Christ as the unique representative and image of God. They seem to echo the muddled comments of Zephyrinus as reported by Hippolytus, 'I know that there is one God, Jesus Christ nor except him do I know any other' (*Adv. haer.* 9. 6), followed by his confession of the impassibility of the Father. This may reflect devotion to Christ as God in a modalist sense as often claimed or a Christocentric access to the Father as God. Both possibilities are evident in the acts of the martyrs. On one hand as often cited there is direct prayer to Christ (*Acts of Carpus*, 41, 47; Wiles 1967: 66; Jungmann 1925/1989: 165), but also prayers through Christ to the Father (*Polycarp*, 14; *Scillitan Martyrs*, 15) or prayer and identification with both God and Christ (*Perpetua*, 12, 15). Even in the passionately Christocentric Ignatius of Antioch prayer is offered both to and through Christ (*Eph.* 4. 2; 18. 2). Given these sorts of ambiguities, the label of 'modalist' for early Christian devotion becomes so broad as to be meaningless, particularly in justifying complex Christological issues.

The evidence of early Christianity therefore in the light of patterns of devotion or in the reconstruction of popular religion is even more historically ambiguous than Wiles claimed in *The Making of Christian Doctrine*. Theologically, the ancient heresiological stereotypes together with the silence of the evidence about popular religion have been commonly used to argue for an implicit orthodoxy of spirituality which underlies the doctrinal formulations. Thus, heretics may be excluded not only for their theological errors, but also for their defective spirituality. This tight connection between spirituality and theology is of course needed to defend the precision of Christian confession and effectively to exclude dissenters. Teachers of orthodoxy such as the Cappodocians or Augustine therefore become benign experts who defend the simple against the impious speculators, but also give a reasoned account of basic beliefs. At times this is indeed true of theologians, but it cannot be used as a universal principle of doctrinal development or historical explanation. This masks not only the creativity of orthodoxy, but the growing élitism of theological and ecclesiastical experts who therefore represent the mind of the people (MacMullen 1989: 511). The unity of popular belief and orthodoxy can hardly be maintained through the medieval period.

Equally important, the language of the danger of speculation which was rooted in heresiological polemics has been accepted uncritically and impoverished our understanding of the role and relation of ancient theologians to their communities. This opposition of simple belief to sophisticated reflection can mask the theological interests of the ordinary and the spirituality of the sophisticated. This of course justifies the teaching of the ecclesiastical hierarchy as suitable for all; Tertullian's fierce polemic against speculation was addressed to all levels of believer in *De praescriptione*. Sadly, this has hidden the unique social and theological unity of earliest Christianity in which the gulf between ordinary and educated believer was lessened in contrast to the larger society.

What difference does it make for modern theology for Eunomius to have been a genuinely religious person? To recapture the unity of spirituality and theology on both sides of theological debate is to admit a broader identity at the heart of Christianity. *Lex orandi, lex credendi* could ultimately be a statement of inclusive flexibility rather than a spiritual guarantee of theological uniformity. Many theologians have used liturgy or devotion as a conservative weight

for theological work or development (Sykes 1978). On the extreme
end this defines theology as a game with set pieces which may be
rearranged in the light of changing culture (Wignall in Sykes 1978).
This position however tends to overestimate the function of
language in the phenomenology of worship. By contrast liturgists
celebrate the metaphorical nature of worship and prayer which
leads the believer beyond 'dull' theology into multiple meanings
and richer experience (Stevenson 1984). Liberation theologies were
nourished by traditional Christian liturgy, but as a result of
changing experience and reflection have begun to revise these
liturgies and theologies to reveal new dimensions of Christianity
(Ro 1990). In this context *lex orandi, lex credendi* curiously protects
the integrity of popular religion in casting suspicion on the
assumption that anyone may ultimately speak for the experience of
all Christians.

In a recent article R. Williams argued against a sense of essential
experience in pre-Nicene Christianity which could effectively
create and maintain a community, but rather focused on the
common telling of and encounter with the historical story of Jesus
(Williams 1989). This approach, which acknowledged plurality of
experience, but located common authenticity and authority in
continued communication about Jesus, offers a more helpful way
of understanding Christian identity not only in the plurality of the
past, but also in the present. The legacy of ancient Christianity is
both the lively history of witness and reflection and the bitter
rhetoric of heresiological exclusion. This traditional construction
of doctrinal certainty is a handicap not only in historical research,
but in the response to the pluralism of modern Christianity. The
revolutionary legacy of credal criticism is therefore to remind us
that theology is not a repeated game with set pieces any more than
a life of faith is a repetition of platitudes. It is the constant and costly
intellectual and spiritual response of a historical humanity to a
living God. To affirm the ambiguities and variety of devotion and
belief in doctrinal development is to open up present theological
reflection to the varied realities of Christian experience. As David
Tracy commented, 'Only by beginning to listen to other voices
may we also begin to hear the otherness within our own discourse
and within ourselves. What we might then begin to hear . . . are
possibilities we have never dared to dream' (Tracy 1987: 79). It has
been the contribution of Maurice Wiles to let us hear the otherness

at the heart of our tradition as our own, and therefore admit that the continued exploration of theological questions is the only foundation of true orthodoxy.

REFERENCES

Brown, P. (1981), *The Cult of the Saints*, Chicago.

—— (1987), 'Late Antiquity', in P. Veyne (ed.), *A History of Private Life*, Cambridge, Mass.: i. 235–311.

Carpenter, H. J. (1963), 'Popular Christianity and the Theologians in the Early Centuries', *Journal of Theological Studies*, NS 14: 294–310.

Davis, N. (1974), 'Some Tasks and Themes in the Study of Popular Religion', in C. Trinkaus and H. Oberman (eds.), *The Pursuit of Holiness in Late Medieval and Renaissance Religion*, Leiden: 308–14.

Frend, W. H. C. (1972), 'Popular Religion and Christological Controversy in the Fifth Century', in G. Cuming and D. Baker (eds.), *Popular Religious Belief and Practice*, Studies in Church History 8, Cambridge: 19–29.

Gallagher, E. V. (1982), *Divine Man or Magician? Celsus and Origen on Jesus*, Chico, Calif.

Gregory, T. (1979), *Vox Populi: Violence and Popular Involvement in the Religious Controversies of the Fifth Century AD*, Columbus, Oh.

Hällström, G. af (1984), *Fides simpliciorum according to Origen of Alexandria*, Commentationes humanarum litterarum 76, Helsinki.

Harris, J. (1989), *Ancient Literacy*, Cambridge, Mass.

Jungmann, J. A. (1925/1989), *The Place of Christ in Liturgical Prayer*, trans. A. Peeler, Collegeville, Minn.

Kannengiesser, C. (1982), *Holy Scripture and Hellenistic Hermeneutics in Alexandrian Christology*, Berkeley, Calif.

Lampe, G. W. H. (1967), *The Seal of the Spirit*, 2nd edn., London.

LeBoulluec, A. (1985), *La Notion d'hérésie dans la littérature grecque IIe–IIIe siècles*, 2 vols., Paris.

Lebreton, J. (1923–4), 'Le Désaccord de la foi populaire et de la théologie savante dans l'Église chrétienne du IIIe siècle', in *Revue d'histoire ecclésiastique*, 19: 481–506; 20: 5–37.

Lienhard, J. (1987), 'The Arian Controversy: Some Categories Reconsidered', *Theological Studies*, 48: 415–37.

MacMullen, R. (1966), 'A Note on *Sermo humilis*', *Journal of Theological Studies*, NS 17: 108–12.

—— (1989), 'The Preacher's Audience (AD 250–400)', *Journal of Theological Studies*, NS 40: 503–11.

Momigliano, A. (1972), 'Popular Religious Beliefs and the late Roman

Historians', in G. Cuming and D. Baker (eds.), *Popular Religious Belief and Practice*, Studies in Church History 8, Cambridge: 1–18.

Norris, F. (1991), *Faith Gives Fullness to Reasoning: The Five Theological Orations of Gregory Nazianzen*, Leiden.

Ro, Young-chan (1990), 'Symbol, Myth, and Ritual: The Method of the Minjung', in S. B. Thistlethwaite and M. P. Engel (eds.), *Lift Every Voice: Constructing Christian Theologies from the Underside*, San Francisco: 41–8.

Snyder, G. F. (1985), *Ante Pacem. Archaeological Evidence of Church Life before Constantine*, Atlanta.

Stevenson, W. T. (1984), 'Is there a Characteristic Anglican Theology?', in M. Darrol Bryant (ed.), *The Future of Anglican Theology*, Toronto Studies in Theology 17, New York: 15–26.

Sykes, S. (1978), *The Integrity of Anglicanism*, London.

Tracy, D. (1987), *Plurality and Ambiguity*, New York.

Wainwright, G. (1980), *Doxology: The Praise of God in Worship, Doctrine and Life: A Systematic Theology*, London.

Wiles, M. F. (1962), 'In Defence of Arius', *Journal of Theological Studies*, NS 13: 339–47.

—— (1967), *The Making of Christian Doctrine*, Cambridge.

—— (1968), 'The Unassumed is the Unhealed', *Religious Studies*, 4 (Oct.): 47–56.

—— (1970), 'Does Christology Rest on a Mistake?', *Religious Studies*, 6 (Mar.): 69–76.

—— (1985), 'Asterius: A New Chapter in the History of Arianism?', in R. C. Gregg (ed.), *Arianism: Historical and Theological Reassessments*, Philadelphia: 111–51.

—— (1986), *God's Action in the World: The Bampton Lectures for 1986*, London.

—— (1989), 'Eunomius: Hair-splitting Dialectician or Defender of the Accessibility of Salvation?', in R. Williams (ed.), *The Making of Orthodoxy: Essays in Honour of Henry Chadwick*, Cambridge: 157–72.

Wilken, R. (1988), 'The Durability of Orthodoxy', *Word and World*, 8/2: 124–32.

Williams, R. (1987), *Arius: Heresy and Tradition*, London.

—— (1989), 'Does it make Sense to Speak of Pre-Nicene Orthodoxy?', in R. Williams (ed.), *The Making of Orthodoxy: Essays in Honour of Henry Chadwick*, Cambridge: 1–23.

Wisse, F. (1986), 'The Use of Early Christian Literature as Evidence for Inner Diversity and Conflict', in C. W. Hedrick and R. Hodgson Jr. (eds.), *Nag Hammadi, Gnosticism, and Early Christianity*, Peabody, Mass.: 177–90.

9

The Theologian as Advocate

SALLIE McFAGUE

Maurice Wiles writes in a deceptively simple sentence, one that underlies both the radical and the creative character of his own work: 'We have no other starting-point than our ordinary experience of the world' (Wiles 1974: 25). The 'making' and 'remaking' of Christian doctrine, which summarizes Wiles's life-long concern, focuses on the dialectic between experience and change. It is the premiss of the present essay that 'our ordinary experience of the world' has changed profoundly during this century; hence, theology must change as well. I will be particularly concerned with the changed stance of the theologian; specifically, towards one of advocacy for the well-being of our planet.

Gordon Kaufman, in his presidential address to the American Academy of Religion in 1982, called on theologians and students of religion, in light of human nuclear capability to annihilate ourselves and most of the rest of living creatures, to turn our attention, *as scholars*, to this issue. He wrote, 'Can we really continue, in the name of "neutrality" and "objectivity," to pursue our academic work in . . . aloofness from the potential disaster that confronts humanity?' (Kaufman 1983: 12). The times are such that, like it or not, we have thrust upon us, Kaufman insists, the responsibility to turn our research programmes towards the deconstruction and reconstruction of the central symbols of the Jewish and Christian traditions—the symbols of God, Christ, and Torah—so that they will help divert rather than court disaster. Just as medical doctors and scientists have professional responsibilities in respect of the crisis confronting us, so do teachers of theology and religion.

I responded to this call and I believe a positive response is justified, not only to this particular issue (which fortunately appears

An earlier version of this essay was published in *Theological Education*, 25 (Spring 1989).

to be receding somewhat from centre stage), but to other pressing ones as well, such as the oppression of peoples due to gender, race, class, or sexual orientation and the ecological deterioration of our earth. (My own work is especially involved with the last issue, but the oppression of people and of the earth are interrelated; hence, the stance of the theologian is the same in both cases.) One of the characteristics of our post-modern world is an apocalyptic sensibility, an awareness that viable living conditions for human beings as well as for other creatures may be ending soon, either through a 'bang' (a nuclear holocaust) or a 'whimper' (ecological deterioration). If one possesses this sensibility—and at the same time sees the triumphalist, monarchical God of the Jewish and Christian traditions as contributing to either militarism (the almighty King who will side with us in the Armageddon against our enemies) or escapism (the powerful Father who will protect his children from disaster)—then one is constrained to become an advocate for radical revision of the tradition's central symbolism. The call to human responsibility for the fate of the earth, and for theologians this must mean *theological* responsibility, becomes inescapable. If the reading of our cultural context is a dire one, in a number of respects, and if the tradition of which one is an interpreter can be credibly shown to contribute to the 'problem', then one *must*, I believe, attempt to see how it might contribute, as well, to a 'solution'.

Am I suggesting that in our perilous times theology must become an advocate in order to help save the *polis*—or in our time, the cosmos—in ways it did not need to in the past, before we had the ability to ruin ourselves and our planet? Is my proposal merely a utilitarian one: theology must at this time contribute to the general good of humankind and the earth, whatever it might have done or been in the past? Yes and no. I do believe that the conditions facing us, a severely damaged ecosystem and massive human suffering, force us to consider what the nature of theology is and ought to be with an urgency seldom experienced in times past. But these conditions may also help us to see more clearly how Christian theology ought to be characterized in our time.

I would like to set my own comments on the nature of theological deconstruction and reconstruction in the context of work at present being done on theology as conversation. While I do not find the metaphor of 'conversation' finally to be adequate to address the crises of our time, it is a suggestive model, especially if qualified and deepened by feminist perspectives, as I will attempt to show.

In a number of works, but most notably in his book *Plurality and Ambiguity* (Tracy 1987), Tracy proposes an alternative to the liberalist–foundationalist assumption 'of a philosophical and theological discourse: a purely autonomous, coherent, unified, and rational self who is capable of grounding all claims to knowledge'.[1] He asserts, and I agree, that the crises of our time minimize all such claims. Quite apart from deconstruction's decentring of liberalist–foundationalist claims, *any* voice claiming certainty and closure is absurd, given the *kind* of issues facing our earth and its inhabitants. No individual thinker and no single tradition is capable of adequately addressing the looming global catastrophe. Tracy, therefore, calls for a plurality of voices, indeed a radical plurality, which takes seriously the otherness and difference of the conversational partners. These conversational partners must include, he claims, those who have hitherto been excluded—the poor, women, the Third World, people of colour, as well as the post-modern thinkers who have written of the way power is organized and manipulated for the benefit of the powerful.[2] Tracy also insists that this conversation face squarely the radical interruption posed by the ambiguities and terors of history: the genocide of six million Jews, the Gulag, Hiroshima, the destruction of North American Indians, apartheid in South Africa. While Tracy focuses this conversation on the interpretation of classic religious texts, what I find most intriguing and important about the model is its potential for interpreting the character that Christian theology should have in our time.

What it suggests initially is the limitation of some current understandings of theology: for instance, the model of theology as an academic discipline concerned mainly with metaphysical claims and epistemological issues, as well as the model of theology as the internal interpreter of its 'story' for its own adherents. Both of these perspectives are too narrow to deal with the situation facing us. We must recognize that many voices, many genres, many tasks are needed if theology is to help address the critical issues of our time. As Tracy insists, we must be able to live in a messy, open-ended situation, willing to listen to the many voices within Christian faith and able to face the historical ambiguities and terrors that our tradition has helped bring about. Whereas in the past it

might have seemed possible to limit theology to academic or
ecclesiastical matters, the global interrelatedness and interdepend-
ence of all human beings with one another and with other living
creatures (as well as the ecosystem that supports us) means that
theology, as is true of other fields of endeavour, is called upon to
understand its task in terms of the entire cosmos. Anything less
than that, whether it be the academy or the church, is a false
limitation and will result in a myopic perspective. To put it as
simply and bluntly as possible: *the* moral issue of our day is the
global one of whether or not we and other species will live or die,
as well as how well we will live. The issue of whether we live or
die must be seen in the context of the quality of life for all of life,
human and non-human: therefore, *the* moral issue of our day is the
tripartite one epitomized in the World Council of Churches'
rallying cry of 'peace, justice, and the integrity of creation'. These
issues, that at one time might have appeared to be separate or even
at odds with each other, must now be seen as profoundly related
if *any* of them is to be adequately addressed. It is a big order to
think morally (and theologically) about *everything that is*, but that
is what we are called to do in these final years of the twentieth
century. Within this context theology must, I believe, define its
role.

There are many different kinds of tasks that need to be done
within this overarching assignment. As Tracy calls for a plurality
of voices and the recognition of ambiguity, I would also insist that
theology embrace a range of genres. While the place of systematic,
philosophical theology will probably always be secure (or at least
as long as universities exist), other genres of theological reflection
are needed. In particular, imaginative experiments with metaphors
and models that can serve as alternatives to the dominant hierarchical, triumphalistic Western ones are called for—and that is the
particular task I have undertaken in my book *Models of God:
Theology for an Ecological, Nuclear Age* (McFague 1987). The point
of this sort of exercise is to attempt to transform sensibilities in a
more ecological, interrelated, cosmocentric direction, and to do so
in a manner in continuity with Christian faith. One of the values of
Tracy's notion of theology as conversation is that it takes seriously
the *different* contributions of many participants while decentring
any *one* contribution as being the absolute or central one. If we
were to see theology on Tracy's model, it would be a far more

collegial, egalitarian, and open affair than it presently is. Individual theologians would see their own work as *one* offering, partial and limited, to the greater work or conversation which is 'theology'. Seldom, I believe, do we think this way. The tendency, rather, is for each theologian to believe she or he must do the whole thing (produce a 'systematic theology') and that this product should supersede or eliminate other contributions.

Theology understood on the model of conversation would be a pluralistic, ambiguous, multi-genre affair, involving many voices and many different tasks. The task that I have elected is focused at the imaginative level of the metaphors and models that both underlie our concepts and profoundly influence our behaviour. In a time when the triumphalistic, hierarchical language of the tradition can be seen as contributing to oppressive dualisms (male/female, rich/poor, black/white, straight/gay, Christian/non-Christian, humanity/nature, etc.), one task needing to be done is the deconstruction of this language and the construction of alternative metaphors and models. This task openly admits to advocacy and is actively engaged in social transformation. All constructive theology, however, advocates, implicitly or explicitly, either for the status quo or for social transformation. Needless to say, this is not the only function of theology, but it is an inevitable one.

We have, up to this point, been focusing on the *nature* of the conversation that is theology and especially on advocational theology that sees itself as involved in the task that Gordon Kaufman called for: the deconstruction and reconstruction of the central symbols of the tradition in relation to their power either to thwart the fulfilment of all forms of life or to help bring about that fulfilment. We need now to turn to a related issue: the 'truth' of such a conversation. The very nature of the theological conversation as suggested here brings up this issue, for with a radically pluralistic, ambiguous, multi-genre conversation the issue of relativism looms large. What possible constraints are there on such a messy, multi-dimensional, open-ended conversation? Can Christian theology in this understanding be what one wishes it to be, what this or that voice says it is, what the majority of voices say it is? And what of the larger issue of how theology's vision of things squares with understandings coming from other disciplines, other fields? Is truth something that one area—say, the sciences—controls or is it also a multi-dimensional affair? We certainly cannot deal with all these issues here, but will focus especially on the question of 'objectivity' and 'relativism'.

I have found the work of Richard Bernstein and other pragmatists helpful at this point (see especially Bernstein 1983). Bernstein attempts to get beyond both objectivism and relativism through the model of conversation. Here we will move from seeing different kinds of theology and theological voices as a conversation (Tracy's contribution) to seeing theology as one conversation partner in the global conversation of all those attempting to make the world a more humane and wholesome place (Bernstein's contribution). Bernstein places the major blame for our foundationalist fixation on the Cartesian insistence on an absolute, indubitable starting-point.[3] This results in objectivism ('the basic conviction that there is or must be some permanent, ahistorical matrix or framework to which we can ultimately appeal in determining the nature of rationality, knowledge, truth, reality, goodness, or rightness'), as well as in its counterpart, relativism ('the basic conviction . . . that all such concepts must be understood as relative to a specific conceptual scheme, theoretical framework, paradigm, form of life, society, or culture') (Bernstein 1983: 8). From the contributions of several thinkers (Jürgen Habermas, Hannah Arendt, Martin Heidegger, Richard Rorty), Bernstein sees a way beyond objectivism and relativism in the model of conversation, for it suggests a different understanding of rationality from either objectivism or relativism. It is more related, Bernstein says, to Aristotle's *phronēsis* (or 'practical' knowledge), which explores the interrelationships among praxis, techne, practical discourse, theoretical concerns, and judgement. Some common characteristics mark the work of these thinkers on the nature of rationality: a historically situated, non-algorithmic, flexible understanding of human rationality; one which highlights the tacit dimension of human judgement and imagination; one that is sensitive to the unsuspected contingencies and genuine novelties in particular situations; one that is animated by a practical-moral concern with the threats to and prospects for human judgement and imagination—in other words, overall, a basically practical understanding of truth and rationality. Understanding rationality in this way undercuts the split between objective and subjective or value-free and advocacy, a split that is no longer supported even in the natural and biological sciences and need not be supported by the humanities, including the theological community. All knowledge is in some sense subjective and interested, at least to the extent that scientists as well as theologians exist in communities structured by major paradigms, paradigms that can and do change. Bernstein believes that the primacy of the practical in relation to truth means that we should not continue to believe that only after 'we resolve the "hard" issues of epistemology and come to grips with scientific knowledge can we turn to the "softer" and "fuzzier" concerns of moral, social, and political philosophy. This is the prejudice that is being questioned in the new conversation about human rationality' (Bernstein 1983: 48).

What is attractive about this understanding of truth and rationality is that it retrieves the 'best' from objectivism and relativism while discarding them as viable positions. That is, 'the new conversation' insists on public criteria, the necessity of a 'starting-point', the importance of logical argument and careful judgement, while refusing the demand for clear and permanent foundations. It also acknowledges that life is often incoherent and contradictory; that imagination and novelty have a place in rationality; that power plays a major role in judgements; and that the well-being of particular communities is a legitimate ground for the conflict of interpretations. In other words, while Bernstein's model of conversation is 'beyond' objectivism and relativism, it includes the major features that have allowed each to make a case concerning 'truth' issues. It is, as well, a particularly helpful model for theology, which has had peculiar and long-term problems with truth, falling often into one or the other camp (into objectivism as with fundamentalism and neo-orthodoxy or into relativism as with some brands of liberalism).

I would like now briefly to suggest how my kind of theology (theology as experimentation with alternative models and metaphors) fits into Bernstein's model—as well as how it does not—and then to indicate even more briefly how I think 'theology as a whole' or the discipline might function in the larger conversation of all those concerned with the well-being of our common life, both human and non-human.

How does one come to accept a model as true? We live *within* the model, testing our wager by its consequences. These consequences are both theoretical and practical. An adequate model will be illuminating, fruitful, have relatively comprehensive explanatory ability, be relatively consistent, able to deal with anomalies, etc. This is largely (though not totally) a functional, pragmatic view of truth, with heavy stress on the implications of certain models for the quality of human and non-human life. A praxis orientation does not deny the possibility of a 'shy ontological claim', but it does acknowledge both the mystery of God and the importance of truth as practical wisdom. Thus, it acknowledges with the apophatic tradition that we really do not *know* the inner being of divine reality: the hints and clues we have of the way things are, whether we call them religious experiences, revelation, or whatever, are too fragile, too little (and often too negative) for heavy metaphysical claims. Rather, in the tradition of Aristotle, truth means constructing the good life for the *polis*, though for our time this must mean for the cosmos. A 'true' model of God will be one that is a powerful, persuasive construal of God as being on the side of life and its fulfilment in our time.

The heavily pragmatic view of truth suggested here is similar to that of some liberation theologians and rests on an understanding of 'praxis' not simply as action vs. theory, but as a kind of reflection, one guided by practical experience. Negatively, praxis is the awareness that human beings cannot rely on ahistorical, universal truths, and positively, it is the realization that human life is fundamentally practical. Hence, in this view, knowledge is not the correspondence of some understanding of reality with 'reality-as-it-is', but it is a continual process of analysis, explanation, conversation, and application with both theoretical and practical aspects. Such knowledge is grounded in concrete history within the norms, values, and hopes of communities. While I would not identify my position with the extremes of pragmatism, it is, none the less, a healthy reminder that religious truth, whatever may be the case with other kinds of truth, is intrinsically concerned with issues of value, of consequences, of the quality of lived existence.

To be more specific now, when a theologian suggests a particular model for consideration in the context of 'truth as conversation', she or he would stand by the 'best' from objectivism—its insistence on public criteria, logical argument, and reflective judgement, as well as the necessity for a 'starting-point'—while at the same time recalling the contributions of relativism—the interested character of all knowledge, the part that power plays in all linguistic enterprises, the role of the imagination, the particular contexts of all constructs. Moreover, the suggested model would abjure any claims to foundationalism, refusing to be seen as permanent or absolute, aware of the limitations and partiality of all models. It would be offered as a possibility for the community (in this case, the church broadly conceived) to consider in its reflections on how to respond to the crises of our day. As Bernstein puts it, 'at a time when the threat of total annihilation no longer seems to be an abstract possibility but the most imminent and real potentiality, it becomes all the more imperative to try again and again to foster and nurture those forms of communal life in which dialogue, conversation, *phronēsis*, practical discourse, and judgment are concretely embodied in our everyday practices' (Bernstein 1983: 229). Truth in this view is a complex matter, orientated towards more humane practices in our public life, and consisting of both theoretical and practical components. While such a conversation needs to take place among and between theologians, theologians and students of religion need also to be part of the larger conversation of all those concerned about the common good.

And here we turn to the second set of reflections from Bernstein's model of truth as conversation: the contribution that 'theology as a whole' should make to the dialogue of voices fighting oppression and attempting to preserve our earth. He feels, as I believe many of us do as well, that the threats upon human and other forms of life in our time are such that we do not have the leisure for *mere* conversation. But the kind of dialogue being suggested here is not *mere* conversation. While conversation alone will certainly not save us from the threatening evils of our time, to the extent that scientists, theologians, philosophers, economists, demographers, physicians, and others have a responsibility, *from within their own fields and bodies of knowledge*, to be on the side of life and its fulfilment, then one of the tasks at hand is to share our knowledge and insights in pursuit of the goal of embodying our best judgements for the conduct of the practical affairs of our public life. As Bernstein says, it is not a theory that will move us beyond objectivism and relativism; that movement beyond must take place in communities—it will occur 'only if we dedicate ourselves to the practical task of furthering the type of solidarity, participation, and mutual recognition that is founded in dialogical communities' (Bernstein 1983: 231).

At this point, however, I find myself pausing—as does Bernstein as well. Where *are* these communities? Bernstein notes that our situation is one in which such communities have little chance of forming; more despairing still is the realization of 'how much of humanity has been systematically excluded and prevented from participating in such dialogical communities' (Bernstein 1983: 226). In other words, are such communities utopian, élitist fantasies that exist nowhere or perhaps only as Tracy poignantly suggests at the University of Chicago (and its look-alikes), where, as he says, 'serious conversation is more often than not a way of life' (Tracy 1987: p. x). Is the model of conversation, both within theology and among various communities with similar concerns, an élitist, utopian one that takes the ideals of the academy as its basic criteria? It is certainly the case that people sharing experiences of oppression, such as those in the base communities of Latin America or the African-American church in the United States have a common ground for conversation that is lacking in theology, let alone among those concerned in other areas.

The unease that I experience with the model of conversation as suggested by both Tracy and Bernstein—its élitist, genteel, academic, and even 'comfortable' character—is due, I believe, to an insufficiently radical understanding of both objectivity and the conversation partners. These issues are related, for, as I will suggest, with a broader mix of partners emerges a different view of objectivity. An instructive illustration of these interrelated points can be found in feminist critiques of that epitome of 'objectivity', the scientific community or 'conversation'. Recent feminist critiques of scientific 'objectivity' have raised the possibility that from a *stronger* view of objectivity (than the one presently operating in science) might emerge an agenda for scientific research that took into account the well-being of a wider range of human beings and even of the planet (see Haraway 1988; Harding 1986; Harding 1991; Harding and O'Barr 1987; Keller 1985). This stronger view of objectivity is dependent, say the feminists, on the mix of conversation partners. The argument, *in nuce*, is that present-day practising scientists, who are largely white, male, middle class, and Western, should admit their partial, biased social location, a location which influences the deep complicity of their research agendas with the needs of the military/governmental/ industrial complex. In order to broaden the base of the conversation, and hence the setting of agendas, other people from other social locations (women, for instance, from different racial, economic, cultural backgrounds) should enter it as equal partners, thus strengthening scientific objectivity by making it more inclusive. If all views, including of course those of women (of whatever race or background), are biased, then acknowledging the limitations of particular social locations by opening the conversation to those from different locations results in a stitching together of various partial perspectives so that a wider, deeper objectivity results. In other words, the issue of objectivity in science (and, I would suggest, in other fields as well, including theology) moves from the end, the testing of a hypothesis, to the beginning: *who* is setting the agenda, the research programmes that will benefit some and not other members of society? The supposition is that the present 'weak objectivity' is a cloak for research programmes that benefit the powerful institutions at the expense of the weak. The question is *who* does science and *for whose benefit* (or who does theology—or any enterprise—and for whose benefit)? The feminist criticism accepts both the political and the empirical character of science; its criticism aims at a greater, not a lesser, objectivity for science, by broadening the base of who participates in setting scientific agendas so that science might be emancipatory, liberating, beneficial for *more* people—and for the planet that supports us all.

The important mix here is situated or embodied knowledge resulting in a stronger objectivity, and therefore the possibility of humane scientific projects. The paradigm for a stronger scientific objectivity is, I would suggest, applicable to the conversation model suggested by Tracy and Bernstein, for it undercuts the implicit élitism and comfortable character of the model by radicalizing the differences among the conversation partners, given their widely varying situated embodiments. The 'view from the body' is always a view from a specific location versus the 'view from above, from nowhere': the former admits to its partiality and accepts responsibility for its views while the latter believes itself universal and transcendent, thus denying its embodiment and limitations as well as the concrete insights that can arise only from particularity (Haraway 1988: 583, 589–90). But when acknowledged, each embodied site can join with others into a network of partial perspectives (or a 'quilt', as feminists put it), in which the good of the many rather than of the few privileged ones emerges as the priority agenda. Needless to say, the emerging agenda involves a radical displacement of any *one* agenda; it is not a matter of 'adding on' perspectives, but of changing the agenda *at the centre*.[4]

This embodied view of objectivity, one that operates from specific sites in order to be of benefit to a more inclusive circle of embodied beings, is at odds with some forms of traditional, Western (male) epistemology. Its two key notions are *embodiment* and *praxis* (vs. disembodiment and theory): knowledge or truth is not concerned with neutral (read 'masked') abstractions corresponding to eternal verities, but with situated, embodied sites of insight and needs, oriented towards their increasing inclusivity and betterment. All embodied projects (in other words, everything that human beings do) are concrete, particular, and partial. Hence, in order for an agenda to gain *any* semblance of being beneficial to the many (many people, animals, plants, whatever), many sites must be included in order for the agenda to be inclusive, one which, in Donna Haraway's words, would be 'friendly to earthwide projects of finite freedom, adequate material abundance, modest meaning in suffering, and limited happiness' (Haraway 1988: 579).

The feminist analysis of the scientific conversation is instructive in deepening and radicalizing the conversation model. Significant conversation in our time would need, at the very least, to be 'collaborative conversation', conversation that was suspicious of conventional rhetoric and accepted social and governmental policies; that was willing to conspire, to work together out of a sense of shared purpose, for a different, perhaps radically different, way of common existence on our planet; that was advocatory in style and substance, rather than polite and merely tolerant. In other words, the conversation model in our time should not imagine its primary context to be the halls of the academy but the streets and alleys peopled with all those working together towards a better existence for all living beings. Such a conversation would be collaborative and advocatory, *because* it emerged from many particular, concrete, different, embodied sites.

In other words, it is necessary for the conversation of our time, within the church, within the academy, and within the world to include as primary partners, setting the agenda and not merely 'adding' to it, the voices that have hitherto been excluded—the voices of women, of people of colour, of the poor, of gay men and lesbians, as well as the 'voiceless majority' of living creatures, the non-human ones. These voices (and those who speak for the voiceless ones) will be openly advocatory, often strident, and not necessarily 'polite', but that is the nature of a collaborative rather than a genteel conversation. From very different embodied sites will emerge radically different agendas, agendas that will be for the benefit of a different and more inclusive community than those presently in positions of power in the church, the academy, or the world. This chastened view of conversation means being willing to stay in communication with voices radically different from one's own; it means embracing heterogeneity as the normal pattern; it means refusing to retreat to the comfort of like-mindedness.

Finally, another value of the model of conversation, especially for understanding the modality of theology, is that it places this traditionally pretentious enterprise in a modest, open-ended context. Conversations are ongoing and seldom issue in dogmatic or absolute dicta. A good conversation assumes that all partners have something to contribute and each makes her or his contribution, knowing it is not the last word or the only word. When the topic of the conversation is a weighty one—as the fate of our earth certainly is—then each person in the dialogue is oriented not primarily to his or her own singular contribution, but, in a collaborative fashion, to whatever will best serve to further the project at hand. While the theologian will always be responsible to both the academy and the church, neither of these contexts is sufficiently broad to serve as a final court of judgement. The issues facing us embrace the entire world, and while no one of us can think 'about the whole' in all the ways that we need to, each of us can be a voice in the conversation about this 'whole', offering our time and talent to advocate its well-being. The part each of us plays in this conversation is necessarily very limited and radically particular, but the goal is unlimited and universal: the well-being of all earth's creatures.

In closing, I would add that the kind of conversation envisioned in this chapter is one predicated on the demise of the Newtonian view of rationality, which emerged from the binary opposition of a discrete self versus its dominated object.[5] That view of rationality is currently under attack from a variety of sources: contemporary biology, the new physics, and feminism. Each of these perspectives in different ways insists that reality is so interrelated and interdependent, with the observer as part of the whole, that subject/

object, self/other kind of thinking is irrelevant and false. We are all part of a whole from which we have evolved and to which we human beings have special responsibilities. What Tracy speaks of in terms of plurality and ambiguity and Bernstein as beyond objectivism and relativism is echoed as well in the emerging vision of reality coming from contemporary science and embodied in the perspective of feminism: we are *all* interrelated and interdependent and, therefore, notions of control, of closure, of absolutes, of dualistic hierarchies, and so on, are not in keeping with reality as understood today. Wallace Stevens expresses poetically what the sciences and feminism affirm as well: 'Nothing is itself taken alone. Things are because of interrelations or interconnections' (Stevens 1957: 25). Or, as Rosemary Radford Ruether says, we must 'convert our minds to the earth', which means following 'the more diffuse and relational logic of natural harmony . . . in a way that maximizes the welfare of the whole' (Ruether 1983: 91).

The conversation which needs to take place must do so within this context and according to the rules coming to us from the new physics and from contemporary feminism. This means that the conversation will indeed not be *mere* conversation, but will be informed and regulated by an insistence that a holistic vision is the *only* permissible one and any conversation that refuses to admit some voices (including non-human ones) or that narrows its dialogue to special, privileged interests is false—that is, untrue to reality as we know it. We circle back, then, to our central theme: the task of theology in our time is to think morally and theologically about 'everything that is', to think about peace, justice, and the integrity of creation.

NOTES

1. The quotation is from Tracy's reply to a review symposium on his book in *Theology Today*, 44 (1988), 515.
2. It is important to underscore that 'plurality of voices' does not necessarily bring with it respect for otherness and difference. Any serious conversation today must underscore that the differences are complex. As Sheila Briggs puts it, 'The various forms of human particularity cannot be contained within a single concept or paradigm of human difference. The analyses of class, race, and gender are not symmetrical . . . The identities of race, gender and class are not

interchangeable in structure or in their historical development' (pp. 12–13 from an unpublished MS entitled 'The Politics of Identity and the Politics of Interpretation'). See also Spelman 1988.

3. To refuse Cartesian foundationalism does not mean that one has no 'starting-point', for there always is one; in the case of this essay, it is the assumption that 'God is on the side of life and its fulfilment'. For a thorough analysis and critique of foundationalism as well as an alternative ('broad reflective equilibrium'), see Schüssler Fiorenza 1984. A helpful comment on foundationalism along these lines is made by Bruce Coriell in an unpublished MS entitled 'A Hermeneutics of Solidarity: A Conversation between Richard Bernstein and Alfred North Whitehead', pp. 13–14:

> The etymological root of the word 'foundation' is the Latin *fundus* or bottom. Thus, the metaphor is primarily a spatial one. Bottom or base can have a descriptive sense in which it identifies a certain location or it can have a functional sense in which the base supports what is above. In a philosophical context, two very different traditions of foundationalism have emerged by appropriating the metaphor of foundation according to these quite different senses.
>
> The type of foundationalism that stresses the functional sense of the metaphor has been consistently developed within the Cartesian tradition (especially in the work of Descartes, Locke, Hume and Kant). The basic units of knowledge which are clear and undoubtable, serve as the support or foundation for a complex system of truth. Knowledge is characterized by theoretical necessity and logical certainty. From this type of foundationalism has arisen philosophical systems of materialism, idealism, and dualism; as well as deductive and inductive methodologies. In our post-Kantian context, most contemporary forms of this tradition can be characterized as transcendental foundationalism, in which the indubitable foundations for truth are the essential human conditions for knowledge.
>
> The type of foundationalism that stresses the descriptive sense of the metaphor is evident in the Greek tradition of Plato and Aristotle. In this tradition, the foundation is simply the beginning (to change from a spatial to a temporal metaphor) of any system of knowledge. Despite the absence of an indubitable starting point, a person must begin somewhere. This dialectical foundationalism maintains that the limited adequacy of any foundation must be continually adjusted in light of conclusions. The process of knowledge is at worst a vicious circle which leads to complete skepticism and at best a helical movement which leads to a provisional approximation of truth. A prominent contemporary form of this tradition can be characterized as

hermeneutical foundationalism, in which any starting point for understanding is recognized as conditioned by human experience and yet discloses truth. In this way, Gadamer and Ricœur follower Heidegger in an ontological move which uncovers the productive aspect of an otherwise vicious hermeneutical circle.

Bernstein (though he might resist the term, 'foundationalism') can be characterized by the Greek, dialectical tradition. Bernstein's insistence on the possibility of knowledge calls for a modest practical rationality akin to Aristotle's *phronēsis*. Just as *phronēsis* presupposes the Greek polis, the foundation of Bernstein's practical rationality is the existence of communities of equality, dialogue and solidarity. The limits of these communities in their actual situations do not provide the ideal theoretical foundation necessary for the indubitability and logical certainty of knowledge. Bernstein envisions a process of hermeneutical self-understanding which continually transforms these communities in such a way that a modest rationality is possible. It is only in this latter dialectical and hermeneutical sense that Bernstein can be called a foundationalist.

4. See the fine analysis of this point by Spelman 1988.
5. For one treatment of this view of rationality, see Donovan 1985.

REFERENCES

Bernstein, Richard (1983), *Beyond Objectivism and Relativism: Science, Hemeneutics, and Praxis*, Philadelphia.

Donovan, Josephine (1985), *Feminist Theory: The Intellectual Traditions of American Feminism*, New York.

Haraway, Donna (1988), 'Situated Knowledges: The Science Question in Feminism and the Privilege of Partial Perspective', *Feminist Studies*, 14 (Autumn): 575–99.

Harding, Sandra (1986), *The Science Question in Feminism*, Ithaca, NY.

—— (1991), *Whose Science? Whose Knowledge? Thinking from Women's Lives*, Ithaca, NY.

—— and O'Barr, Jean (eds.) (1987), *Sex and Scientific Enquiry*, Chicago.

Kaufman, Gordon D. (1983), 'Eschatology and the Study of Religion', *Journal of the American Academy of Religion*, 51/1 (Mar.): 3–14.

Keller, Evelyn Fox (1985), *Reflexions on Gender and Science*, New Haven, Conn.

McFague, Sallie (1987), *Models of God: Theology for an Ecological, Nuclear Age*, Philadelphia.

Ruether, Rosemary Radford (1983), *Sexism and God-Talk: Toward a Feminist Theology*, Boston.

Schüssler Fiorenza, Francis (1984), *Foundational Theology: Jesus and the Church*, New York.

Spelman, Elizabeth V. (1988), *Inessential Woman: Problems of Exclusion in Feminist Thought*, Boston.

Stevens, Wallace (1957), *Opus Posthumous*, ed. S. F. Morris, New York.

Tracy, David (1987), *Plurality and Ambiguity: Hermeneutics, Religion, and Hope*, New York.

Wiles, Maurice (1974), *The Remaking of Christian Doctrine*, London.

10

Doctrinal Development: Searching for Criteria

JOHN MACQUARRIE

When I was teaching theology in the United States in the 1960s I often felt bewildered by the sheer multiplicity of options that were competing for allegiance in the theological world of those days. As well as the mainstreams of opinion, new fashions had arisen, and one heard of the death of God, the secular city, black theology, and many other 'new theologies' that claimed to show the way forward. I had to wonder how one could judge among the competing claims.

Perhaps that particular decade was a more than usually unsettled time. There have been many such times in the history of theology, and it looks as if there will be many more. The idea that there exists a 'faith which was once for all delivered to the saints' (Jude 3) seems very questionable when we glance back over the history of Christian doctrine. Current New Testament scholarship stresses the diversity of views already circulating in the first century, in contrast to the biblical theology of even a generation ago, when the unity of the Bible was a major theme. No up-to-date dictionary of theology omits to have an article on 'Development of Doctrine', although this topic scarcely appears in earlier reference books. It is true, of course, that the place of tradition has always been recognized, but whereas today the word 'tradition' is understood as the *activity* of passing on doctrines or practices, it was formerly considered to be an unchanging 'deposit', carefully preserved from generation to generation. In the 1990s the theological situation seems just as much in flux as it was a generation ago, except that now the fact of theological change is very widely accepted, except among 'fundamentalists', both biblical and doctrinal. So that question about how one judges among the competing claims is still with us, even intensified. Development is not just something that occasionally happens in theology, it belongs to all theology even if it is more obvious at some times than at others. Because it belongs to all theology, it is itself a topic for theological study and has its place on the theological agenda.

Obviously the factors entering into this development are numerous and complex. I wrote a moment ago that development does not just 'happen' and by that I meant that it is not just a fate originating outside theology and then determining its course. Yet that is only partially true. To some extent, theological development is influenced by the cultural and historical conditions in the midst of which theological studies are pursued. Perhaps the theologian could make a strenuous effort to empty his or her mind of the presuppositions of the particular society or epoch in which theological reflection was taking place, but it is doubtful how far such presuppositionless thinking can be achieved. To a large extent, we are irreversibly determined by the prevailing culture, even if we may reject some elements of it. In the modern world, we cannot escape seeing and understanding things as post-Enlightenment men and women, and this inevitably conflicts with the way in which people saw and understood events in New Testament or patristic or medieval or Reformation times. So, to the extent that Christian doctrines incorporate presuppositions derived from those earlier times, we find that our minds are inhospitable to them. Many years ago, Rudolf Bultmann wrote: 'It is impossible to use electric light and the radio and to avail ourselves of modern medical and surgical discoveries, and at the same time to believe in the New Testament world of demons and spirits. We may think we can manage it in our own lives, but to expect others to do so is to make the Christian faith unintelligible and unacceptable to the modern world' (Bultmann 1953: 5). Many others had said something similar long before Bultmann. When such a situation arises, either we have to give up Christian faith or its doctrines have to be developed in new ways to take account of the new knowledge.

Everyone knows that in the past two or three hundred years great multitudes of people in the Western world have in fact given up Christian faith as irreconcilable with the presuppositions of the scientific age. But it is also the case that many people have continued to be Christians. They have believed that there is something precious and irreplaceable in Christianity and they have sought ways of re-expressing its teachings in the post-Enlightenment age. (I say nothing about what some people are now calling the 'post-modern' age.) Those who continue to hold the Christian faith believe that it has within itself resources for renewal. Development is not just forced upon it by cultural changes in the world around, it is at the same time a theological task to be carried out in response to changing situations. Great ideas and great movements of the human spirit have a life and creativity of their own, so that they grow and develop in the course of history. It is in this sense that the development of doctrine is to be understood not just as a fate that determines theology from outside, but as itself a theological task. If the theologian and the ordinary Christian believer are right in holding that with Jesus Christ a new revelation came to the human race, that is to say, a novel, profound, and revolutionary understanding of humanity and its relation to God, then they accept as an imperative the need to rethink the meaning of Christianity in relation to the world in which they live. Christian faith has within itself an inner dynamic which is always in search of new and more adequate ways of expression—not only theological and intellectual, but also moral, social, liturgical, and so on.

A word which has been used quite often by New Testament scholars in recent years (see Robinson and Koester 1971) and which helps to express what I mean is 'trajectory'. Of course, the biblical scholars use it in a more technical sense than I am doing, but it does supply a useful metaphor for what I am trying to say. The metaphor comes from artillery. When a shell is fired from a gun, it follows a certain path. This path depends on a great many factors—the weight of the projectile and its velocity as it leaves the gun, the pull of gravity and the effects of air resistance, the atmospheric conditions prevailing at the time, and so on. If anyone feels that the comparison of Christian doctrine with an explosive shell is inappropriate, one could equally well express the idea by comparison with a golf ball being driven from the tee. The path described by that ball through the air will be determined partly by the skill of the player, who will have to calculate (though tacitly, one might almost say instinctively) how much force he has to put into his stroke and how much elevation he has to impart to the ball in order to counteract the force of gravity and cause the ball to travel as close as possible to the green. But allowance has also to be made for factors not originating with the player, such as the wind blowing across the fairway and the humidity or dryness of the atmosphere. All in all, even this simplified description indicates a highly complicated situation. If one then seeks to move from the physical image of the shell or the golf ball to the subtler notion of a doctrine or theory moving through historical time, it is obvious that the factors operating are even harder to identify.

It may be worth quoting some words of the New Testament scholar Patrick Henry on this model of trajectories. While acknowledging that 'any application of models from one realm of discourse to another presents problems as well as new opportunities, and missiles and space ships moving through their trajectories are not the same thing as ideas and persons moving through history,' he nevertheless sees the importance of the comparison in the suggestion that 'ideological tendencies and psychological states have a kind of independent life which can be plotted along historical graphs' (Henry 1979). The point is that ideas—or, at least, some ideas—have a kind of inherent dynamic. Scholars have spent much time and effort in trying to discover where ideas have come from, but the trajectory model suggests that one has to be equally concerned with where these ideas are going.

There are, of course, very different ways in which this view that ideas may follow particular trajectories can be interpreted. We have noted that many complex factors may go into the determination of the trajectory. Some of these may be described as impersonal or even accidental—the idea is deflected from its original direction by, let us say, political or cultural changes. But that is never the complete explanation and may not even be the major explanatory factor. The dynamic creativity of the idea itself, to say nothing of the intelligent contribution of those who are seeking to propagate it, may ensure that the idea survives and even flourishes in a new form within the new milieu in which it has arrived. Perhaps this sounds too idealistic, even a new version of the ancient saying, *Magna est veritas et praevalebit* (3 Esdr. 4: 41, Vulgate). The widespread occurrence of so-called 'heresy' in the Christian Church and the very title of this essay are plain evidence that truth does not always prevail or that Christian doctrines have no immunity from corruption. On the other hand, the intellectual or spiritual strength of an idea or teaching is surely a factor in determining whether it is going to survive and even flourish in spite of political machinations or cultural hostilities. I suppose a Marxist historian, if he stuck closely to orthodox Marxist theory, would claim that Christian doctrines belong only to the superstructure of history and are finally determined by economic factors that lie more deeply. There are also many positivist historians who would think on rather similar lines. But if the human being is not himself simply a natural phenomenon wholly determined by the forces of the physical world, then such reductionist accounts of human history are not adequate. I am not of course denying that they have the merit of drawing attention to important phenomena that do shape human destiny and that were often overlooked in a more idealist era when the course of events was in too facile a fashion interpreted as the action of God or the self-realization of the human spirit.

The remarks made in the last paragraph or two show us just how important are our presuppositions when we consider such a topic as the development of doctrine. That development is itself one aspect of the history of the Christian Church, and I doubt if ecclesiastical history (or any kind of history) can be studied apart from some presuppositions, which cannot be dismissed out of hand as mere prejudices. I did in fact acknowledge earlier that people in our own time cannot help perceiving and thinking under the influences of the Enlightenment. But I think we are now at a sufficient distance from the Enlightenment to be able to think about it critically. It would in fact be a betrayal of the Enlightenment if we were to accept slavishly and uncritically everything that it has bequeathed to us. If its challenge, as Kant put it, was 'Dare to know!' (Kant 1867: iv. 159), then we must be prepared to become enlightened about the Enlightenment itself and to criticize where necessary some of its presuppositions.

Let me say a little more about this subject of ecclesiastical history, of which the development of doctrine is a part. Is it possible to write ecclesiastical history without some prejudices, either for or against Christianity? Would a positivist or, perhaps even more, a Marxist understanding of history be free of prejudice or in any sense truly scientific? Some years ago, when I was thinking about some of these questions, I asked a distinguished ecclesiastical historian whether ecclesiastical history differs from general history in any important respects. The scholar in question had in fact taught general history in a famous university before he took up teaching in the special field of ecclesiastical history. He answered the question in very moderate terms. He saw a great deal of common ground between general history and ecclesiastical history. Both have to ascertain as accurately as possible what we call the 'facts' of the matter. There are ways of doing this which are recognized by all kinds of historians, and the rules governing such investigation have to be respected if the work of the historians concerned is to have integrity. But even when the 'facts' have been uncovered—and it can be questioned whether there are any bare facts—questions about the causation, interrelation, and interpretation of these alleged facts have to be answered. Indeed, we seem to be forced into a deeper enquiry into the ulterior, if not ultimate, factors operating in history.

Let me give an illustration of what I have in mind. About ten years ago, I was lecturing in Chicago and my host kindly told me that he had arranged for me to have an evening's relaxation at the opera. He mentioned (or rather, I *thought* he mentioned) that the work to be performed was Verdi's *Otello*, with Sir Georg Solti as conductor. On the day of the performance, I discovered that the work in question was actually *Attila*, a rarely performed work of Verdi composed nearly forty years before *Otello*. A famous incident in the career of Attila is incorporated into the opera. About the year 452, Attila and his army of Huns came down from northern Italy and threatened the city of Rome itself. Something, however, happened to change the actions of Attila and his Huns. Instead of attacking Rome, they turned around and went off elsewhere. Rome was saved. But what had happened? Three explanations have been offered.

The traditional and popularly believed explanation was that Peter and Paul, the patrons of the city martyred there under Nero nearly four hundred years earlier, appeared in the sky, and scared off Attila and his host. This scene was vividly presented in the opera with the aid of modern theatrical effects. A second explanation was that the pope of that time (Leo the Great of Chalcedonian fame) went out of the city gate to plead with Attila and to reason with him about the merits of Christianity. This scene too was suitably depicted. I was just sinking into what Coleridge called 'that willing suspension of disbelief for the moment' when a glance at the programme notes acquainted me with a third explanation. According to the author of these notes, the 'real' explanation of Attila's retreat from Rome was that there was an acute shortage of supplies for the army and that simultaneously there had erupted an outbreak of plague. These programme notes must have been written by some hard-headed positivist or Marxist historian, for whom material events are the 'real' causes of historical happening!

So how does one 'explain' why it was that Attila retreated from Rome? Let us go back to my friend the ecclesiastical historian, for we heard only the beginning of his reply to the question about the difference between ecclesiastical and general history. He would be at one with the secular historian in rejecting the legendary or mythological explanation of the event as due to a supernatural intervention by the apostolic guardians of the sacred city. But he would have recoiled equally from the belief that one needs to look for the cause in some material factor, shortage of food or the scourge of disease. He would have attached most importance to the conversation between Leo and Attila. As he expressed it to me, he claimed that the ecclesiastical historian in seeking the motivation behind historical happenings allows a weight to such matters as faith, spiritual aspiration, religious belief—a weight which many secular historians would not allow at all. One might think that this particular argument had been fought out many years ago in the work of Max Weber. In deliberate opposition to the Marxist view that our beliefs, including our religious beliefs or even especially them, are determined by economic factors, Weber produced a vast array of evidence to show that the modern European capitalist system was the product of the developments in Christian doctrine at the time of the Reformation. Weber was too wise to think that the changes of belief wrought by Protestantism constituted the only cause for the rise of capitalism, and in this he would be in agreement with the modest claims of my ecclesiastical historian. The complex web of history contains many threads, probably far more than historians ever identify. But especially if we are thinking of intellectual history, including development of doctrine, we must recognize the role of intellectual and spiritual factors and not suppose that the 'real' explanation has to be sought in the politics of the Emperor Constantine or of the German princes who supported Luther.

We must, I think, be careful to avoid one-sidedness in attempting to explain how something so complex as the development of doctrine takes place. I have just been criticizing reductionist attempts to explain in what may broadly be called 'naturalistic' terms. The influence of power politics, wars, plagues and famines, economic policies, and so on cannot and should not be excluded, but to try to make these the sole or even the major influence is surely exaggeration and reveals the reductionist presuppositions of those who offer such explanations. Something similar, I believe, can be said about those who, at the opposite extreme, see the development of doctrine in 'supernatural' terms. I do not mean just the crude mythology of those who are inclined to fundamentalism and hold that the doctrinal truths of Christianity are supernaturally preserved by divine action or inspiration. Even if one accepts that Christianity has its origin in a revelation, in the impact of the life and career of Jesus Christ on his first followers, the revelation has been humanly packaged and humanly transmitted, first in the oral proclamation, then in the reduction to scripture, then in the further processing into creeds and dogmas. Although we sometimes talk loosely of 'revealed' theology—perhaps contrasting it with 'natural' theology—it is not the theology itself that is revealed. The theology is the result of human meditation and criticism directed at material which, in Christian belief, constituted a revelation. Even scripture is not considered to be revelation, but the attestation or record of the revelation, as it was perceived by human agents. But although nowadays responsible theologians would shy away from claims that they can perceive the divine activity at work in preserving and developing Christian truth in the face of threats to its integrity, some highly responsible theologians and historians try to construct more sophisticated theories of history in which God has his part, though this does not exclude what we might call the 'naturalistic' factors in history. For instance Pannenberg claims that history is given a unity by God and that it is to be seen as eschatological, moving toward an all-embracing end. But he denies that this means that he is upholding a 'supernaturalist' philosophy of history. 'Proper theological research into history must absorb the truth of the humanistic tendency toward an "immanent" understanding of events. It may not supplant detailed historical investigation by supernaturalistic hypotheses' (Pannenberg 1970: 79). Whether Pannenberg has himself abided by the principle he lays down here I must leave to the reader to judge.

Another sophisticated illustration from recent theology is supplied by Hans Küng. He too seeks a way that lies between supernatural-ism on the one side and a naturalistic positivism on the other. The massive work in which he expounds this is called *The Incarnation of God* and is subtitled *An Introduction to Hegel's Theological Thought as Prolegomenon to a Future Christology*. As this descriptive subtitle indicates, Küng has gone back to Hegel for his inspiration, though we have still to see whether he will ever carry out his implicit promise of writing a christology which would take Hegel's thought as its prolegomenon. It has to be said at once that Hegel is not popular at the present time, and has indeed been very unpopular among Christian theologians for a long time. The reasons for that are not hard to seek, and I think Küng himself is aware of the difficulties that would arise from any uncritical following of Hegel. But it could be the case that a critical attention to Hegel would be of help to the theologian, and not least in this matter of the development of doctrine. For was not the development and unfolding of ideas at the very centre of Hegel's interest? I am not saying that the Hegelian dialectic offers any short cut to solving the theologian's problems, but I think that Küng has helped to reopen a line of enquiry that had been too quickly abandoned. Hegel was certainly no supernaturalist in the pejorative sense of the word, while on the other hand he exposes the weaknesses of any materialistic or positivist philosophies. Marx, of course, took over many of his basic ideas from Hegel, but claimed to be standing Hegel's philosophy on its head. What he meant by this claim touches very closely on the problem with which we are engaged in our present discussion. Marx retained the Hegelian dialectic and the principle of development included in it, but he 'stood the philosophy on its head' in the sense that he transferred the source of the dialectic from spirit to matter. But did that make any sense? Hegel saw *Geist* (a German term which embraces the connotations of both 'spirit' and 'mind' in English) as the final reality of all that is, and as a reality which is above all active, developing, and structuring. Hegel's idealism, however, was not of the subjective type which denies reality to matter, but he did think of matter as deriving its structures and its regular behaviour from spirit. Marx, on the other hand, wanted to make matter itself the active, structuring, dialectical principle which operates both in the world and in our thinking. For the orthodox Marxist, matter was no longer conceived as it had been traditionally, that is to say, it was no longer conceived as dead, inert, mindless stuff, the 'chance collocations' of which might in course of time give rise to ordered worlds and even to living and thinking beings. The conception of 'matter' in orthodox Marxism exalted it into a creative being, almost, one might say, into a god. In fact (although I think he exaggerates) there is some truth in the complaint of the Canadian scholar Arthur Gibson, 'I believe that Lenin's matter is closer to the theist's God than Hegel's Absolute could be' (Gibson 1968: 117).

There are, I believe, some periods in the development of doctrine which are amenable to analysis in terms of the Hegelian dialectic. A good illustration of this is offered by the course of Christian doctrine in Germany from about 1790 to 1830. The rationalism of Kant and his contemporaries came into conflict with the appeal of Schleiermacher to feeling, and these opposing views were at least partially reconciled in Hegel's own wider conception of spirit. But if one tries to extend the pattern as some nineteenth-century Hegelians tried to do, either backward into earlier times or forward into later, it all becomes too complicated and one gets the impression that enthusiastic dialecticians end up by imposing their pattern willy-nilly on the historical data. To revert to the metaphor which we used earlier, one would have to say that the trajectory of the ideas has not worked itself out in terms of strict logic, and they have been blown off course by various extraneous influences. So although acknowledgement of the dynamic of ideas is needed for an explanation of the development of doctrine, it falls short of being a sufficient explanation in a universe where ideal realities have to exist in the midst of natural facts.

Let us at this point pause and try to sum up how far we have come in our enquiry. We began by accepting the fact that Christian doctrine does in fact develop, and may look very different at one period from what it did at another. We were unwilling on the one hand to believe (at least, in any naïve way) that this development is guided and safeguarded by the Holy Spirit of God; for even if we felt able to acknowledge, with Vincent of Lerins, that there is 'a great increase and vigorous progress in the individual man as well as in the whole Church as the ages and the centuries march on, of understanding, knowledge and wisdom' (*Commonitorium*, 23. 28) (and perhaps many people would not acknowledge this!) we might think that there have been too many lapses and ambiguities to make it easy to believe that the Holy Spirit has been in charge. On the other side, we were equally unwilling to see the progress (or sometimes regress) of doctrine as brought about only by extraneous influences, ranging from economic upsets to scientific discoveries and even to the machinations of ambitious politicians. That all these influences may have some part in the complex process I freely acknowledge. But I come back to the point that the thrust of the process lies in the dynamic of the doctrines themselves, as derived originally from the Christ event and as continuously unfolded in the theological activity of the community. To say this is to assert that there must be some discoverable continuity between the later developments and the original source. Christianity, or, indeed, any movement which possesses a body of teaching, is bound to become diversified in the course of history, yet there are limits to what it can become without losing its identity. Christianity cannot become just anything. In his well-known study of the formation of doctrine in the early Church, Maurice Wiles claims, 'The idea of radical discontinuity in doctrine is not strictly conceivable' (Wiles 1967: 167). This is surely a claim that would be almost universally accepted. I suppose a deconstructionist might disagree and would question the whole attempt to find criteria for determining what is and what is not to be considered a legitimate development. But deconstructionism is still *sub judice* and it looks as if, like earlier types of scepticism, it will end by abolishing its own theories. As Kevin Hart has written after a lengthy and not unsympathetic examination, 'the enterprise of deconstruction always in a certain way falls prey to its own work' (Hart 1989: 158).

But how, in turn, does one judge continuity, and how much continuity must there be? Continuity cannot mean just repeating doctrinal formulae from the past. The question is rather, whether some new formula says in different words and employing different categories what the old formula said in its words and categories. To qualify as continuous, it would, I think, have to avoid reductionism, but it might very well eliminate some of the language or categories that seem to be the heritage of a pre-Enlightenment way of perceiving things. Let me offer an illustration. Christology, the doctrine of the person of Jesus Christ, is quite central in Christian theology. It has for many centuries found expression in a doctrine of incarnation, and for a great many Christians (though not all) that doctrine of incarnation has been embodied in the Chalcedonian definition. But as the leading Catholic theologian of the last generation, Karl Rahner, was bold enough to say, 'We have not only the right but the duty to look at [the Chalcedonian formula] as end *and* as beginning' (Rahner 1961: 150). The formula solved some of the problems that were vexing the Church in the fifth century and in that sense was an end, but history was going to continue and theological reflection was going to continue and a time was bound to come when Chalcedon would no longer be saying clearly what the Church then and the Church now wants to say about Jesus Christ as the centre of its faith and of its knowledge of God. I believe we do not want to say *less* about Jesus Christ than the Chalcedonian fathers said—we do not want to be reductionist— but for many of our contemporaries, that language about 'two natures' and even the word 'incarnation' may be stumbling-blocks.

Let me now set side by side two contemporary statements concerning Jesus Christ. One comes from Maurice Wiles and was published two years after *The Myth of God Incarnate*. He seems to regard it as 'an acceptable alternative' to incarnational christology, and he has rigorously excluded the traditional incarnational language. The statement runs as follows:

[Jesus] was not just one who had taught about God; he was not just one who had lived a life of perfect human response to God. He had lived a life that embodied and expressed God's character and action in the world. As prophets in the past had expressed the word of God that had come to them not only in speech but in symbolic action, so in a far more comprehensive way did Jesus. The impact not merely of his teaching but of his whole person communicated the presence and the power of God with an unprecedented sense of directness and finality. (Wiles 1979: 24)

This does to me seem to be an adequate statement of the Church's faith in Christ, and I would personally find it acceptable as saying all that was important in the Chalcedonian formula, or all that is implied in the notion of an incarnation. The last sentence in particular is almost like an echo or an exposition of the famous Johannine verse, 'And the Word was made flesh and dwelt among us' (John 1: 14). Wiles's statement is, in my view, not reductionist. But while I could subscribe to his statement and acknowledge its usefulness for teaching the meaning of Jesus Christ in our time, I would still want to hold on to the older formulations for liturgical and some other purposes, as I shall explain in a moment.

Meanwhile, let us look at another contemporary statement, this time coming from John Robinson, the former bishop of Woolwich. He did not shy away from the word 'incarnation' but he under- stood it in terms very like those of Wiles, terms which again I would find acceptable. Incarnation, in his view, does not necessarily imply the pre-existence of a supernatural being who at a given time takes flesh. He wrote:

I believe that the word can just as truly and just as biblically (in fact, more truly and more biblically) be applied to another way of understanding it. This is: that one who was truly and utterly a man—and had never been anything other than a man or more than a man—so completely embodied what was from the beginning the meaning and purpose of God's self-expression (whether conceived in terms of his Spirit, his Wisdom, his Word, or the intimately personal relation of Sonship) that it could be said and had to be said of that man, 'He was God's man' or 'God was in Christ' or even that 'He *was* God for us.' (Robinson 1973: 179)

I do not think there is any major difference between what Wiles affirms about Jesus Christ or what Robinson affirms or what I would affirm myself. If I want to retain the ancient credal formulae, it is to emphasize the continuity with the Christian community. The Niceno-Constantinopolitan Creed, in particular, is the most ecumenical document that we have, and when we recite it in the liturgy, it links together great masses of the faithful through space and time. But if someone were to ask me to explain what it is saying about Jesus Christ in more up-to-date language, I would find Wiles's words both illuminating and adequate.

Although we noted that development of doctrine has always been going on in the Church, we have also seen that it has been attracting special attention in the modern period. The credit for bringing the problem of development to the notice of theologians is usually given to Cardinal Newman. He had been thinking about the problem for several years before he published *An Essay on the Development of Christian Doctrine*. This book was first published in 1845, the year of Newman's conversion from Anglicanism to Roman Catholicism, and the thinking behind it was not simply that of an academic historian but very much the existential concern of a man wrestling with the difficulties that stand in the way of faith. He had begun the book while still a priest of the Church of England but it was published only after his conversion. The definitive edition of the work did not appear until a generation later, in 1878, and by that time the essay itself had undergone considerable development. In turning to Newman's important work in the final part of this essay, I shall not be appealing to him for solutions to the problems of development. Indeed, some of the things already said have distanced us quite a bit from Newman's position. Newman, for instance, claims to have perceived in the development of doctrine a 'superintending Providence and a great Design' and has perhaps paid too little attention to less exalted factors which affected the course of doctrine. I would also find it difficult to go along with his idea that, from the apostles onward, the Church had 'fullness' of knowledge although some of this knowledge was only unconsciously lodged in its memory. But he is cautious in dealing with these matters, and I do not intend to get into dispute over them. I want rather to draw attention to what may be called the practical consequences of Newman's teaching, occupying the final two-thirds of his definitive text. These practical consequences are seven notes (he originally called them 'tests') by which developments are to be assessed. Newman offered these proposals quite modestly and they are not all of equal value, but I think they are still useful in judging the novel claims that keep arising in the history of Christian theology. We shall not expect to find everything that Newman has written about the notes acceptable, but perhaps we shall be able to discern at least the outline of a programme.

To do justice to Newman's arguments would demand a treatment going far beyond what is possible here. He himself gives a summary statement of the notes in about forty pages of his book, then devotes a further 200 pages to evidences for the validity of each note, drawn from the entire history of the Church down to his own time. Here I shall select what I take to be the more important of Newman's notes, and the ones which seem to be most relevant to our own needs in the late twentieth century.

Newman's first note is 'preservation of type' (Newman 1989: 171). He explains this by means of a biological analogy. A development in doctrine is (to use his own word) 'genuine' if we can discern an underlying type in various manifestations. A butterfly, for instance, preserves the type of its species, even if it begins as an egg and at a later stage of its development is a caterpillar and very unlike a butterfly in its mature form. Newman gives as an ecclesiastical illustration an institution rather than a doctrine, namely, priesthood. Christian priests have looked and acted very differently at different times in the history of Christianity, but there is a persistent type whom we can recognize in Chaucer's medieval parson and again in Goldsmith's Anglican vicar of 400 years later.

The idea of a persistent type recurring in many manifestations appears more recently in Hans Küng's book *Why Priests?* (Küng 1972).

I pass on to Newman's third note, 'the power of assimilation' (Newman 1989: 185). New knowledge, even if it may seem at first sight hostile to Christian doctrine, may turn out to be amenable to assimilation. It is indeed the accumulation of new knowledge in the past two or three hundred years that has been one of the major pressures calling for rethinking of Christian doctrines. The example is not Newman's, but I suggest that the theory of evolution would illustrate this third note very well. Darwin's *Origin of Species* appeared in 1859, roughly half-way between the first edition of Newman's book and the definitive edition. To many people, evolution seemed to be the refutation of Christianity. But looking back from our own time, we see that the Christian doctrine of creation was able to come to terms with the new knowledge and has even become more impressive in the light of the new vision of things that science has afforded us.

Newman's fourth note is 'logical sequence' (Newman 1989: 189). In spite of his use of the word 'logical', Newman seems to be thinking not of straightforward deduction of new truths from others already held but rather of a slow growth of knowledge through meditation on a few basic ideas. One may think, for instance, of the growth over three or four centuries of the idea of the triune God. This was not logical deduction in the sense of a deliberate inference, and I do not think either that it could be described as making explicit knowledge that was already implicit. I quote an illustration from Newman which leaves a measure of vagueness over just what mental processes are involved. He writes: 'Justin or Irenaeus might be without any digested ideas of purgatory or original sin, yet have an intense feeling, which they had not defined or located, both of the fault of our first nature and the responsibilities of our nature regenerate' (Newman 1989: 192).

The seventh and last of Newman's notes is 'chronic vigour' (Newman 1989: 203). This appears to be a pragmatic mode of judging. False developments, Newman believed, have a transitory character, whereas the genuine development shows vigorous and continued growth. This may well be too optimistic a view. After all, Arianism flourished around the Mediterranean basin for a long time after the Church had disowned it, and Nestorianism had likewise a flourishing aftermath in central Asia and as far afield as China. It looks as if Newman accepted the *magna est veritas* idea. But while a too facile acceptance of that ancient maxim would be wrong, there is some value in it, as we learned from the imagery of ideal trajectories.

Newman did not think that his list of seven notes is a complete one—he speaks of 'seven out of various notes'. In any case, we have glanced at only four of them. But I think they still have something to teach us as we try to find a way through the multitude of competing developments that abound in contemporary theology.

REFERENCES

Bultmann, Rudolf (1953), 'New Testament and Mythology', in H. W. Bartsch and R. H. Fuller (eds.), *Kerygma and Myth*, London.

Gibson, Arthur (1968), *The Faith of the Atheist*, New York.

Hart, Kevin (1989), *The Trespass of the Sign*, Cambridge.

Henry, Patrick (1979), *New Directions in New Testament Studies*, London.

Kant, Immanuel (1867), *Sämtliche Werke*, Leipzig.

Küng, Hans (1972), *Why Priests?*, London.

Newman, John Henry (1989), *An Essay on the Development of Christian Doctrine*, Notre Dame, Ind.

Pannenberg, Wolfhart (1970), *Basic Questions in Theology I*, London.

Rahner, Karl (1961), *Theological Investigations I*, London.

Robinson, James M., and Koester, Helmut (1971), *Trajectories through Early Christianity*, Philadelphia.

Robinson, John A. T. (1973), *The Human Face of God*, London.

Wiles, Maurice (1967), *The Making of Christian Doctrine*, Cambridge.

—— (1979), *Explorations in Theology 4*, London.

11

Revelation Revisited

BASIL MITCHELL

In March 1980 *Theology* published a short dialogue between Maurice Wiles and myself entitled 'Does Christianity Need a Revelation?' It seems worthwhile, in a volume devoted to the recognition of Maurice Wiles's work, to return once again to this subject, the more so as the discussion has since been carried further by two authors who developed their ideas while working in Oxford in response to Wiles's thinking (Abraham 1981, 1982; Brown 1985).

In that original debate Wiles wrote, with characteristic courtesy, 'Professor Mitchell seems to me to see the points I want to make so well and to present them so fairly, it is a real matter of surprise that he does not agree with them' (Wiles 1980: 109), and it has to be said that my reaction to his own contribution was very much the same. So in what follows I shall try to state the case fairly for a comparatively 'strong' doctrine of revelation and to show why Wiles's alternative account remains in my view unsatisfactory or, at least, incomplete.

My main claim was that a statement of Christian doctrine which omits revelation fails to be fully coherent. The concept of revelation, I suggested, depends upon the analogy of one person communicating to another truths about his character, purposes, and intentions which that other would not otherwise be in a position to know. I argued:

1. that the arguments of natural theology do not enable us to infer God's purposes except in somewhat general and religiously inadequate terms;
2. that God, as understood in natural theology, would have reason to communicate with those of his creatures who were able and willing to receive his message;
3. that the Bible is most naturally interpreted as the vehicle of God's revelation of himself.

I noted as an addendum to (1) that the need for some kind of 'divine speaking' is especially evident in relation to divine forgiveness and divine promises, for both forgiving and promising require performative utterance. If I am to know that you forgive me or that you promise me something, it is not enough that I draw inferences from your behaviour; you must *pronounce* forgiveness and *enunciate* promises. And in an endeavour to explain the related concept of divine inspiration I appealed to an analogy with the way in which a teacher can inspire a pupil.

Dr Brown largely endorsed this line of argument (as presented by myself and Abraham) while criticizing certain features of our presentation of it, and made it the basis of his own positive account of revelation as a divine–human dialogue, in the course of which 'God progressively unveils the truth about himself' (Brown 1985: 70):

A setting of revelation in a wider context that I believe preserves a strong sense of divine initiative is a model which may be characterized as that of a divine dialogue. This may be briefly summarized as follows: revelation is a process whereby God progressively unveils the truth about himself and his purposes to a community of believers but always in such a manner that their freedom of response is respected.

Brown's talk of a 'divine/human dialogue' has the great merit of emphasizing the importance of the human response and so of doing justice to the enormous variety of social contexts, literary genres, historical situations, and personal characteristics to be found in the biblical record. The extent of this variety and complexity as displayed and analysed by historical and literary critics is one very persuasive reason why theories of divine revelation have seemed less and less plausible to modern scholars. The notion that God would or could communicate in propositional form certain truths about himself which we could not otherwise learn makes, it has been thought, too little allowance for individual creativity and cultural development; it makes human beings into passive recipients of a timeless message in a way which fails to take the historical process seriously. And certainly the Bible does not read like the medium of such a message.

However, Bishop Butler's warning requires to be heeded:

As we are in no sort judges beforehand by what laws or rules, in what degree, or by what means, it were to have been expected, that God would naturally instruct us, so upon the supposition of his affording us light and instruction by revelation, additional to what he has afforded us by reason and experience, we are in no sort judges by what methods and in what proportion it were to be expected, that this supernatural light and instruction would be afforded us. (Butler 1896: 220)

Brown's dialogue model with its stress on the human response to a divine initiative avoids the over-simple and excessively abstract concept of revelation which many theologians have taken to be the only one possible, and yet takes account of the overwhelming impression which the Bible conveys (especially but not only the New Testament) of an *irruption* into human history which, at various times and in different ways, disturbed and transformed the existing culture. Taking this seriously involves recognition of two things: (1) the admixture of error in what is claimed to be of divine inspiration; (2) the extent to which revelation is conditional upon the stage of intellectual and spiritual development achieved at any given time by the community which is being addressed.

However, given this general framework, within which Abraham, Brown, and I are prepared to work, there are certain problems about the relationship between the divine and human partners to the dialogue. In particular there is the problem, to which Wiles calls attention, of how to do justice to the human element in revelation without in effect conceding the deist's claim that the whole process can best be accounted for in terms of purely human inspiration. This claim is reinforced by an epistemological challenge: how is it possible to distinguish the divinely revealed message from the merely human interpretation which is rightly seen to be a necessary condition of its reception. How the problem arises may be seen in Brown's discussion of his dialogue model. God, he suggests, might have a moral reason for never imposing a particular viewpoint upon a recipient 'but always wishes that it should become, as it were, internalized or, putting it another way, experienced as the recipient's own insight' (Brown 1985: 72). If this is to be taken as more than a suggestion, it would be open to two objections: it would make it very much more difficult to *tell* whether God was speaking or not—a deist interpretation would become distinctly more plausible—and it weakens the argument, which Brown elsewhere stresses, that the prophets and other 'inspired' writers regularly refer their utterances to God and not to their own unaided processes of thought.

I think, therefore, that his position is better expressed in the more moderate formula 'but always in such a manner that their freedom of response is respected'. This was one of the things I wanted to capture in my use of the teacher–pupil analogy. If we suppose the teacher to be developing some original idea which the pupil unaided could not have thought of alone, it remains the case that the pupil needs to have his or her own capacities stretched to the full in order to understand it. Understanding could not be a purely passive process; and an essential test of understanding is the pupil's capacity to 'go on from there'—to express what has been taught in other words, to draw out its implications in fresh contexts, etc. The force and originality of the teacher's instruction does not obliterate but rather engages and enhances the pupil's intellectual powers. This is entirely compatible with the pupil's sometimes making mistakes, so that if we had access only to the pupil's notes, we could reasonably discount certain inadequacies as due to the pupil's limitations.

There is also, of course, an important disanalogy to which Brown also calls attention. We do not have direct, independent access to God's speech and actions as we normally do to those of a human teacher. Nevertheless we can easily suppose a situation in which the only access we have to a teacher's thought is through the writings of his pupils, and this would be not unlike that envisaged in the divine dialogue model. The problem of discovering the thought of Socrates is a celebrated historical example, in which the task is complicated by our having to rely on three witnesses, one of whom, Xenophon, is too limited; another, Aristophanes, too irresponsible; and the third, Plato, too inventive to be wholly dependable.

The teacher–pupil analogy is, in fact, only one way of illustrating Brown's model of the divine–human dialogue. One might call it the divine tutorial model. At the risk of over-elaboration it may be worthwhile trying to develop it just a little further. There are, after all, different ways of conducting a tutorial. I will mention three in particular:

1. *Authoritarian.* The tutor simply tells the pupil what she or he needs to know.
2. *Socratic.* The tutor gives nothing away: he confines himself to eliciting suggestions from the pupil which are then subjected to criticism.

3. *Dialectical.* A structured discussion takes place between tutor and pupil which may tend either in the authoritarian or the Socratic direction. In the former, the tutor takes the lead; in the latter the pupil is encouraged to take the initiative. In either case, if the pupil's understanding is to be increased, the tutor must either advance opinions himself or indicate clearly whether and to what extent the pupil's suggestions are acceptable.

To bring the comparison into line with the divine–human dialogue we have to suppose that the tutor is conveying to the pupil some of his own beliefs, purposes, and intentions—matters on which he is a unique authority. He is, let us say, telling him what he was getting at in some of his own published work or how he was proposing to develop some of his ideas. Of course students of the subject are in a position to hazard opinions, more or less informed, as to what he is up to and may do so with greater or lesser insight, but he himself must be allowed the last word. I remember a graduate student of mine, who had just come from a seminar of Sir Peter Strawson's, recounting with amusement how one of the graduates present had speculated at length as to what Strawson *would* say in response to a particular objection, while that notably modest philosopher remained silent, to the manifest disappointment of the class.

Now it is, of course, conceivable that the graduate student in question might have been entirely right as to what Strawson actually thought and then the case would allow of a 'deistic' interpretation. Similarly, by dint of purely human experience or inspiration, man may hazard a guess, or work out carefully, what God's intentions might be and, as it happens, get it right. This, indeed, the deist argues, is what must always be supposed to happen in the divine–human case, because *ex hypothesi* God does not intervene but maintains throughout a dignified Strawsonian silence. And if this *is* what happens, he will urge, in what way are we worse off? How, after all, on any construction of the matter, do we know that what purports to be divine revelation is what it purports to be? Only by applying tests of consistency and coherence: is this statement of God's purposes internally consistent; does it cohere with what we otherwise have reason to believe about the divine nature? But, in that case, as Brand Blanshard (Blanshard 1962: 54) exclaims: 'What is the difference, after all, between one who takes reason as the guide of life and one who, taking revelation as the guide, imposes the test of reason on the candidates to revelation?'

Wiles (Wiles 1982: 107) makes substantially the same point with specific reference to morality:

There can be little doubt that Moses, Isaiah, Jesus and Paul all made substantial contributions to the development of our moral awareness. But the form in which their teaching comes to us is not such that we can accept it as morally binding, simply on the ground that they taught it or that God is believed to have inspired their teaching. In every case their teaching comes to us in forms that are neither wholly clear, consistent or convincing. We have to use our moral judgement to determine in what respects it is morally binding upon us.

Blanshard and Wiles are both victims of the same confusion. There have been in human history moments of genuine originality when new truths were discovered which no one before had had the insight to discern. To recognize them as truths presupposed the capacity on the part of those who received them to appreciate just how they illuminated what had previously been known. That is to say a power of rational judgement (including, where appropriate, moral judgement) was required. But it does not in the least follow that those who possessed this power of critical thought were *ipso facto* endowed with the creative gift which the discovery itself demanded. Similarly it requires thought to recognize a revelation for what it is, but the thought that suffices for that is not of itself enough to anticipate the revelation (Mitchell 1982: 144–8).

I had tried, in my earlier essay, to reinforce the case for revelation by arguing that there was a particular kind of 'divine speaking' which was peculiarly resistant to deistic interpretation, namely that which involved performative utterances. I claimed that such central Christian concepts as those of divine forgiveness and the promises of God were intelligible only if occasions could be identified on which God pronounced forgiveness or enunciated promises. These could not take the form simply of events capable of being considered deistically as 'divine behaviour' or 'God in action', because behaviour unaccompanied by speech remains inherently ambiguous.

This proffered assistance to his argument Brown rejects (in the form in which it is stated by Abraham). He declares roundly:

Indeed on this question of forgiving, commanding and promising we can
. . . say that he [Abraham] is quite wrong. Thus in the case of forgiveness,
even in the human case, words are often unnecessary to indicate this. I see
that I am forgiven in virtue of the kinds of acts that are done towards me.
So similarly, in God's case: a particularly loving action would seem to
suffice, for example, the continued experience of divine aid even after some
dreadful deed of which one has repented. (Brown 1985: 56)

Now I concede at once that we (Abraham and I) generalized
rashly. I can, for example, forgive with a smile or apologize with
a gesture. J. L. Austin when he introduced 'performatives' maintained that they were, characteristically, verbal, but allowed that
they could be on occasion non-verbal. Thus at one stage in his
argument he says: 'another test [for an expression's being per-
formative] is whether one could really be doing it without saying
anything, for example in the case of being sorry as distinct from
apologizing, in being grateful as distinct from thanking, in blaming
as distinct from censuring' (Austin 1962: 79). The suggestion is
that, if one could, the expression is not being used performatively.
But later on he casts some doubt on this as a way of distinguishing
illocutionary from perlocutionary acts:

We can persuade etc (i.e. perform perlocutionary acts) non-verbally.
However this alone is not enough to distinguish illocutionary acts, since
we can, for example, warn or order or appoint or protect or apologize by
non-verbal means and these are illocutionary acts. (Austin 1962: 188)

We clearly have to be more discriminating. Let us, then, take
forgiving and promising and consider them in relation to both the
human and the divine cases.

1. *Forgiving in the human case.* I can clearly forgive without ever
saying so. 'Have you forgiven me?' 'I forgave you long ago.' Even
if it is insisted that forgiveness presupposes repentance, repentance
too can be signalled non-verbally. In the parable of the Prodigal
Son, the prodigal's repentance is in fact expressed in words,
'Father, I have sinned and am no more worthy to be called thy
son,' but it need not have been, and the father does not need to
say, 'I forgive you.' His actions make that clear.

2. *Forgiving in the divine case.* Brown suggests that God could
make it clear that he no longer held it against the offender by
continuing to shower blessings upon him after he has repented, but
here the problem of ambiguity surely does arise. God sends the rain

upon the just and the unjust; and if the repentant sinner always did prosper, and God's attitude could legitimately be inferred from this, why should it be interpreted as forgiveness rather than magnanimity? What lesson we should learn from experiences of prosperity and adversity is a matter of great uncertainty as the Psalms and the Book of Job amply testify.

No doubt God could bring it about that the repentant sinner experienced an inner peace which was proof against disturbance by memories of his offence; or he could plant a conviction in him that he was indeed forgiven. Along these lines Brown develops his own account of revelation in terms of religious experience. But, as we shall see, this is not to abandon the theme of divine speaking.

3. *Promising in the human case.* It is very much harder to see how promises can be made non-verbally. Of course someone can ask me, 'Do you promise to read my thesis?' and I can nod my head in assent, but the promise has to be articulated by someone. One can conceive of a ritual, such as a marriage ceremony, in which promises are understood to be made non-verbally, but could its interpretation be unambiguous unless it had been set up initially in words?

4. *Promising in the divine case.* It is even harder to see how God could promise non-verbally. In developing his case against deism Brown rightly insists that belief in an after life is hard to justify save on interventionist principles. What, then, of God's promise of eternal life—a gift which it is in his sole power to offer or withhold? Or God's promises to Abraham? Indeed the whole notion of covenant is one that requires a clear expression of commitment on both sides.

I suggest, then, that Brown's critique of my own appeal to the role of performatives does not succeed, for divine forgiveness and divine promises are both of them essential to the Judaeo-Christian revelation and neither of them is capable of entirely non-verbal expression. Brown's insistence that revelation takes the form of divine–human dialogue rather than of divine monologue does not render that appeal otiose but rather reinforces it. For forgiveness as requiring repentance and promising as requiring acceptance naturally take the dialogue form. Consider, for instance, Isaiah 6:

And, said I, Woe is me. For I am undone; because I am a man of unclean lips: for mine eyes have seen the King, the Lord of Hosts.

. . . he laid it upon my mouth and said, Lo this hath touched thy lips; and thine iniquity is taken away, and thy sin purged.

Confession: forgiveness.

I hope that the outlines of this approach to revelation are now clear. The case is partly negative—designed to show that revelation need not be conceived in the abstract, somewhat mechanistic manner that has led theologians and biblical scholars to distance themselves from the idea; and partly positive—concerned to insist that the relationship between God and man to which the Bible bears witness cannot adequately be conceived unless genuine communication is understood to take place between them. Any critique of this approach will be similarly twofold. It will be argued that revelation as now conceived in the form of a divine–human dialogue is still unsatisfactory; and that the main weight of biblical teaching can be fully sustained without recourse to it.

The most serious objection will have occurred to readers at a very early stage. The entire discussion, it will be felt, has been conducted in unduly anthropomorphic terms. The very procedure of seeking to elucidate the relationship between God and man by analogy with that between one human being and another is suspect; and the particular example chosen for development is absurdly inadequate and quite ludicrously culture-bound. Oxford colleagues may find it natural to think of a divine–human dialogue as a sort of never-ending tutorial in which a God of liberal sensibilities releases the truth in instalments with anxious care for the autonomy of the recipients, but this has little in common with the God of Abraham, Isaac, and Jacob. If the notion of encounters with God, which is undoubtedly present in the Bible, is to be taken seriously, they are, for the most part, far more terrifying and mysterious as well as far more various than the model suggests; while, if one is as sensitive as one ought to be to the limitations of all such analogies, it will be necessary to withdraw from anthropomorphism altogether.

A lot will depend on how the divine–human dialogue model is to be construed. Even in cases where God is said to speak, he does not literally speak, whether in monologue or dialogue. It is the prophet or other inspired individual who says 'Thus saith the Lord', and the most that can be said of him literally is that he has the subjective experience or conviction of having been addressed by God. Perhaps not even that, for, it may be suggested, 'Thus saith the Lord' may in his culture be the accepted way of adding emphasis to one's words, comparable to the Platonic 'certainly' (*panu men oun*). In ordinary human communication others can always in principle hear the words spoken; in the case of God they cannot; they are wholly dependent on the prophet.

This being so, Wiles may say, the interpretation of episodes of this kind (which suit the model best) is bound to be problematic. It makes sense to look for the best overall explanation of them and, in so doing, to rely on what we otherwise have reason to believe about God. God is unchanging and transcends our comprehension. His activity sustains everything all the time; and, if men sometimes feel that God speaks to them, even that he promises or forgives, the most plausible construction to put upon it is that they have become momentarily aware of his creative and sustaining presence and, as a result, have become convinced that all will be well, indeed that fundamentally and eternally all *is* well. Nothing would be more natural than to construe this conviction in manageable human terms. The degree of assurance that accompanies the experience is such as, in ordinary human intercourse, could be adequately conveyed only by the use of 'performatives'—although a moment's reflection suffices to show that promising makes sense only among creatures whose intentions can otherwise not be relied upon, forgiveness among those whose loving response is in doubt. Performatives can have no place in the life of God, but are devices to palliate human imperfection.

How is the theist to respond to this criticism? It seems to me that he will have to insist on the analogy between human and divine communication and indicate more clearly the respects in which it does and does not hold. This can best be understood by following Brown's positive thesis about revelation further. This thesis is, as I understand it, that revelation occurs primarily by way of certain kinds of religious experiences—and it is characteristic of these that they involve 'numinous experience or sensory phenomena (auditions, visions, etc.) or mystical experiences of union'. Such experiences, he believes, resist interpretation in non-personal terms:

Only theism can offer a non-reductionist account of mystical and sensory experience, i.e. an account which takes seriously the way in which the recipient perceives his experience, *viz* as personal communion and interchange or direct confrontation with some spiritual reality. (Brown 1985: 82; cf. Davis 1989: 170–1)

Now it is not clear that the deist cannot allow 'direct confrontation with some spiritual reality'. Indeed he claims that religious experience is essentially a confrontation with a spiritual reality which is always there but only occasionally recognized for what it is. What he denies is that, when such confrontation occurs, it involves any *special* activity on God's part. The deist need not deny that it may take the form of 'personal communion and interchange'. Many years ago I used from time to time to be invited to interviews with an Indian mystic, which consisted in my sitting in his presence for a period, during which he remained silent and motionless. Dialogue in any ordinary sense it was not, but his followers would certainly have claimed that it was 'personal communion and interchange'. He was very possibly unaware of my presence, but it was open to me to share in his meditation and to benefit from it.

To have made it anything like dialogue or at any rate *enough* like dialogue, something more would have been required. It need not have involved spoken or written words, but there would have to have been something about the experience which justified me in saying, 'he told me such and such' or 'he told me to do such and such'. It might have been enough that I came away from the interview with some problem resolved, convinced, as I had not been before, that a particular course of action was the right one, so long as I had reason to believe that he was responsible for my having acquired that conviction.

The same requirement emerges if we consider what Brown has to say about what he calls 'thematic experience'. The occasion for this is some event, which is in principle capable of a natural explanation, but which the prophet sees as a divine action. Brown prefers not to commit himself as to whether in such cases there is need to appeal to divine causality (Brown 1985: 77), but he insists that 'if revelation occurs at all, it can only properly be said to begin to occur at the point of interpretation of the event' (Brown 1985: 62). Thus 'the decision to see the Exile as a divine act at all was the important "revelatory" contribution (if revelatory indeed it was), but this was hardly the only possible interpretation of the situation' (Brown 1985: 63).

A better example for our purpose than the Exile might be Hosea's inspired insight into the unwavering love of God for unfaithful Israel. Brown has instanced the limitlessness of God's love as something that natural reason could not grasp unaided so here, one might agree, *is* a case of revelation. The experience is 'thematic' in that it is an event—Hosea's continuing love for the unfaithful Gomer—which provides the clue to God's unfailing love for Israel. It is Hosea's interpretation of this event, his seeing it as a clue to the nature of God's love, which is the point at which revelation begins; and for it to *be* a revelation it is necessary that Hosea should have reason for taking the conviction that developed in him about the nature of divine love as a communication from God.

God does not literally speak. Is, then, 'God spake by the prophets' to be taken as mere metaphor or, as modern theologians like to say, 'myth'? To concede this is to give too much to the deist. I have from time to time used the word 'communicate' which is employed in a broader sense than 'speak' normally is—though 'speak' itself may be stretched to cover more than the use of vocal chords to frame words in a natural language. For someone to communicate with me there must be an intelligible message which I have reason to ascribe to a particular conscious agent, and it does not matter in what form the message is cast so long as I have good enough grounds for interpreting it as I do.

By what criteria, then, are we to tell whether what purports to be a communication from God is one or not? Brown provides us with the tests we need:

1. There must be sufficient discontinuity. What is offered must be something which goes beyond what the individual could have attained to unaided. It may be either something that natural reason as such could not have reached on its own or something which was not attainable at a particular state of cultural development.

2. There must be sufficient coherence with what is known independently—either from natural reason or from a religious tradition based on other well-authenticated religious experiences.

3. There will characteristically be—but it would be going too far to say that there *must* be—a sense of otherness, invasiveness, associated with the experience. Brown recognizes this when he says (Brown 1985: 82) that 'The "inspiration" of the religious genius is no mere metaphor. For he claims to be able to identify the source of his inspiration as another person.' This is not entirely consistent with his earlier claim that 'God

always wishes that it should become, as it were, internalized, or, putting it another way, experienced as the recipient's own insight' (Brown 1985: 72). His own examples show clearly enough that God does not always proceed in this way—the Resurrection, Pentecost, the conversion of St Paul. The latter in particular represented a catastrophic invasion of St Paul's personality.

Mere mention of these examples is enough to illustrate the dilemma which attends any attempt to make sense of revelation. The concept would be altogether unnecessary if the religious history of mankind were a smooth continuum in which a steady process of increasing enlightenment could be discerned. There would be no need for any divine–human dialogue if the human mind unaided could make steady and indubitable progress towards a fuller understanding of God's purposes. As it is, the actual history, full of conflicting claims and hinting at unfathomable mystery, while it shows the limitations of human reason, also casts doubt on attempts to make sense of 'revelations' in terms of a single conceptual framework. Somehow a balance has to be struck. If a divine reality is always breaking in, challenging human pretensions at some points, while reinforcing them at others, we cannot maintain complete autonomy, but must endeavour to respond in some appropriate way. The responses in human terms have assumed the forms of religious traditions in which a consistent attempt has been made to discern God's purposes and to do his will. The use of these words presupposes that God is, as Temple used to say, 'at least personal', so that the relationship between God and man is, in a sense, personal.

Once this is granted, the language of dialogue becomes inescapable because this is pre-eminently the form of relationship between persons. Repentance/forgiveness, promises/trust are the modes of the deepest encounters between people and how are we to think of our relationship with God except in these terms?

It is, of course, true that we are not in a position to know what forgiveness or promising are in the life of God, but we can be sure that they are not, as it were, automatic responses that can be read off from the divine attributes of charity and faithfulness—*pardonner c'est son métier*. No doubt we must think away all sorts of anthropomorphic associations when we dwell upon God's love for sinful men, but we cannot think away his concern for the erring individual as the very person he or she is, the one sheep out of a hundred that is lost, without reducing that love to something that is less than human. This is why it is not possible to treat the persistent conviction of the biblical writers and those of whom they write that they are recipients of truths rather than discoverers of them as a culture-bound phenomenon comparable to, say, belief in demonic possession (Wiles 1980: 114).

The importance, in human relationships, of something's actually being said on certain occasions, even if it is already known, is well understood; so is the importance of not presuming on another's attitude even when it can reasonably be inferred. Why should God be denied the resources for personal communication which human beings take for granted?

The charge of anthropomorphism may come from two different directions. It may spring from a conviction that the fundamental attributes of God cannot be personal ones, a conviction classically formulated in terms of Platonic philosophy. For God is changeless and eternal and all the attributes we associate with personhood involve change of some kind. Hence only by remote and strained analogies can we ascribe to God the qualities of love, mercy, justice, forgiveness which we reverence in human beings. Or it may derive from the thought that, although God is indeed personal, we are in constant danger of ascribing to him personal characteristics which are found in human beings in a certain form, but which cannot, on reflection, be supposed to belong to the person that God is. Someone who objected to the use of the expression 'divine tutorial' earlier in this essay might quite properly complain that it carries with it connotations that belong to a very particular, rather limited, social situation. But the critic might go further and claim more generally that 'God cannot be said to have aims and motives in precisely the way that we do, nor does he disclose them to us in the way that we do to one another' (Wiles 1982: 29).

Wiles does not rely on the classical concept of God, but, as this last quotation indicates, warns us rather against ascribing to God in too literal a way language which is at home in particular human situations. The question at issue, then, in relation to revelation, is whether to talk of God as having purposes and intentions and as disclosing them to mankind is an instance of such improper transference, or whether, by contrast, it is so bound up with the idea of personhood as to be inseparable from it. That is to say, is it merely a contingent feature of those persons we are most familiar with, human beings, that they have purposes and intentions which are only incompletely manifested in their overt behaviour and which, therefore, can be known to others only in so far as they choose to avow them; or is this something that we could think away and still be dealing with what is fully a person, capable of being responded to not less but more completely than we respond to human beings?

The model of a divine–human dialogue (of which the divine tutorial was a particular, domestic, illustration) draws its strength from its capacity to acknowledge those things which Maurice Wiles constantly seeks to emphasize on the human side of the encounter while at the same time doing justice to the primacy of the divine initiative. I do indeed agree with all that he has so illuminatingly said about the enhanced sensitivity of particular persons in varying times and situations to the divine presence, but remain to be persuaded that this alone suffices to account for the overwhelming impression of being addressed by God to which so many of them bear witness.

REFERENCES

Abraham, William J. (1981), *The Divine Inspiration of Holy Scripture*, Oxford.
—— (1982), *Divine Revelation and the Limits of Historical Criticism*, Oxford.
Austin, J. L. (1962), *How to Do Things with Words*, Oxford.
Blanshard, Brand (1962), 'Symbolism', in Sidney Hook (ed.), *Religious Experience and Truth*, London.
Brown, David (1985), *The Divine Trinity*, London.
Butler, Joseph (1896), *Analogy of Religion*, ed. W. E. Gladstone, Oxford.
Davis, Caroline Franks (1989), *The Evidential Force of Religious Experience*, Oxford.
Mitchell, Basil (1982), *The Justification of Religious Belief*, Oxford.
Wiles, Maurice (1980), 'Does Christianity Need a Revelation?', *Theology*, 83 (Mar.), 109–14.
—— (1982), *Faith and the Mystery of God*, London.

12

A Priori Christology and Experience

SCHUBERT M. OGDEN

I

If anything can be said to be 'Christian doctrine', it is christology; and so 'the making and remaking of Christian doctrine' must at least mean, whatever else it means, the making and remaking of doctrine about Christ. More broadly, it must mean the making and remaking of doctrine about Jesus who is said to be the Christ, as well as any number of other things that are functionally equivalent to 'the Christ' and interchangeable with it.

To be sure, the distinction between 'making' and 'remaking' is hardly absolute, since what could be reasonably described from one standpoint as an instance of the first could be quite properly analysed from another standpoint as a case of the second—and vice versa. Thus, even within the comparatively short period of time documented by the New Testament writings, we find not only the making of christology, but the remaking of it as well, in the sense of reformulating still earlier thought and speech about Jesus in his decisive significance for human existence. But there are also good reasons for the not uncommon use of the distinction absolutely to designate two main phases in the whole long history of christological developments. The first phase, which is taken to be the making of christology, can be reckoned to include all the developments from the earliest Christian witness reconstructible from the writings of the New Testament to the classical definition of orthodox christology by the Council of Chalcedon. The second phase, then, is the remaking of orthodox christology that was carried out by the revisionary theologians of the late eighteenth and nineteenth centuries, in their struggles to find a new middle way between orthodoxy and the Enlightenment. Clearly, if the distinction between making and remaking christology is to be given more than a merely relative meaning, this use of it has a strong claim to express that meaning.

No less clear, however, is that the process of remaking christology that was begun by an earlier revisionary theology now has to be carried forward so as to include a remaking of this revisionary christology itself. In other words, from the standpoint of our own theological situation, the absolute distinction between making christology and remaking it is once again relativized. This is because both of the usual types of christology, revisionary no less than orthodox, have now proved to be incapable of solving the christological problem as it arises out of our theological situation today (cf. Ogden 1982: 1–19).

One way of demonstrating this is to do the main thing I propose to do in the remainder of this essay—namely, to show that both orthodox and revisionary christologies are vulnerable to the same fatal objection to any proposed solution to the problem of christology. Having done this, I then want to show that a third type of christology, which I should want to defend, is free from this objection and is, therefore, strong at the very point where the two usual types have been shown to be weak. In this way, I hope to indicate the remaking of christology, and thus of Christian doctrine, that now seems to me to be called for if Christian theology is to continue to play its proper role.

II

If we ask just what Christian theology's proper role is, my answer is that it is critical reflection on the Christian witness of faith so as to validate the claims to validity that bearing such witness necessarily makes or implies. This answer presupposes that Christian faith is a particular mode of human self-understanding, even as bearing witness to this faith by all that one thinks, says, and does is a particular form of human life-praxis. Precisely as life-praxis, however, bearing Christian witness is a matter of leading one's life, or living understandingly, and therefore of necessity involves either making or implying certain distinctive claims to validity. Specifically, it involves the two claims that the 'what' of one's witness, in the sense of what one thinks, says, or does to bear it, is adequate to its content and that the 'that' of one's witness, in the sense of the act of bearing it, is fitting to its situation. Actually, the first of these two claims is itself duplex in that it involves the two further claims that the 'what' of one's witness is appropriate to Jesus Christ and that it is credible to human existence. Consequently, there are three claims to validity that bearing Christian witness either makes or implies and that may well need to be critically validated as and when they become problematic.

The proper role of Christian theology in general, as a field of critical reflection, is to provide such necessary validation. Central to playing this role is the discipline of systematic theology, whose task is to validate critically the claim of Christian witness to be adequate to its content and, therefore, both appropriate to Jesus Christ and credible to human existence. Systematic theology can perform this task, obviously, only by presupposing the critical interpretation of Christian witness that its sister discipline, historical theology, has the task of providing, even as it must leave to its other sister discipline, practical theology, the further task of critically validating the claim of witness to be fitting to its situation. But if systematic theology neither is nor can be the only theological discipline, it is none the less at the centre of Christian theology in critically validating the claims to validity that are perforce made or implied in bearing Christian witness.

Thus to understand its role, however, is not to imply that Christian theology is to be done merely critically and retrospectively, with a view only to such Christian witness as has already been borne. Of course, constituted as it is, as critical reflection on Christian witness, it would be neither possible nor necessary but for the prior existence of this witness and the continuing activity of bearing it. But the point is that bearing Christian witness *is* a continuing activity and that the whole purpose of Christian theology, finally, is to perform a service necessary to bearing it validly. Consequently, Christian theology not only may, but also must, be done constructively and prospectively as well as critically and retrospectively, with a view to the Christian witness of the future as well as the Christian witness of the past. This means that systematic theology has to formulate as clearly and coherently as possible what any future Christian witness has to be if it is to be adequate to its content—what it must think, say, and do to be both appropriate to Jesus as Christians have experienced him and credible to the men and women who now need to hear it.

To do this, however, systematic theology must satisfy the specific requirements of both appropriateness and credibility as these arise out of our theological situation today. Of course, appropriateness and credibility themselves remain constant as the two criteria of adequacy, being as situation-invariant as the corresponding claims to validity that are necessarily made or implied in bearing Christian witness. But just what these criteria require is not constant but variable, being as situation-dependent as human life-praxis generally is bound to be. Thus what is required today if Christian witness is to be appropriate depends upon what is now to be defined both in principle and in fact as the formally normative instance of Christian witness by which the appropriateness of all other instances has to be determined. Likewise, the requirements that must be met today if Christian witness is to be credible depend upon what is now to be accepted in fact as well as in principle as the truth about human existence.

In our theological situation today, an essential requirement of credibility is that any valid formulation of Christian witness (as well as, naturally, of Christian theology) must be capable in some way of verification by common human experience. I do not mean to imply by this that the requirement that Christian witness be verifiable somehow by experience is something completely new or peculiar to the immediate present. On the contrary, I hold that one of the lasting achievements of revisionary theology right from the beginning is to have shown that the credibility of Christian witness can be validated, finally, only by appeal to what anyone is capable of experiencing simply as a human being. Thus, for something like two hundred years, Christians and theologians, like their contemporaries generally, have been justified in rejecting all appeals to mere authority as in the nature of the case insufficient to validate the credibility of their witness and theology. Indispensable as such appeals certainly are to validating claims to appropriateness, they can do nothing whatever towards validating claims to credibility until such authority as they appeal to can in turn be verified by direct appeal to experience.

Because this is so, however, the problem of christology that arises out of our theological situation today is, in large part, the problem of validating the credibility of christological formulations in experiential terms. This is not the whole of the problem, because systematic theology, now as always, must also be concerned—and concerned first of all—with validating the appropriateness of christological formulations. And in this respect, also, the specific requirements of the criterion, given our situation, make for certain problems, not least in validating the usual types of christology. But even after a christological formulation is validated as appropriate, there remains the question whether it is also credible; and in our situation today, the very least that 'credible' can mean is 'verifiable somehow in terms of human experience'.

By the same token, it must be a fatal objection to any formulation proposed to solve the christological problem that it cannot be verified in experiential terms. It would be fully credible, of course, only if it were to be, in fact, verified in some way by common experience. But unless it at least *can be* so verified, the question of whether it *is* verified and, therefore, 'credible' in the relevant sense could not even be asked, much less answered positively.

III

Having now clarified the significance of 'experience' for my argument, I turn to the other main concept, 'a priori christology'. This concept has recently enjoyed a certain currency in Christian theology, thanks especially to the work of Karl Rahner. While I could readily appropriate much, if not all, of what Rahner means by it, my own use of it, at least for the purposes of this essay, is much more easily explained. To clarify what I mean by it, I want to consider, first, what is properly meant by 'christology' simply as such, or by what I take to be the somewhat more precise term, 'the constitutive christological assertion'.

In its obvious literal sense, 'christology' means *logos* about *christos*, or thought and speech (including the speech of actions as well as of words) about Christ. But 'Christ' here is evidently used not so much as a concept or a title as a proper name—to refer to the particular person Jesus whom the thought and speech of christology are all about. This is clear from the fact that, as we noted at the outset, 'christology' is commonly used more broadly to refer to any thought and speech about Jesus who is said to be the Christ, even where what is asserted about him may be formulated in terms other than the particular concept or title 'the Christ'. Thus even where Jesus is said to be such different things as the Son of Man or the Lord, the Word of God or even God, we unhesitatingly recognize clear cases of 'christology' in this broader sense of the word.

Moreover, it is evident from the New Testament and the church's creeds that predicating such honorific titles of Jesus is not the only way in which Christians have formulated what they have to think and say about him in their witness and theology. They have followed no less frequently the different, if closely related, way of asserting his decisive significance by narrative formulations that have to do with his origin and destiny or the course of his earthly life, and that we can understand today only as mythological or legendary. Thus, whether Jesus is said to be conceived by the Holy Spirit and born of the Virgin Mary or to be risen from the dead and ascended into heaven, the assertion thus formulated mythologically is clearly the same christological assertion that the various honorific titles otherwise function to formulate. And the same is true of the legendary formulations that are also familiar from the New Testament, when different authors think and speak of Jesus' precocity among the teachers in the temple (Luke 2: 41–9), his faithfulness to his vocation and submission to God's will (Matt. 4: 1–10 par.; Mark 14: 32–42), his godly fear and obedience (Heb. 5: 7–9), his exemplary endurance of suffering (1 Pet. 2: 21–3), and his being sinless and made perfect (Heb. 4: 15, 5: 9, 7: 26–8; 1 Pet. 2: 22). These formulations, also, are rightly reckoned to be christological because they clearly function to do what all christology properly does—namely, to formulate what I call 'the constitutive christological assertion'. By this I mean the one assertion, however formulated, that Christians make or imply about Jesus that constitutes not only christology but the Christian witness of faith itself explicitly as such.

Because it is thus constituted by an assertion about Jesus, however, christology simply as such is by its very meaning a posteriori. Just as Jesus himself is a historical fact, so the assertion of his decisive significance, however formulated, must also be, in one important part, a historical assertion. And this means that it could not be made or implied at all except after the fact of his appearance in history and on the basis of particular historical experience, mediate if not immediate, of this fact.

On the other hand, the christological assertion is like any other, historical or not, in asserting a certain predicate of its subject.

Relative to its particular subject or any other of which it could be meaningfully asserted, the predicate as such is a priori. Not only what it means, but also what conditions need to be fulfilled in order to assert it truthfully of any subject, can, and in a sense must, be understood before the fact of this or that particular assertion of it, whether of Jesus or of someone else. This would be true, indeed, even if the christological assertion were nothing more than a historical assertion. But this it cannot be, because it does not assert that Jesus *was* thus and so, but that he *is* the Christ, or, in some functionally equivalent and interchangeable formulation, that he is of decisive significance for human existence. As such, it is also, in important part, what is commonly called 'an assertion of faith', or, as I prefer to say, 'an existential assertion'. This I take to mean that, although it could indeed arise only after the historical fact of Jesus' appearance and on the basis of particular experience of this fact, it also makes a certain valuation of Jesus in relation to the existential question that we human beings typically ask about the meaning of ultimate reality for us. To be exact, it makes a valuation of Jesus as himself the decisive answer to this existential question and as, therefore, the explicit primal source authorizing the authentic understanding of ourselves and others in relation to the strictly ultimate reality of the whole.

It lies in the nature of the case, however, that the existential assertion of christology can no more be truthfully made about Jesus than about anyone else unless certain conditions are fulfilled that are necessary and sufficient for truthfully making it. In other words, the valuation that christology makes of Jesus is not merely a subjective preference, but rather necessarily implies an objective claim—to the effect that Jesus fulfils all the conditions that are necessary to anyone's being the decisive answer to the existential question and, therefore, of decisive significance for human existence. But this means that it must be possible to stipulate these necessary conditions a priori—before the fact of Jesus, even as before every other fact of which 'the Christ' or any functionally equivalent christological predicate could be meaningfully asserted.

What I mean by 'a priori christology', then, is just such a stipulation. Even as christology simply as such is the explicit assertion, in some formulation or other, of the decisive significance of Jesus, so a priori christology is the explicit stipulation, again, in some terms or other, of the conditions that need to be fulfilled in order to make or imply the same kind of assertion about any subject whatever.

Among the other implications of this comparison is that a priori christology, also, can be implied even when it is not made explicit. As a matter of fact, it belongs to the very logic of a christology simply as such that it necessarily presupposes *some* a priori christology. To assert or imply that Jesus is of decisive significance for human existence could not be meaningful at all unless it presupposed some stipulation of the conditions necessary to asserting this truthfully of any possible subject. But, then, there are the best of reasons for making this implied stipulation explicit as an a priori christology. For whether or not a proposed christo-logical formulation can be critically validated as credible depends, finally, upon whether or not the a priori christology that it necessarily presupposes allows for at least its possible validation.

IV

This brings us to the main task of my argument: to show that christological formulations of either of the two usual types are open to the same fatal objection to any proposed solution to the problem of christology today. I will consider the two types of christology separately but will proceed in each case by taking the same two steps. After briefly characterizing each type, I will first explicate the a priori christology that it necessarily presupposes, and then I will explain why this a priori christology precludes even the possibility of critically validating the christology itself as credible, if this means, as it must mean today, verifying its formulations in experiential terms.

I begin with the type of christology that I call 'orthodox'. If the classical formulation of this type was provided, as I have said, by the Chalcedonian definition, it is arguable that the two main approaches to christology that the definition sought to hold together were already present in the New Testament writings themselves (cf. Chadwick 1983). These approaches can be characterized suffi-ciently for our purposes by nuancing the distinction I made earlier between mythological and legendary ways of asserting Jesus' decisive significance by narratives about his origin and destiny or the events of his earthly life. In point of fact, there was not simply one mythological way of doing this but two. On the one hand, there was the presumably earlier and more traditional Jewish way of representing Jesus as in every respect a human being, but a human being who had been specially sent or commissioned by God, or whom God had in some special way elected or adopted, whether by inspiring him with the divine Spirit or by raising him from the dead. On the other hand, there was the later and more typically Hellenistic (and Hellenistic-Jewish) way of representing Jesus as himself in some respect a divine being, whether an ideal figure like the Jewish Wisdom or Word of God, whose only pre-existence was God's own, or, rather, a real figure somehow pre-existing alongside God, who could become incarnate as a human being to effect the salvation of all other men and women.

If the first of these ways was relatively strong in more clearly attesting to the full reality of Jesus' humanity, it was relatively weak in not so clearly witnessing that he was God's own decisive act of salvation. But the reverse was true of the second way, whose relative strength and weakness were exactly opposite, in that it more clearly witnessed to Jesus as God's own decisive act, even while less clearly attesting to his being really and fully human. Essentially the same was true, then, of the later, more fully developed forms of these same two approaches between which the Chalcedonian definition attempted to effect a consensus. On the one hand, there was the *logos-anthropos* christology of Antioch, which was strong in its witness to Jesus' humanity, even if weak in attesting to him as God's own act of salvation. On the other hand, there was the *logos-sarx* christology of Alexandria, which was strong in attesting to Jesus as God's own saving act, even though weak in witnessing to him as really and fully a human being. By holding these two christologies together, the Chalcedonian definition, in its way, summed up the whole development of christology that had begun even before the New Testament writings, thereby providing the guide-lines for the church's witness to Jesus that it is the proper function of doctrine to provide (cf. Norris 1966, 1980).

If we ask now what this orthodox type of christology necessarily presupposes in the way of a priori christology, the answer seems clear enough. It presupposes that, for any possible value of x, x can be truthfully asserted to be of decisive significance for human existence if, and only if, x is not only really and fully a human being but also actualizes God's unique possibility of acting decisively to save all other human beings. By God 'acting' here, I mean, just as orthodox christology clearly means, what is commonly understood to be a divine 'intervention'. We rightly speak of such an intervention whenever God intentionally produces a state of affairs by causally altering the way things would have gone otherwise, if the only causes involved had been natural or non-divine. Orthodox christology evidently takes for granted that, just as any special act of God would be an intervention in this sense, so the same must be true *a fortiori* of God's decisive act of salvation in the human being Jesus. This means, then, that the a priori christology that orthodox christology presupposes stipulates just such a divine intervention as among the necessary conditions that any value of x must fulfil if he or she is to be truthfully said to be of decisive existential significance. If, and only if, a being who is really and fully human at the same time actualizes God's possibility of intervening decisively for human salvation, can he or she be truthfully asserted to be the Christ or any of the other things that are functionally equivalent thereto.

The great weakness of this a priori christology, however, is that nothing in common human experience could ever verify that any really and fully human being at the same time actualizes an intervention of God, much less God's decisive intervention for human salvation. For all experience could possibly show, any assertion to this effect about any human being whatever would be merely that—merely an assertion, unverifiable by appeal to experience and to be accepted, if at all, solely by appeal to authority.

This should not be confused with the objection that the general concept of God's intervention is either unclear or incoherent or without any basis in experience. There are, indeed, certain well-known difficulties with the concept, theological as well as philosophical, which have led many revisionary theologians to abandon it (cf. Wiles 1986). But other, more traditionalist theologians and philosophers continue to defend the concept as viable on the grounds that it is necessarily implied by any Christian witness or theology that is appropriate to Jesus Christ and that the usual revisionary arguments against it do not, in fact, provide sufficient reasons for abandoning it.

Thus one of the most common objections against the concept is that divine intervention is incompatible with the strict naturalistic determinism widely held to be at once assumed by modern science and confirmed by its continuing successes. But, as William P. Alston has effectively shown, this objection has little weight. Aside from the fact that appeals to what science is held to assume or confirm are really only appeals to authority, neither the procedures of science nor its results warrant the conclusion that 'every event in the universe is strictly determined to be just what it is by natural factors'. On the contrary, 'all our evidence is equally compatible with the idea that natural causal determination is sometimes, or always, only approximate', and 'particular divine actions would not jeopardize, or otherwise adversely affect, anything fundamental to science' (Alston 1990: 7–8). As for the other common objection that the concept of God's intervention entails violating laws of nature, Alston replies convincingly that this all depends on how we think of laws of nature and that we have no good reason to think of them in the particular way that warrants the objection. The only such laws we have reason to accept do not specify the sufficient conditions of certain outcomes without qualification, but only within 'a system closed to influences other than those specified in the law'. Thus, 'since the laws we have reason to accept make provision for interference by outside forces unanticipated by the law, it can hardly be claimed that such a law will be violated if a divine outside force intervenes; and hence it can hardly be claimed that such laws imply that God does not intervene, much less imply that this is impossible' (Alston 1990: 9–10).

Alston recognizes, significantly, that it is one thing thus to defend the general concept of divine intervention, something else again to validate claims arising from applying it to particular cases. In this connection, he makes a brief response to the classical formulation of objections to such claims in David Hume's chapter on miracles in the *Enquiry Concerning Human Understanding*. He observes, first of all, that 'it is not generally the case that alleged divine interventions go contrary to our experience'; and then, secondly, that 'the likelihood of a report of miracle is profoundly influenced by one's background religious and metaphysical assumptions. If these include the principle that the world is created and governed by a being who has reasons to intervene from time to time, this will materially increase the probability of some such reports being correct, though it does not, of course, establish the correctness of any particular report' (Alston 1990: 10–11). Consistent with this concluding admission, Alston expressly disavows any concern 'to determine how we should go about identifying divine interventions', assuring his reader that he is concerned 'only to argue for the viability of the concept' (Alston 1990: 11).

Alston's sense of the limitations of his argument is fitting. Even if an alleged divine intervention does not generally go contrary to our experience, so as to justify a strong experiential argument against its occurrence, nothing simply in experience either does or can suffice to identify it as the divine intervention it is alleged to be. An occurrence *contra naturam* is, for all experience could ever show, simply that, since whether it is a divine intervention, or is to be explained instead by other forces likewise unspecified by the relevant laws of nature, can never be determined simply be appealing to experience. As for Alston's second observation, careful inspection discloses that it subtly begs the question. That a God conceived to be the all-good and all-powerful creator and consummator of all things *may have* reasons to intervene from time to time does indeed seem to follow. But from background religious and metaphysical assumptions which include the principle that the world is, in fact, created and governed by a God so conceived it in no way follows that God actually *has* any such reasons sufficient to increase the probability of at least some reports of God's having so intervened correct. Whether God, in fact, has such reasons can no more be decided by a principle included in one's background religious and metaphysical assumptions than can the question of whether God has, in fact, intervened. Nor are we ever in a position to answer the first question any more than the second simply by what we can experience as human beings.

Viable, then, as the concept of divine intervention may be, there is not the least reason to suppose that we could ever be justified in so applying the concept through experience as to identify any particular divine intervention. There cannot be a valid inference from the general concept to a particular application, because *a posse ad esse non valet consequentia*. But, then, even if God did in fact decisively intervene, no assertion to this effect could ever be verified in experiential terms. Because this is so, however, any christological proposal of the orthodox type is open to the fatal objection that its formulations of the christological assertion cannot be experientially verified. The a priori christology that it necessarily presupposes explicates a condition for truthfully making the assertion that no experience could possibly verify as fulfilled. Consequently, whatever may be said for the appropriateness of such a christology, its claim to be credible cannot be validated in the way in which our situation today requires.

V

The same is true of the other usual type of christology that I distinguish as 'revisionary'. Since I have already extensively criticized this type elsewhere, I will consider it more briefly here and refer the reader to other writings for fuller discussion (Ogden 1982, 1984).

If there is any single formulation of revisionary christology that can be rightly regarded as classical, it must surely be that of Friedrich Schleiermacher in *Der christliche Glaube* (Schleiermacher 1960; cf. Faut 1904). But here, too, the type was already anticipated in a way in some of the christological formulations documented by the writings of the New Testament. I referred earlier to these writings as evidencing a legendary way, alongside the two mythological ways, of asserting Jesus' decisive existential significance by narrative formulations concerning his origin and destiny and the course of his earthly life. Whereas the mythological ways, as we have seen, both represent Jesus, in some terms or other, as God's own saving act, and hence as actualizing God's unique possibility to intervene decisively for human salvation, the legendary way thinks and speaks of Jesus, again, in different terms, as actualizing the unique possibility of a human being to exist authentically and even perfectly in relation to God—to be utterly and completely open to God, and to both self and all others in God, and to lead his or her whole human life accordingly. It is significant, however, that this legendary way of representing Jesus, which is evident already from the New Testament, traditionally had its place only in the context provided by one or both of the other mythological ways. Thus, while the Chalcedonian definition undoubtedly continues the legendary way, also, by explicitly attesting to Jesus' sinlessness, the claim thereby implied for the perfection of his human existence is in no way independent of his being God's decisive intervention but rather follows logically from it.

It is quite otherwise, however, with the revisionary christology of Schleiermacher and of all who have continued to follow his lead right up to today. Here the legendary way of asserting Jesus' decisive significance has been taken out of its traditional context in one or both of the mythological ways and then pursued by itself as an independent type of christology. This is evident from the fact that all references to God's unique intervention in Jesus are construed as equivalent to references to Jesus' unique perfection as a human being. Thus Schleiermacher can say that 'it is exactly one and the same to ascribe to Christ an absolutely powerful God-consciousness and to attribute to him a being of God in him' (Schleiermacher 1960: ii. 45 (§ 94)). When Schleiermacher speaks of 'God-consciousness', he is simply referring to authentic human existence, so as to formulate the ideal of human perfection as a God-consciousness that is 'absolutely powerful'. But however this ideal may be formulated—and revisionary theologies have formulated it in many different ways—the claim typical of revisionary christologies from Schleiermacher to the present is that Jesus is of decisive existential significance because, and only because, he actualized this ideal in his own existence as a human being.

The reason for this, of course, is that revisionary christologies are all of a single type precisely because they necessarily presuppose one and the same a priori christology. They presuppose, to be explicit, that, for any possible value of x, x can be truthfully asserted to be of decisive significance for human existence if, and only if, x is not only really and fully a human being but also actualizes his or her unique possibility of attaining a perfect human existence. By 'a perfect human existence', I understand the ideal, or unsurpassable, actualization of authentic existence—of what any human being is at least implicitly authorized to be in every moment of his or her existence by God, in the sense of the strictly ultimate whole of reality in its meaning for us. This means, then, that a human being can be truthfully asserted to be the Christ, or any of the other things that Jesus has been asserted or implied to be if, and only if, there is no moment in his or her entire existence in which he or she fails to actualize the possibility of thus existing authentically. In this sense, a sinless human existence not only implies, but is also implied by, a perfect human existence; and only the actualization of such an existence could warrant truthfully asserting of any human being what christology asserts of Jesus.

But the great weakness of this a priori christology, also, is that no such assertion, about Jesus or anyone else, could ever be verified by direct appeal to experience, as distinct from some authority, itself in need, finally, of experiential verification. Nothing that any one human being could possibly experience could ever verify that another, equally really and fully human, actualizes even authentic existence, much less attains perfection or sinlessness. Consequently, even if a human being did in fact attain perfection, an assertion to this effect could not be verified experientially, but could be accepted as true solely on the basis of authority.

Once again, however, there is no need in saying this to object to the very idea of perfection, or to even the possibility of someone's attaining it. Just as the concept of a divine intervention can be allowed to be viable, so the idea of a human perfection can also be accepted as sufficiently clear and coherent to refer to something at least possible. But this in no way meets the objection that experience cannot possibly determine whether any human being has attained a perfect existence. Even if one could judge from the thoughts, words, and deeds of a person, instead of only from the witness thereto of others, there would still be no way of inferring from what one can thus experience about the person to a self-understanding that in the nature of the case one cannot experience. Nor can such an inference be mediated by a warrant to the effect that if one has, in fact, understood oneself authentically or attained perfection, one will think, say, and do certain things, while avoiding certain other things. What the inference logically requires is the converse of this warrant; and for all that any experience could possibly show, its converse is nothing but the formal fallacy that it gives every appearance of being. Moreover, the data base that would be needed to infer the attainment of perfection so far exceeds what any one human being could possibly experience of another that any attempt to acquire it can be dismissed at once as a practical absurdity.

Because this is so, all christological proposals of the revisionary type are vulnerable to the same fatal objection that must be made to any of the orthodox type. Their formulations of the christological assertion are experientially unverifiable, because they, too, necessarily presuppose an a priori christology that stipulates a condition for truthfully making or implying the assertion that no experience could ever show to be fulfilled. Therefore, even if the claim of revisionary christologies to be appropriate could be critically validated, their further claim to be credible in terms of human experience cannot.

VI

If the argument to this point is sound, it should now be clear that both of the usual types of christology, orthodox and revisionary, are incapable of solving the christological problem that arises out of our situation today. The question, then, for Christian theology, and for systematic theology in particular, is whether there is some alternative proposal for solving the problem. Is there a third type of christology whose formulations can be critically validated as credible because they at least can be verified in some way by common experience?

The answer to this question depends, as we have seen, upon whether there is another a priori christology that allows for at least the possible experiential verification of any christological formulations necessarily presupposing it. This an a priori christology can allow only if fulfilment of the conditions that it stipulates for truthfully asserting the decisive significance of Jesus or of anyone else can be verified somehow experientially. I now want to show that there is such an a priori christology and that, therefore, there is also a type of christology whose formulations can be critically validated as credible in terms of human experience.

The a priori christology I have in mind stipulates the following as the conditions that need to be fulfilled in order truthfully to assert of anyone what christology asserts or implies about Jesus. For any possible value of x, x can be truthfully asserted to be of decisive significance for human existence if, and only if, x is not only really and fully a human being but also decisively re-presents the meaning of ultimate reality for us and, therewith, our unique possibility of authentic existence. By 're-presents' here, I mean simply 'makes explicit'. My assumption is that the meaning of ultimate reality for us, including our unique possibility of existing authentically, is and must be presented implicitly to each and every one of us as soon and as long as we are human beings at all. But what is thus presented at least implicitly in all our human experience can also become present again, a second time, and in this sense be *re*-presented explicitly through specific persons and things and through the specific concepts and symbols by which we grasp and express their meaning.

There is the further possibility, then, that someone or something will not only thus make the meaning of our existence explicit, but will do so 'decisively', by explicitly answering our existential question, thereby authorizing our decision between all other re-presentations. In other words, if *x decisively* re-presents our possibility, *x* is not simply one authority among others, but rather functions as the explicit primal source of all authorities because it explicitly authorizes them as well as the authentic understanding of ourselves and others in relation to the whole. This means that if, and only if, a being who is really and fully human at the same time decisively re-presents our authentic possibility, and thus functions as just such a source of authority, can he or she be truthfully asserted to be of decisive existential significance.

The great strength of this a priori christology, compared with both of the others we have considered, is that whether or not this condition is in fact fulfilled is at least verifiable by human experience. That a person decisively re-presents our authentic possibility depends entirely on what he or she thinks, says, and does, and on what others think, say, and do, including, not least, the others who bear witness to his or her meaning for us. But all of this can be directly experienced, mediately if not immediately, and there is no need to depend upon authority to validate the credibility of formulations asserting or implying his or her decisive significance for our existence.

This is not to deny that there is an important difference between verifying that someone, in fact, re-presents a certain possibility and verifying that the possibility thus re-presented is, in truth, our unique possibility of authentic existence. To verify the second may also be—and I believe is—a matter, finally, of experience. But the experience required to verify it is not simply the particular historical experience required to verify the first, but is the existential experience of our own existence with others in relation to the whole. This means that it also requires properly metaphysical and moral procedures of verification that go beyond all of the procedures required to verify strictly historical assertions (cf. Ogden 1982: 82–5, 127–68). But in this respect, the other a priori christology is in no way different from the two usual accounts, both of which likewise involve their own metaphysical and moral presuppositions. After all, it would not make any sense to talk about a divine intervention were there not a God who has the possibility of intervening; and unless the strictly ultimate reality is a God of whom a human being can and should be conscious, there could be no meaningful talk of human perfection being an absolutely powerful God-consciousness. The great strength of the other a priori christology, however, is that, once its metaphysical and moral presuppositions are shown to be true, whether Jesus or anyone else is of decisive existential significance can be verified forthwith by appeal to particular historical experience such as anyone might possibly have. It does not stipulate conditions that no one could ever possibly experience to be fulfilled, whatever his or her background metaphysical and moral presuppositions.

That there is this other a priori christology, however, means that there is also a third type of christology, whose formulations can be critically validated as credible because they at least can be verified experientially. According to these formulations, Jesus is of decisive existential significance, not because he actualizes either God's possibility of intervention or his own possibility of perfection, but because he decisively re-presents our possibility of authentic existence. That he in fact does this, however, is experientially verifiable, whereas the reasons formulated by the two usual types of christology are not. Consequently, the third type of christology can be critically validated as credible in terms of experience, and thus is strong at the very point at which the other types are weak.

Of course, this is not the only point at which a proposal must be strong if it is to solve our christological problem. Today as always, such a proposal must be appropriate as well as credible, and this means appropriate to Jesus as Christians have experienced him ever since the constitutive experience of the apostles. Whether the third type of christology is appropriate in this sense is not a question I can answer here, any more than I have argued that it is, in fact, credible. But even in this respect it may validly claim a certain strength, relative to the orthodox and revisionary types. Whatever else Christians may have experienced Jesus to be and mean, they could not possibly have experienced what no person is ever in a position to experience about another. Therefore, the usual types of christology can no more validly claim to be appropriate to Jesus as Christians have experienced him than to be credible to human existence as all of us experience it.

On the other hand, the third type can still prove to be as appropriate in terms of specifically Christian experience as it is credible in terms of human experience generally. There are good reasons to look to it, then, for the remaking of christology, and thus of Christian doctrine, that our situation today requires.

REFERENCES

Alston, William P. (1990), 'Divine Action: Shadow or Substance' (unpublished MS).

Chadwick, Henry (1983), 'The Chalcedonian Definition', in *Actes du Concile de Chalcédoine, Sessions III–VI: La Définition de la foi*, trans. A. J. Festugière, Geneva: 7–16.

Faut, S. (1904), *Die Christologie seit Schleiermacher: Ihre Geschichte und ihre Begründung*, Tübingen.

Norris, Richard A., Jr. (1966), 'Toward a Contemporary Interpretation of the Chalcedonian Definition', in Richard A. Norris, Jr. (ed.), *Lux in lumine: Essays to Honor W. Norman Pittenger*, New York: 62–79, 177–8.

—— (1980) (ed.), *The Christological Controversy*, Philadelphia.

Ogden, Schubert M. (1982), *The Point of Christology*, London.

—— (1984), 'Rudolf Bultmann and the Future of Revisionary Christology', in Bernd Jaspert (ed.), *Rudolf Bultmanns Werk und Wirkung*, Darmstadt: 155–73.

Schleiermacher, Friedrich (1960), *Der christliche Glaube nach den Grundsätzen der Evangelischen Kirche im Zusammenhang dargestellt*, ed. Martin Redeker, 7th edn., Berlin.

Wiles, Maurice (1986), *God's Action in the World*, London.

13

The Supposedly Historical Basis of
Theological Understanding

DAVID A. PAILIN

Throughout his theological writings Maurice Wiles has acknowledged the historical basis of the Christian faith, investigated the history of its development, and sought to identify what can credibly be claimed about 'acts' of God in history, while in all three issues he has sought to take fully into account the proper nature of historical understanding and the results of historical criticism. In the first respect he states, for example, that 'it is a fundamental feature of traditional Christian faith to see in its past history, and in the history of Jesus in particular, the determinative and distinctive element in that faith. . . . Christianity sees itself as rooted in history in a unique way' (Wiles 1976a: 99). In a later essay, considering how the Bible is 'an indispensable resource rather than a binding authority' for theological reflection, he quotes John Barton's remark that the Bible is, among other things, 'the "primary evidence for the events that lie at the source of Christian faith"' (Wiles 1987a: 51–2). His interest in the second matter is manifest in his studies of the sources and factors involved in the 'making' and the 'remaking' of Christian doctrine (Wiles 1967, 1974) as well as in his later involvement in the debate about the so-called 'myth of God incarnate' (Wiles 1977, 1979) and (at the time of writing) his unfinished study of Arianism (for which Christ Church library provides him with an enviable resource of seventeenth- and eighteenth-century texts).

In relation to the third issue, he describes 'the language of God's action' as being 'both central and problematic' for Christian practice and understanding. While, therefore, he affirms that 'we live in a world in which God is continually active as creator and redeemer, a world of whose existence he is the purposive initiator and continuator', he also calls for 'more careful and thorough exploration than it commonly receives' of what is meant by talking of 'God's acts in history' (Wiles 1989: 199–201). The conclusion of his own reflections on the problem can be seen, for example, in his Bampton Lectures, *God's Action in the World*. He recognizes, however, that some may query whether his understanding of the retrospective nature (cf. Wiles 1986: 64, 83, 89) of identification of the 'all-pervasive and sustaining presence' of 'the living God' can satisfy their notion of a God who plays an active role in the world (ibid. 108). That notion, however, may owe more to human wishes for superhuman interventions when things get into a mess than to credible perception of the reality of God.

A comment in a recent review reflects Maurice Wiles's recognition of the importance of the results of historical understanding. Here he states that 'modern biblical scholarship has certainly not said the last word about the Bible. But it has said things to which anyone who wants to make a serious contribution to theology must address him or herself' (Wiles 1991: 108). Not only have his own remarks about the Bible consistently met this requirement; in his theological work he has also met the parallel requirement in relation to historical scholarship. In this he stands in the British intellectual tradition from John Locke (and Anthony Collins) and David Hume which insists that conclusions and convictions be controlled by the evidence which justifies them.

In his works Maurice Wiles also takes careful account of what historical investigations disclose about 'historical relativism' (Wiles 1976*b*: 157). What he means by this phrase does not entail a denial of realism in historical judgements, nor the incommensurability of different cultural ages. As he understands it, 'historical relativism' has three aspects. On the one hand it means that past forms of Christian thought and practice must be recognized to belong to 'the particular limited circumstances of their time and place' (cf. Wiles 1976*b*: 157; 1974: 45). Secondly, it means that in principle there is a 'large measure of uncertainty about' historical judgements in general and about 'the founding events of the [sc. Christian] faith' in particular (Wiles 1989: 53; cf. 1974: 47–9). Maurice Wiles consequently warns theologians not to expect more from historical scholarship than what historical enquiry can in principle produce (cf. Wiles 1976*a*: 35). Thirdly, it means that 'there are no bare historical facts' because 'the writing of history involves a degree of interpretation which depends in some measure upon the personal standpoint of the historian and problems of his age' (Wiles 1967: 175).

When Maurice Wiles discusses the function of references to past events and to the results of historical investigations in arriving at theological understanding that is reasonable because it is both coherent and credible (cf. Wiles 1987*b*: 48), his remarks show that he is well aware (some of his critics might be tempted to say 'too well aware' if it did not disclose their obscurantism) of these problems of 'historical relativism'. Nevertheless there is a further and fundamental problem to which he has devoted much less attention. This is the problem of how believers and theologians move from historical judgements to faith in and claims about the reality of God. It is a problem which Maurice Wiles is not alone in neglecting. Although Lessing identified it in 'On the Proof of the Spirit and of Power' (cf. Lessing 1956: 51), it has generally been bypassed rather than attacked (cf. Pailin 1975).

In the long tradition of the 'quest' for the historical Jesus, for example, it appears to have been widely assumed, especially in British studies, that if only the 'historical Jesus' could be identified, the Christian theologians' basic task would be complete. All that would remain to be done would be minor titivating and current applications of the faith thus established. In reality, the fundamental problem for Christian faith and its theological self-understanding would remain. The problem would be to show how it was originally and is now both credible and coherent to move from what happened historically (i.e. from events which happened to persons because of the agency of persons and were observed by persons) to claims about the reality of God. This Gordian knot cannot, furthermore, be cut by recognizing that the historical Jesus is indiscernible because the records which we have about him present the witness of faith to Jesus as the Christ (cf. Knox 1958, 1963; Ogden 1982: 51–6; 1986: 60–2). While this is a valid point about the records, it does not solve the fundamental problem but poses it in a new way. How, if that be the case with the supposed evidence about Jesus, are we to hold that it is coherent and credible to accept that those who present the witness of faith have correctly interpreted (and in this sense understood) what they claim to 'have seen and heard' (1 John 1: 3)?

This is the problem which I wish to consider in my contribution to these essays honouring Maurice Wiles. In attempting, however, to cast a little light into one of theology's dark corners, I do not pretend to solve the problem. My aim is less ambitious. It is to suggest that reflection on the relationship between events, records, and faith indicates that Christian theological understanding ultimately depends upon metaphysical convictions.

In *Religion in the Making* Alfred North Whitehead states that 'religion requires a metaphysical backing'. Only so can it claim rationally credible authority in contrast to 'the emotions which it generates' (Whitehead 1927: 71; cf. 43, 53, 73–4). This does not mean that theology must become a kind of metaphysical musing which is pursued prior to or, at any rate, for the most part independently of any consideration of the actual facts of contingent reality. Such speculations may produce neat, schematic systems but, as the fate of Leibniz's thought in the hands of Dr Pangloss reminds us, they are also likely to be judged to be abstract theorizings rather than reliable insights into the ultimate nature of reality. According to Whitehead it is the 'genius' of Christianity that it first points 'at the facts' and then asks for 'their systematic interpretation' (ibid. 40; cf. Whitehead 1978: 4–7). The 'facts' in his view are particularly those of the sayings and deeds of Jesus; the 'interpretation' is the 'generalization' into 'final truths' of what was 'first perceived as exemplified in [these] particular instances'. Truths derived from particular events are thus 'amplified into a coherent system and applied to the interpretation of life'. They are then verified (or falsified) by their success (or failure) in providing a significant 'meaning, in terms of value, for our own existence, a meaning which flows from the nature of things' (Whitehead 1927: 110).

While, however, the doctrines of 'rational religion' arise from what is perceived to have been said and done on particular occasions, the interpretation and establishment of those doctrines as having 'universal validity' for 'the ordering of all experience' (ibid. 21) is a product of metaphysical understanding. Historical events may evoke or provoke the insights but historical investigations cannot justify the religious interpretation of those events nor its truth. Whitehead accordingly remarks that 'it is a curious delusion that the rock upon which our beliefs can be founded is an historical investigation'. He holds that it is crucial to appreciate that 'history presupposes a metaphysic' (ibid. 72). Although in this latter passage Whitehead is primarily concerned with the way in which historians' understanding of past events is determined by their current understanding of contemporary reality, the quotation sums up his general view of the relationship between past events and religious beliefs. The occurrence of certain events may in practice lead to certain beliefs about God and the fundamental processes of reality. Nevertheless, the significance and credibility of those beliefs does not, in the end, depend upon historical investigations into the events. The crucial appeal in the case of theological understanding is not to the historians' researches but to the metaphysicians' tests of 'logical coherence, adequacy, and exemplification' (ibid. 76; cf. Whitehead 1978: 5).

These remarks about the relationship between past events and religious belief raise fundamental questions about claims that the Christian faith is 'an historical religion' and that it is 'based upon history'. When such claims are made, it is generally not to make such trivial points as that Christianity is a faith with a history, nor that its origin can be given an approximate date, nor even that its believers practise their faith in the historical world and that their beliefs are conditioned by their world. They are made to assert that the 'happenedness' of certain events is a *sine qua non* of the Christian faith and that the content of that faith is, in some respects at least, dependent upon what actually happened in them.

These claims about the Christian faith may seem to be warranted by the authoritative summary of its beliefs in the Apostles' Creed. Even when references to the virginity of Mary and to the resurrection of Jesus are recognized to be theological and not historical affirmations, the second article of the Creed contains several items whose reference is historical. 'Jesus', 'born', 'suffered under Pontius Pilate', 'crucified, dead and buried' are names and verbs which refer to past persons and events.

G. E. Wright understands theology in this way. In *God Who Acts* he states that 'Biblical theology is *the confessional recital of the redemptive acts of God* in a particular history, because history is the chief medium of revelation' (Wright 1952: 13). He admits that the 'history' from which faith's understanding is derived is not what the (secular) historian might immediately recognize: it is rather to be designated as 'history interpreted by faith' (ibid. 128). Nevertheless, in his view faith's interpretation of events does not foist meaning upon what happened; it elicits its authentic significance. He thus asserts that 'the realism of the Bible consists in its close attention to the facts of history and of tradition because these facts are the facts of God' (ibid. 38).

In claiming that past events have a fundamental role in the Christian faith and its theological self-understanding, some theologians do not deny that there is a limited contribution from metaphysical reflection. They insist, however, that a historical element, appropriately interpreted, is an essential part of a genuinely Christian form of theological understanding. Wolfhart Pannenberg, for instance, maintains in relation to Christology, the defining doctrine of Christian theism, that reference to past events is essential. Citing Schleiermacher, Tillich, and Bultmann, he attacks theologians who derive their understanding of Christ from the present experience of salvation. Instead, he argues, 'Christology must start from Jesus of Nazareth, not from his significance for us. . . . The significance of Jesus must be developed from what Jesus actually was then' (Pannenberg 1968: 48). John Macquarrie makes the point more generally. When discussing the significance of the historical Jesus, he puts it that 'this actual human figure who lived at a particular time is indispensable to a full statement of Christian faith and theology' (Macquarrie 1966: 256–7).

Other theologians are more hostile to metaphysics. They reject any contribution to theological understanding that is based on metaphysical considerations. In their view historical events alone are the primary and normative foundation of authentic theological understanding. Karl Barth, for example, states that

When the Christian language speaks of revelation and God it means a reality which is very insignificant looking and outwardly most unpromising; it speaks quite simply of a single concrete fact in the midst of the numberless host of facts and the vast stream of historical events; it speaks of a single human person living in the age of the Roman Empire . . . (Barth 1954: 211)

Similarly Thomas F. Torrance asserts that Christian theological understanding is based on events that occurred in the past. The 'eternal Truth' is encountered 'as *temporal fact*'. Hence, while 'theological thinking' is more than 'historical thinking', it is such not 'by leaving the historical behind, but through participation in the eternal which has entered into the historical and gathered it into inalienable relation to the Truth in Jesus Christ' (Torrance 1969: 154).

Further examples of the claim that the Christian faith and its theological expressions are based on historical events are not hard to find. The vast majority of Christian theologians—some claim all authentic Christian theologians—see their understanding of God as crucially dependent on things that happened, and particularly on the events of the life of Jesus. For most of them it follows that the so-called quest for the historical Jesus (or, with appropriate variations, for the apostolic witness to Jesus as the Christ) according to the methods of historical investigation from Lardner and Reimarus to Schillebeeckx and Sanders has been concerned with a fundamental issue for the Christian faith. While, however, this view of the quest is widespread, questions must be raised about its justifiability, especially when it is considered to imply that ultimately the knowledge of God is a product of historical investigations. On reflection it appears that Whitehead is nearer the truth when he suggests that any theological significance found in historical investigations into past events and in the events themselves is primarily dependent upon some form of metaphysical understanding.

What is it, however, that makes the relationship between faith and history problematic? The fundamental problem for establishing a credible relationship between past events, their historical apprehension, and theistic faith is not that posed by what Clement Webb once described as 'the rise of a new ideal of historical knowledge' which casts 'doubt upon the historical value of the traditional account of the origins of the Christian faith and life' (Webb 1935: 49). If this were the problem it could probably be overcome by recognizing that faith is a matter of commitment in the face of acknowledged probabilities rather than a matter of building upon indisputable facts. It should be recognized, however, that this response to historical uncertainty may be less comfortable than many theologians seem to appreciate. As Maurice Wiles points out, there is 'an oddity' in both affirming of a certain person 'that he is the embodiment of the divine' and 'acknowledging that our knowledge about him in himself is at every point tentative and uncertain' (Wiles 1974: 49). Nevertheless, while the development of historical rigour may create a problem for theologians, it is not this which poses the crucial problem for reaching theological understanding from historical investigations.

As was mentioned earlier, the crucial problem confronting any attempt to derive a knowledge of God from history is that pointed to by Lessing when he spoke of the 'ugly, broad ditch' between two kinds of understanding, that of history and that of theistic faith. The ditch marks, in Aristotle's phrase, a *'metabasis eis allo genos'*—a logical type-jump—which apparently prevents any rationally justifiable way of deriving the latter kind of understanding from the former (cf. Lessing 1956: 55; cf. 51–6). It is unfortunate that most responses to Lessing's insights into the problem of history and faith concentrate on his initial discussion of the problem—which he describes in terms of the problem of basing necessary truths of reason upon the accidental truths of history—and consider it to pose the question of the proper confidence to be given to faith based on historical judgements in view of the fact that the latter can never be more than probable. Such responses miss the much more disturbing point of Lessing's use of the accidental/necessary distinction. This is to identify the fundamental problem posed by the relationship of faith and history as that posed by the difference in logical type between beliefs about the reality of God and assents to claims that certain events happened in the past (cf. Pailin 1975, 1992; Michalson 1985).

Although it is notoriously difficult to prove such a negative thesis as that historical events (or reports of them) cannot provide a knowledge of God that is significantly independent of metaphysical understanding, in the remainder of this essay I want to consider briefly six ways of understanding past events (or reports of them) in order to suggest that none of them provides a satisfactory way of deriving theistic significance from such events (or reports) so far as they are matters of *historical* understanding. If there be a seventh way of historical understanding which does satisfy the theological requirement, I do not know of it. The following discussion thus supports the claim that Christian faith and theology ultimately depends not on certain historical events but on metaphysical understanding which determines the significance of those events.

In this examination, it must not be forgotten that references to 'past events' are to occurrences which act as regulative ideas for historical descriptions and understanding of them. An event happens but the act or acts of apprehending what happened, as well as the further stages of understanding it, involve successive stages of interpretation. To ask and to reply to the question of any event 'What happened?' can never in practice be wholly unprejudiced.

The specification implied in the 'what' of the question and in any appropriate answer to it are to some extent determined by pre-supposed structures of understanding. We may exchange one structure for another in order to apprehend an event in a different way, and we may hold that one way of apprehending it is better than another because it includes or excludes certain characteristics, but we can never check how we grasp an event against that event itself. Bearing this in mind, then, what are some of the ways in which events are interpreted and how may those interpretations be justified?

The first way to be discussed uses a distinction which has played an important role in twentieth-century theology, namely that drawn between *Historie* and *Geschichte*. One use of these German words is to distinguish between the bare happenedness of an event (that it occurred and is, as we might say, a 'historical' event) and the event as being important for its own or later times (and as such might be described as a 'historic' event). An event may thus be said to be *geschichtlich* because its occurrence has important consequences for following events—as, for instance, Abraham's decision to leave Harran or the German decision to give Lenin a safe conduct to travel to Russia in 1917 may be regarded as having had more or less lasting repercussions on later events when we consider the occupation of Palestine for four millennia or the political state of Europe for much of the twentieth century.

The interpretation of a 'historical' event as being 'historic' (i.e. the shift from an event seen as *Historie* to the same event recognized as *Geschichte*) is a matter of its identification as having something akin to causal influence. Such an interpretation can be justified by historical examination even where, as sometimes is the case, the historical 'cause' is not so much what actually occurred as what was believed to have occurred. The effects of some *geschichtlich* events, that is, are the products of *historisch* events in human understanding rather than of occurrences that were publicly observable.

Although this interpretation of the distinction between *Historie* and *Geschichte* has some theological value, it does not solve the problem of the relationship between past events and theistic faith. While this distinction is useful in that it highlights the significance of some events (of the kind 'because this once happened, that and that happened later'), it does not show why it is legitimate to derive a set of theistic beliefs from a set of events (or reports of events).

Rather than explain the nature of the theistic derivation and show that it is rationally justified, it merely offers a particular way of describing the problematic relationship.

A different way of using the terms *Historie* and *Geschichte* is to distinguish between what happened and a person's existential appropriation of and response to what happened (or to what that person considered to have happened). When used in this way, the distinction again highlights rather than solves the problem of eliciting justifiable knowledge of God from past events. It leaves us with the question 'On what grounds and with what justification should one react in such a way to this or that event, seeing it as illuminating the nature of ultimate reality and indicating an appropriate way of life?' Many kinds of event may evoke this type of response in individuals and in groups, but the fact that it happens does not explain why it happens nor whether it is a justifiable response to an event.

The *Historie–Geschichte* distinction thus either fails to raise the problem of the relationship between history and the knowledge of God (because it is concerned with the effects of certain events upon others) or merely provides a way to state the relationship that constitutes the problem. We need to look elsewhere for a solution.

A second way of relating events and their interpretations is in terms of the distinction between an 'outward' occurrence and an 'inward' intention expressed thereby. This distinction trades on the way in which we claim to be able to discern a person's character through observing what that person says and does. Similarly it is considered reasonable to claim that past events which were empirically observed and recorded are able to provide evidence whereby we can come to conclusions about the character and motives of the agents involved in them, whether those agents be individual human beings or the 'corporate persons' which we refer to when we speak of 'the German nation' or 'the Labour Party'.

Our ability to produce such interpretations of events depends, however, upon a prior understanding of the ways in which such agents act, and of the relationship between their acts and their character or intentions in the case in point. I can, for example, only come to conclusions about the ways in which Mary's actions reveal Mary's character and intentions by assuming that the relationship between the 'outward' and the 'inward' in her case is significantly comparable to what I understand to be the case in my own self-awareness. Similarly warrantable judgements about how its Party Manifesto reflects the character of the Labour Party depend upon having some basic understanding of the forces at work in constituting such a corporate person as that which is called 'the Labour Party', and of how the character of such a body is expressed through those forces.

The necessity for such pre-understanding is the reason why the distinction between 'outward' occurrence and 'inward' intention *by itself* fails to solve the problem of the relationship between past events (or historical knowledge of them) and theistic understanding. Even if we wish to maintain in principle that events can be significant for faith because in them we can perceive the agency and hence the nature of God, we can only reach conclusions about God's nature and will from past events on the basis of a prior understanding of the relationship between God's agency and the observable course of events. Such understanding, however, cannot be the product of examining past events alone since it is this understanding which provides the basis for identifying which events are to be interpreted as expressing theistic agency and for determining how they are to be thus interpreted. Even if it be recognized, as it probably should be, that the relationship between the events chosen and the theistic interpretation of them is reciprocal or circular, the problem remains. According to the model used, the basic problem is either how to justify starting the reciprocal interaction or how to get into the theistic hermeneutical circle in the first place.

By itself, therefore, the distinction between the 'outward' and the 'inward', when applied to historical events and religious faith, fails to show how we can bridge the ditch between these two modes of understanding.

The problem of the relationship between events and their theistic interpretation is not solved, thirdly, by reference to another form of relationship disclosed by studies of history. This is the relationship between what happened in the past and what later was taken to have happened. The distinction indicated here is a warning against presuming that a person's response to an 'event' is always a response to what actually happened. Since, however, the reference to 'what actually happened' is to a regulative absolute, we should perhaps put it that while people respond to what they take to have occurred, critical investigations sometimes give solid grounds for holding that what actually occurred was significantly different. There may, for example, be great differences between what a constitutional historian of the thirteenth century would now claim to have been established by the signing of Magna Carta at the time of its signing, and what has been held to be the significance of that event in later constitutional struggles. The 'Magna Carta' which ensured the barons a share of the spoils of power is a far cry from the 'Magna Carta' which is supposed to protect the rights of Englishmen to rule and tax themselves!

Where such differences are found, the justifiability of an interpretation of an event's significance is to be judged by two criteria. One is its appropriateness to what seems in terms of the original context to have happened then. The other is the authenticity of developments in the understanding of that event and of its significance in relation to later circumstances. In the latter case, however, the decision must always be provisional. As Wolfhart Pannenberg points out, the final determination of an event's full significance must wait until the end of history (cf. Pannenberg 1971: 1–27).

In so far as the interpretation of an event belongs to the same logical type as the event itself (e.g as both the event of Magna Carta as perceived by those involved in signing it and later views of what happened belong to the realm of political rights), comparison of what the event was later taken to have established with evidence about what initially was effected may justify or undermine the later interpretations of its significance. Either way both the relationship and the procedures for checking it are straightforward. This does not, however, apply to cases where the logical type changes—for example, when the change is from understanding an event as a historical occurrence to a religious understanding of its significance. Here again the problem remains of how to find a rationally justifiable way of crossing the logical ditch between historical understanding of an event and claims about the reality and will of God supposedly derivable from it. The distinction between what happened and what was taken to have happened merely complicates the problem by reminding us that if it is found to be justifiable to hold that religious faith is based on history, the 'history' that it is based upon may not be what actually occurred but what is reasonably to be regarded as a misunderstanding of what happened.

It should be noted that an unjustified interpretation of an event (i.e. so far as historical scholarship is concerned, a misunderstanding of it) may persist in spite of the evidence about it. This sometimes occurs when the (mis)interpretation expresses insights which are both important in themselves and enshrined in traditional views of the event. Such is the case with the popular tradition in England that has for centuries linked the establishment of the supposed rights of Englishmen to the signing of Magna Carta. In such cases it is the principle expressed by the interpretation and not the event itself which is the decisive factor in determining how the event is understood.

Where historically unjustifiable interpretations of events persist in spite of the evidence, what is considered to be established by those events may be only accidentally related to the events to which popular understanding has attached them. In such cases both the relation of an event to its 'interpretation' and the validity of what is asserted in that 'interpretation' are not justified by historical investigations into the original event. Consequently, while the distinction between an event and what is believed to have happened is important in studying reports of historical events, it does not help us to perceive how to bridge the gap between interpretations of different logical types—and hence between events and theistic understanding which is held to be derived from them.

Appreciation of the distinction between what is believed to have happened and what historical research indicates happened does, however, have some significance for theological understanding. What the distinction indicates is that the relationships between events, historical understanding of them, and any theistic understanding that is held to be derived from them are complex and variable. While, therefore, theologians may presume that any knowledge of God which they consider they can justifiably derive from 'history' must be derived from what actually happened in the past, in practice the basis for such derivation is what they consider to have happened. The two may differ significantly.

At one extreme believers might consider that their faith was mortally wounded if historical research showed that the evidence concerning certain events is incompatible with the understanding of them that provides the basis for their faith. Henry Rack described this position in a letter to me about this problem:

if it could be shown that Jesus really was, drastically, morally different from what we have thought, I think it would in practice make a difference to him as the focus of Christian theology and piety. For I suspect that in the end people form a personalized ideal and the ideal *as so conceived* would not easily survive detached from the person visualized if he were shown to be quite other than he is usually supposed to have been.

At the other extreme believers might respond to alleged historical falsification of the supposed ground of their faith by continuing to affirm the idealized picture of its ground independently and in spite of historical research, treating the picture (whether consciously or not) as the true reality. So far as such believers were troubled by historical arguments which seemed to undermine the story on which their faith rested, they might attempt to excuse—they might even say 'justify'—their position by suggesting that historians, perhaps because of their secular prejudices or because of the inconclusive state of the evidence, have got it wrong! In practice, however, believers generally adopt neither of these extreme positions. Their response to historical investigations that challenge the foundational events of their faith takes the somewhat messy form of an attempt to find a middle way, partly by modifying their theistic understanding to fit its supposed historical basis and partly by doubting the reliability of some of the troublesome conclusions of historical study.

Discussion of the difference between what critical investigation may establish to have happened and what is widely believed to have happened draws attention to the interpretative character of reports about the past, both in the original sources and in later historical understanding of them. This suggests a fourth model for understanding the relationship between events and their interpretation, namely the relationship which is identified by the recent combination of the words 'fact' and 'fiction' to produce the word 'faction'. This term is used, for example, to describe certain documentary programmes or books like Alexander Solzhenitsyn's *August 1914*. The significance of the term is to acknowledge that its authors have combined imaginative inventions with authentic source materials in order to convey what in their opinion 'really' happened or what it was 'really' like to be there. What faction seeks to present is not fiction because its authors' aim is to represent what occurred in order to make its significant elements live for their audience. Neither is it fact (at least not in the common and naïve sense of that term) because what is presented includes materials which the authors have invented in order to make up gaps in the source materials.

In the case of theology, faction may be considered to be an appropriate description of what is presented by much (if not all) of the so-called 'historical' material within the Bible which is not simply fiction. The authors of the Pentateuchal narratives and of Judges, Samuel, Kings, and Chronicles use whatever sources they may have had to tell a theological story about a people and its relationship to God. In such acts of worship as that at Passover the central 'events' in this story were recited and symbolically re-enacted in order to bring home to the people their living significance. Whatever may originally have happened in, say, the departure of a group of people from Egypt and in the occupation of Palestine, the biblical narrative was presented by its authors to disclose the 'real' significance of (and therefore the true 'reality' of) these events. In the New Testament the Gospels confess that they are such, namely 'gospels' (cf. Mark 1: 1) written 'in order that you may hold the faith that Jesus is the Christ' (John 20: 31). Those, therefore, who hold that Christian theologians do not have evidence for identifying the historical Jesus but only for determining the character of the apostolic witness to him as the Christ should not be regarded as sceptical radicals. They are taking seriously what the material says about itself.

The notion of 'faction' is a useful way of drawing attention to the presence of imaginative input in some representations of past events and in the interpretative expressions of their significance. It does not, however, provide a way to solve the problem of the relationship between past events and the contents of theistic faith. Rather, as with the previous ways of understanding the past which have been discussed, it merely presents that problem in a particular way. How, for example, and with what justification was it that the people of the Old Testament came to interpret their history in terms of particular acts of divine providence? The Angles, Saxons, and Normans never, so far as I can discover, claimed similar divine warrant for their conquests of England, and theological justifications of British (or French or German or Dutch or Russian or American) imperialist rule in the past two centuries are now generally—and justifiably—seen as embarrassing attempts at rationalization. Why is the Old Testament story different? The supposed history as given does not provide the answer but poses the question. Similarly, if it be recognized that the authors of the Gospels were not writing something akin to modern secular biography (which itself involves selection and interpretation of material to portray its subject) and that their materials contain imaginative additions which arise from their concern to communicate their faith's understanding of the significance of Jesus (even if those additions are not as large-scale as David Friedrich Strauss suggested in *The Life of Jesus*), to describe what they produced as faction only draws attention to the problem of the move from event to faith. How did those whose faith's understanding of Jesus is there presented bridge the gap between what was seen and heard by some people in Palestine and confession of Christ and God? If, therefore, contemporary theologians who refer to the Gospel material to justify the historical basis of the Christian faith are not to beg the fundamental question by accepting the faith-interpretation which determines that material, they must justify their claim that the theistic interpretation of the material discloses the significance of the original events. Reference to 'faction', however useful in some respects, leaves the basic problem of the relationship between past events and theistic faith unsolved.

A fifth relationship between events and their interpretation is that between a story and the moral which it is used to illustrate. Here the story may be clearly fictional (as with La Fontaine's fables) or apparently factual (as with the story of George Washington and the cherry tree) but in either case the truth of the moral is independent of the factual status of the story. It is dangerous to listen to flatterers whether or not a crow ever lost its cheese to a fox; it is good to be honest whether or not George Washington did own up. The value of such stories is not that they report what actually happened on some occasion but that they vividly illustrate the point of the moral or effectively evoke the desired ethical insight.

The happenedness of the event described may give psychological 'punch' to the moral which it is being used to teach but that happenedness itself is irrelevant to the 'truth' of that moral (cf. Braithwaite 1955 on this view of the function of stories in ethical commitments and religious beliefs). Consequently, while the truth of a story as a report of a past event may be investigated by those interested in conducting such historical research, the truth of the moral drawn from it is a distinct matter which will only be established by the methods appropriate to the content of the moral. A story may thus be found to be historically accurate and the moral false, or vice versa, or both true in their respective realms, or both false.

When applied to the 'ditch' between the reports of past events and theological understanding, this view of the relationship between events and interpretation suggests that Lessing is correct in holding that there is a logical type-jump between events and the religious understanding derived from them but wrong in expecting to find a rationally justifiable way of bridging the gap between them. The logical distinction between historical and theistic ways of understanding must be recognized to be radical. While psychologically or traditionally there may be ways of explaining why certain events (or the reports of them) evoke or express certain insights into the reality and will of God, no amount of historical investigation can justify those insights. They can only be justified by the appropriate method for claims about the nature of ultimate reality—that is, by metaphysical tests such as those of consistency, coherence, ultimacy, and universality.

Some of Maurice Wiles's remarks seem to come close to this way of understanding the logical relationship between events and faith. In *The Remaking of Christian Doctrine*, for example, he writes of 'particular events' as 'occasions which arouse in us . . . a sense of divine purpose. But that sense does not necessarily entail any special divine activity in those particular events' (Wiles 1974: 38). Unsympathetic critics of his position might also consider that it makes more sense of the radical implications of this view of the retrovident nature of the identification of God's action in the world than his affirmations of God's general, non-specific influence on what happens (cf. Wiles 1986: 64, 83, 89). In any case, however well or badly the cap fits Maurice Wiles, this view of the relationship between events and faith holds that illuminating events are to be regarded as stories expressing or evoking insights into the reality of God but that those insights must be independently (and metaphysically) verified. This does not, however, mean that what is thereby perceived may be grasped or communicated adequately apart from a story about events. It may be that God's nature, especially in the case of the personal mode of theism typical of Jewish, Christian, and Islamic theological understanding, severely limits the extent to which abstract metaphysical statements are satisfactory media for conveying knowledge of the divine.

If, furthermore, it is justifiable to hold that the narrative form is the proper mode for conveying theistic understanding of God as personally agential (cf. Hans Frei's *The Eclipse of the Biblical Narrative* and the narrative theologies influenced by Frei's ideas), it may also be held that historical (or quasi-historical) stories rather than timeless myths are the most appropriate or even the only way of conveying a satisfactory knowledge of the divine. Consequently the (quasi-)historical character of a 'story' (whether as a 'factual' report of actual events or as a constructed 'faction' of quasi-actual events) may be indispensable for apprehending any metaphysically justified insights into the reality and will of God. If this be so, the story form itself is not (*pace* some Hegelian comments) replaceable in theological understanding. Although any particular story or set of stories re-presents what in principle is independently communicable and ascertainable, it may be replaced in any satisfactory form of theological understanding only by another story or set of stories.

Stories, furthermore, may not only provide an indispensable medium for metaphysical understanding of the reality of the divine. They are also important for the practice of faith since they enable believers to identify with the object of their faith and to respond appropriately. It may be no accident that Jesus brought people to awareness of God through parables derived from their experiences and, to move from the lofty to the mundane, that the most effective parts of sermons are usually their illustrations! And if it be stories that effectively communicate the insight and inform the practice of faith, it may be that abstract theological descriptions of that insight and practice primarily make sense by being reminders of—and parasitic upon—those stories. Nevertheless, whatever the hermeneutical indispensability of stories, the truth of the understanding which is thereby communicated cannot be warranted by reference to the historical basis (if any) of the stories themselves. Some form of metaphysical justification of their theological references and truth is required.

A sixth way of considering the relationship between events and interpretation is the contrary of the fifth. Theologians and believers who seek to put it forward generally regard the fifth way as unacceptable since it implies that there is no intrinsic or necessary relationship between the happenedness of certain events and the knowledge of God which is supposed to be derived from them. They maintain, on the contrary, that the happenedness of certain events is not accidental to the validity of the theological understanding derived from them, at least in some crucial cases. While, for example, aspects of God's concern may be satisfactorily illustrated through the fictional stories of Jonah and of the prodigal son, insights into the nature of the divine as all-embracing love are justified as well as evoked by the actual occurrence of at least some of the events reported about Jesus of Nazareth. This is because in some significant way God is to be identified as an effective agent in those events.

Those who endorse this sixth way maintain that the relationship between certain events and the knowledge of God, at any rate in some fundamental instances so far as theistic understanding is concerned, is not parallel to the story and its moral relationship. It resembles, rather, the way in which a person's character is held to be revealed by actions in which she or he is an intentional agent— or, since individual human agency is probably to be judged to be too anthropomorphic and particular to be a satisfactory model for divine activity (cf. Wiles 1986; Pailin 1987, 1989, especially ch. 9), by the way in which the nature of the regulating structures of political and economic processes may be held to be discerned through the study of political and economic history.

This way of understanding the relationship between events and their interpretation has many similarities to the second view of the relationship which was discussed earlier. The difference from that earlier position is that now it is being maintained that just as a human being's character is expressed by that persons' actions, or as political history reveals the character of political structures, and economic history reveals the nature of economic structures, so certain events reveal God because they are to a significant extent the result of divine agency. Indeed some theologians claim that it is *only* by so observing God's activity that we can justifiably claim to discern God's actual nature.

Just as historians uncover the basic nature of past personal agents and of political and economic structures by studying appropriate past events, so insight into the nature and will of God is held to be achieved by studying the history of events, and particularly those in whose occurrence God's agency was a prominent, if not a determinative, factor. Believers have accordingly claimed to

discover what God is like by considering the exodus of the
Hebrews from Egypt, or their exile in Babylon, or the life of Jesus,
or the history of the Church, in a way that is similar to that by
which others claim to uncover the character of Cromwell by
studying his actions, or the nature of politics by studying political
history, or the principles governing economic activity by examining its history. What is important to note is that whereas in the fifth
position, the happenedness of events is accidental to the justification of the insights derived from them, in this case it is essential.
The fact that the events occurred as they did is considered to make
the theistic insights derived from them genuine perceptions of the
nature of ultimate reality rather than speculative suggestions.

This view of the relationship between events and their interpretation may well be deemed as satisfactory for such matters as political
and economic understanding as it is for discerning a person's
character. Any attempt to derive understanding of the nature and
will of God from the effects of divine activity in historical events
depends, however, upon answers being found to three fundamental
questions. First, how is the nature of divine agency in historical
events to be understood? Secondly, which events are to be investigated as particularly displaying divine agency? And thirdly, how
are we to assess the significance of any divine agency which can be
identified? Satisfactory answers to all these questions are necessary
before this sixth way of understanding the relationship between
history and theism can be regarded as credible. Reflection on these
questions, however, also makes it clear that answers to them are
not obtainable solely through historical investigations. Both the
questions and answers to them involve metaphysical understanding
for they concern the validity of a particular way of understanding
the fundamental character of all reality.

There are three possible responses to the problems posed by this
understanding of the relationship between events and theistic
belief. One is to hold that the supposed relationship is inappropriate
because divine agency is not analogous to the agencies of other
forces, particularly that of personal agents, in affecting what
happens. If it is also held that no other significant way of understanding God's agency is conceivable (in contrast to ways of talking
about divine agency which convert it into a cipher for what
happens because of the activity of other forces), this response
expresses a metaphysical understanding of the ultimate nature of

reality which, *inter alia*, indicates one way in which God's agency is *not* to be understood. It leaves the only acceptable relationship between past events and theological understanding as that of story and moral.

A second response seeks to give credible answers to the three questions. Since, however, God's omnipresent reality is ultimate in being, value, and rationality, this response depends upon metaphysical reasoning. It involves arguments to show what meaning can be given to the notion of divine agency as intentional activity, and how that agency can be identified among the other recognizable forces involved in bringing about historical events. Evidence about the nature of past events will have an important role in such arguments but historical investigations by themselves will be unable to provide the desired answers. This is because it is those answers which will determine what is and what is not a proper way to understand past events as providing sources of insight into the activity of the divine as the ultimate and universal reality which functions agentially in events of history.

The fact that contemporary historians typically presuppose that references to divine agency are not to be included in any acceptable way of understanding the course of past events should not be allowed to rule out this second response in principle. The secularist presuppositions of current historical study may be, as Keith Ward has suggested (Ward 1990), a metaphysical prejudice which blinds historians to forces shaping events just as much as the 'leaders, politics and battles' approach of older historians blinded them to the importance of social and economic factors in influencing what happened. When, however, contemporary historians hold that it is important to take account of social and economic factors in investigating certain events, they justify their position by arguments to show that only so are such events, whether past or present, adequately understood. On the other hand, similar arguments cannot be produced to justify in a rationally convincing way holding that the position of the planets is a significant factor in understanding the course of events. In a similar way those theologians who wish to refer to divine agency in past events must show that there are sound reasons for including it among the explanatory factors for understanding what happened. This, however, can only be done by metaphysical arguments about the ultimate nature and fundamental structure of the processes of reality. They alone can show how and with what justification the notion of divine agency may be used in understanding past events—and hence in gaining insight into the divine reality from what is so understood.

A third response to the problems posed by the attempt to treat God as agent starts by recognizing that no satisfactory argument has yet been produced to show how the agency of God in historical events is to be directly identified. At the same time it does not deny the actual efficacy of divine agency. What this response does is to advance a complex argument which maintains, first, that God is to be thought of as an intentional agent with a particular character and will; secondly, that since God has this character and will, it is appropriate to regard certain events as due, in part at least, to the influence of divine agency; and, thirdly, that aspects of the divine intention (for example, that human beings should be free, responsible persons) require God to act incognito.

The basis of this argument may be an insight into the divine nature which is derived from musing upon certain events but which is initially considered to be only accidentally related to those events—as a moral may be to its story. Metaphysical reflection, however, may conclude not only that the insight is rationally justified but also that it is rationally justifiable to regard the initial event which evoked the insight as itself affected, if not effected, by divine agency.

Alternatively metaphysical reflection, while provoked by certain events, may lead to the conclusion that we are in no position ever to determine where, how, and to what end God acts. As the uniquely universal individual, God exists as the one who necessarily is present to each event, influencing its actualization and subsequently influenced by its concrete form. Since, however, God is omnipresent to all events, the divine reality and purpose is not discernible by differentiation through comparing different events (cf. Whitehead 1978: 4). While we may learn about Cromwell by contrasting what happened in events in which he was involved with other events in which he was not involved, we cannot so learn about God's reality. The divine reality is primarily to be discerned, if at all, by metaphysical reflection.

It seems, therefore, that metaphysical considerations are fundamental to and presupposed by any attempt to derive knowledge of God from past events and probably also provide the basic content of such knowledge. In spite of the way in which believers and theologians have traditionally asserted that their knowledge of God is based upon history (and so, according to the more naïve among them, upon fact), consideration of the relationship between history and theistic understanding suggests that while references to past events may indicate where and when certain theological insights emerged, the identification and justification of such claims to understanding rest upon metaphysical reasoning. Such reasoning either approves the knowledge directly (if the relationship to events be seen as having the story and its moral form) or holds that some events at least are to be understood as being due in part to divine agency. What is important to note is that in both cases the fundamental judgement is not that of history but that of metaphysical understanding.

If, therefore, Lessing's 'ugly, broad ditch' between history and theistic belief can be bridged, it can only be through metaphysical insights which show how God is to be discerned as agent in specifiable ways in specifiable events for specifiable purposes. If no such metaphysical case can be produced, there seems to be no way of basing the knowledge of God upon the happenedness of certain events. The relationship between the two has to be seen as the accidental one that certain events, as observed or as reported from a particular standpoint, just happen to evoke or illustrate insights into the nature and will of God which must be independently confirmed to be true.

Surprising, then, as it may seem to those who emphasize the historical basis of the knowledge of God and the historical foundations of Christian belief, the material as well as the formal content of that understanding is primarily a product of metaphysical reflection. As Whitehead remarks, 'the ages of faith are the ages of rationalism' (Whitehead 1927: 73).

REFERENCES

Barth, Karl (1954), *Against the Stream: Shorter Post-War Writings, 1946–1952*, London.
Braithwaite, Richard B. (1955), *An Empiricist's View of the Nature of Religious Belief*, Eddington Memorial Lecture, Cambridge.
Knox, John (1958), *Jesus Lord and Christ*, New York.

—— (1963), *The Church and the Reality of Christ*, London.

Lessing, Gotthold E. (1956), *Lessing's Theological Writings*, ed. H. Chadwick, London.

Macquarrie, John (1966), *Principles of Christian Theology*, London.

Michalson, Gordon E., Jr. (1985), *Lessing's 'Ugly Ditch': A Study of Theology and History*, University Park, Pa.

Ogden, Schubert M. (1982), *The Point of Christology*, London.

—— (1986), *On Theology*, San Francisco.

Pailin, David A. (1975), 'Lessing's Ditch Revisited: The Problem of Faith and History', in R. H. Preston (ed.), *Theology and Change: Essays in Memory of Alan Richardson*, London.

—— (1987), 'History, Humanity and the Activity of God', *Religious Studies*, 23/4 (Dec.): 435–56.

—— (1989), *God and the Processes of Reality: Foundations of a Credible Theism*, London.

—— (1992), 'Faith and History: Is it a Mistake to Hold that the Christian Faith Rests on History?', *Epworth Review*, 19/3 (Sept.): 39–49.

Pannenberg, Wolfhart (1968), *Jesus: God and Man*, trans. L. L. Wilkins and D. A. Priebe, London.

—— (1971), *Basic Questions in Theology*, vol. ii, London.

Torrance, Thomas F. (1969), *Theological Science*, London.

Ward, Keith (1990), *Divine Action*, London.

Webb, Clement C. J. (1935), *The Historical Element in Religion*, London.

Whitehead, Alfred North (1927), *Religion in the Making*, Cambridge.

—— (1978), *Process and Reality: An Essay in Cosmology*, ed. D. R. Griffin and D. W. Sherburne, New York.

Wiles, Maurice (1967), *The Making of Christian Doctrine: A Study in the Principles of Early Doctrinal Development*, Cambridge.

—— (1974), *The Remaking of Christian Doctrine*, London.

—— (1976a), *What is Theology?*, Oxford.

—— (1976b), *Working Papers in Doctrine*, London.

—— (1977), 'Christianity without Incarnation?' and 'Myth in Theology', in John Hick (ed.), *The Myth of God Incarnate*, London.

—— (1979), 'A Survey of the Issues in the *Myth* Debate' and 'Comment on Lesslie Newbigin's Essay', in Michael Goulder (ed.), *Incarnation and Myth: The Debate Continued*, London.

—— (1986), *God's Action in the World*, London.

—— (1987a), 'Scriptural Authority and Theological Construction: The Limitations of Narrative Interpretation', in Garrett Green (ed.), *Scriptural Authority and Narrative Interpretation*, Philadelphia.

—— (1987b), 'The Reasonableness of Christianity', in W. J. Abraham and S. W. Holtzer (eds.), *The Rationality of Religious Belief: Essays in Honour of Basil Mitchell*, Oxford.

—— (1989), 'In what Contexts does it Make Sense to Say, "God Acts in History"?', in P. Devenish and G. Goodwin (eds.), *Witness and Existence: Essays in Honor of Schubert M. Ogden*, Chicago.

—— (1991), review in *Epworth Review*, 18/2 (May): 107–8.

Wright, G. Ernest (1952), *God Who Acts: Biblical Theology as Recital*, London.

14

Doctrinal Criticism: Some Questions

ROWAN WILLIAMS

'Doctrinal criticism is the critical study of the truth and adequacy of doctrinal statements.' With this quotation from a highly influential essay by G. F. Woods (Woods 1966), Maurice Wiles, in 'Looking into the Sun', his inaugural lecture at King's College, London (Wiles 1976), signalled the opening of his own discussion and development of Woods's programme. This programme he summarizes as including the following:

Examination of the relation of any doctrinal statement to its historical situation; the analysis of any doctrinal statement into its component parts; investigation of the varying uses of analogy in the various terms employed in any doctrinal statement; distinction of the differing types of proof to which appeal is made; recognition of the variety of ways in which doctrinal statements are combined into systematic wholes; consideration of what point has been selected as the fundamental starting-point of a doctrinal system and for what reason. (Wiles 1976: 152)

The task is clearly conceived, by both Woods and Wiles, on the analogy of biblical criticism; we have lost our innocence in respect of the biblical text, and have learned to look beyond the surface of narrative and rhetoric. We have become sensitive to the varieties of genre and idiom, to the historical interrelation of different texts and portions of texts, to the process by which texts are produced and the social and ideological conflicts they embody and encode. The text tells us both more and less than we thought: more about the history of its own production and about its world of reference, less about what it *purports* to tell us of a distant or relatively distant series of events. A critical reading is one which knows what sort of information to look for. So, it is suggested, with the 'text' of Christian doctrine as well. We must lose our innocence, learn to see what doctrinal propositions really tell us (about the conditions of their production, about what counted as argumentation in the context in which they were produced, what connections between different bits of Christian language appeared natural and obvious and why, and so on), and what they cannot tell us (facts about a transcendent and intangible realm). But the Christian theologian undertaking this task is not trying to dissolve the substance of the believer's central commitment, any more than the biblical critic— properly understood—is a threat to faith. He or she is only pointing out that traditional doctrinal formulations, rooted as they are in social and intellectual milieux that are not ours, cannot tell us authoritatively what they purport to tell us: 'I am not in a position either to affirm them or to deny them; I cannot give any satisfactory sense to them *in that form*' (Wiles 1976: 161). But the analytic enterprise yields 'insights' about the character of belief and the object of belief, insights which may be profitably brought into conversation with the theologian's 'patient, continuing study of the world around' him or her (ibid. 162).

This inaugural lecture exemplifies all that is most attractive and stimulating in Maurice Wiles's work. It says a great deal in a brief space, with complete clarity and an absence of what might be called intellectual tribalism (the sending out of signals by the use of jargon). It both commends and embodies a commitment to honesty, patience, and humility in the study of the evolution of Christian language. It is reticent, for the most part, about its author's own confessional position, yet somehow indicates a paradoxical but perfectly real loyalty to an enterprise which is certainly conceived as being in continuity with the thought and prayer of earlier ages. Its programme has been variously worked out in Wiles's later writings, all of which exhibit the same qualities —rare enough in theology to command much gratitude. For there can be no doubt that Wiles has succeeded in placing on the map of Anglophone theology a set of issues of the first importance, largely by the care and tentativeness of his own style. Anyone now discussing theological method in the British context—to mention no others—will sooner or later have to come to terms with the Wilesian question, a question which might be summarized like this: if, as is surely the case, traditional doctrinal statements make claims about what is actually true about the universe, how do we respond to those claims in an intellectual climate in which they cannot possibly be *legitimated*? This is a different issue, I think from that of the possible *verification* of religious claims by agreed secular methods: Wiles is not a positivist with a pious gloss, looking for simple, universal proofs. The problem is rather that an examination of the history of Christian doctrine uncovers a bewildering range of criteria appealed to in establishing the validity of credal or confessional statements, few if any of them recognizably resembling the kind of appeals we might now allow in testing the validity of inferences.[1] If this is so, then whatever doctrinal statements tell us, we cannot assume that it is simple information about states of affairs. But (and this is where the paradoxical loyalty comes in) Wiles will have no truck with the idea that doctrines were never meant to convey propositional truths in the first place: he has expressed considerable scepticism about the proposal that we should treat doctrine as 'regulative',[2] seeing in this the prospect of another and deeply corrupting sort of positivism, a passive assent to the *de facto* deliverances of ecclesiastical authority.

The issue of doctrinal criticism is thus a position formally agnostic about the truth-claims of particular classical doctrinal statements—but in practice sceptical or negative. For if a doctrinal statement might be telling us the truth, but we were incapable of articulating any coherent criteria for deciding whether it were doing so or not, the one thing the doctrine surely could *not* be telling anybody would be 'saving' truth. Assuming that any truth which purported to be of decisive and transforming relevance should be capable of being *known* to be true, of being asserted with confidence in its sustainability or legitimacy, the truth claims of doctrinal utterances, in so far as they employ means of legitimation unrecognizable or unacceptable to us, must be at best matters of secondary interest. What is significant now is the experiential impulse behind the doctrinal formulae. In the case most frequently discussed by Wiles—the doctrine of the Incarnation—we can say that the doctrinal enterprise reveals, not the propositional veracity of what it actually claims, but the 'transforming impact' of the life, death, and resurrection of Jesus (the phrase is used in Wiles 1974: 52): as Wiles admirably puts it, the first believers were not 'rationalist theologians, drawing firm deductions from fixed and detailed patterns of expectation; the categories in which it was natural for them to think of Jesus were extended and outgrown by the immensity of the experiences in which they were caught up, and which they associated with him as risen Lord' (ibid. 53).

The critical study of doctrine, then, delivers two things: nega-tively, an awareness of the fragility of the epistemological foundation on which doctrinal claims may rest; postively, an enhanced appreciation of the intensity of an experience dramatic enough to produce such extraordinary, strained, and finally unsustainable claims. The impulse is to maximize the status of Jesus so as to ground ontologically the sense of a 'transforming impact'; but the pressure towards such an ontological grounding is not necessarily derived wholly or even primarily from the nature of faith itself. It owes a great deal to factors in the intellectual culture in which Christian faith developed. This point is explored in some detail in the celebrated essay of 1970, 'Does Christology Rest on a Mistake?' (Wiles 1976: 122–31). Here the commitment to Jesus' ontological uniqueness is seen as dictated by prior assumptions about the punctiliar character of the creation[3] and the fall. The action of God and the condition of sinful humanity are taken to be bound up with identifiable episodes in the history of the universe: thus the saving action of God reversing the fall is understood analogously. But the former linkage is mythological—indeed, *fallacious* (Wiles 1976: 125, 127); thus the consequence is equally an error about logical entailment. Similar readings of the roots of incarnational doctrine recur, though their emphasis is more generally on the effect upon Christian language of current expectations of decisive (punctiliar) divine intervention (see, for example, Wiles 1974: 54; 1977: 4). I have a strong suspicion that Wiles came to recognize that the way in which the point is made in the 1970 essay is vulnerable to a number of serious criticisms, from the viewpoint of New Testament theology (can Paul's second Adam typology be the source of quite so much and bear so much weight in the argument? and does anyone in the early Christian period actually, concretely, *argue* like this?), and from strict logic (is the linkage of fallenness with a historical fall actually a *logical* question at all, and can we then convict Paul or whoever of mistakes about logical necessity?). None the less, the overall point is clear enough: there are factors quite extrinsic to Christian commitment as such which lead to the confusions of classical incarnational language. The Church may long have 'felt the need to say something more' (Wiles 1976: 129) than that Jesus opens our eyes supremely or decisively to the nature of God's relation to the world, 'illuminating, as no other life, the significance of the whole story' (Wiles 1976: 128; cf. 1974: 113–15; 1977: 161), but that feeling rests on a sort of category mistake, the search (prompted by adventitious circumstances) for a clear ontological substrate beneath the naturally exuberant expressions of devotion which emerge in response to what the life of Jesus effects—and which remain quite legitimate in their proper sphere (Wiles 1977: 9).[4] That there *is* a sort of ontological substrate Wiles is prepared to grant, rather surprisingly;[5] but its relation to the mythological or metaphorical language of the doctrinal tradition is oblique.

This summary does less than justice to a wide-ranging, flexible, and always elegantly expressed case, but I hope it accounts for its main themes. I believe that something like the task identified as that of the doctrinal critic is indeed a proper theological job; but I shall argue in the rest of this essay that Wiles's version of it will not quite do. My queries fall under four main headings. First of all, I have doubts about the brisk assimilation here of doctrinal to biblical criticism. Second, I find the actual definition and categorization of classical doctrinal statements unsatisfactory. Third, I think that Wiles's account of the relation between doctrine and experience contains a substantial *petitio principii*. And finally, I have a question about the whole model of critique and the concept of establishing legitimacy employed by Wiles and a good many others in discussing doctrinal truth claims. If I can at all emulate Wiles's fairness and patience with positions other than his own, I shall be paying him tribute enough.

1. *Doctrinal and biblical criticism*

Biblical criticism can operate at several levels, but, for the purposes of the present discussion, I want to focus on two major aspects. At the simplest level, a 'critical' reading of the biblical text is any reading that is capable of discerning things over and above 'surface' meaning; and, in this sense, biblical criticism goes back to the earliest ages of the Church. To read comprehensively and adequately is to know something of how a text works in its setting—to be sensitive to idiom and genre, so that we do not mistake metaphor for literal description or deliberate fiction for reportage.[6] Apparent absurdities are thus removed, and the text is allowed to establish its own world of reference instead of being forced into ours and judged inadequate by standards it does not set out to meet (on this see Ricœur 1976: ch. 4, and 1981, especially ch. 4). This is the common coin of patristic and medieval hermeneutics: modern criticism works on much the same basis, though with a far sharper sense of the radical nature of historical and cultural difference. The main point of this exercise, whether in its classical or its modern form, is to make sure that we do not derive from the text information it is not designed to give. The more sensitive we have become to the genre and location of various bits of scriptural narrative (aetiological myth, wisdom tale, catechetical pericope, etc.), the less we shall look for bare documentation—in other words, the more sceptical we become about simply reading all scriptural narrative as historically veracious in the modern sense, though scholars may reasonably differ quite widely over how much history they can recover. Most of the familiar styles of biblical criticism (source criticism, *Formgeschichte*, redactional analysis) assume that this sensitivity to genre is a substantial part of their task, even if it is not the only one.

However, they also have a more complex agenda, which has come increasingly into focus in the twentieth century (though it is anticipated, albeit crudely, by Reimarus, Baur, and others). This is what is sometimes called *Tendenzkritik*—though it might also be seen as *Ideologiekritik*. In whose interest does this text work? On whose behalf is it claiming authority (whom does it legitimate)? Although this has been an element in most modern critical discussion, it has now emerged with far greater clarity in the hermeneutics of liberation theologies—most recently in feminist exegesis (cf. examples accessibly collected in Loades 1990: part I; Russell 1985). Form criticism, in looking at narratives from the point of view of the needs of communities in specific situations, and redaction criticism, asking about the shaping influence of authorial theologies, both employed the notion of reading with an eye to *Tendenz*; but it has taken the more robust and controversial methods of liberationist hermeneutics to draw out the potential consequences of such reading. A surviving text is a successful text, on the whole—which means that it has served what turned out to be a successful interest. To understand it fully, we need to be aware of what it does not say, what it controverts, what it represses or suppresses. We must do some (potentially subversive) decoding, and we can turn our first-level skills at reading with a sensitivity to idiom and genre into tools for this tougher and riskier task. And while 'first-level' criticism has a pedigree stretching back to the patristic era, this latter style is more obviously the result of the post-Enlightenment challenge to non-accountable authority. Its only classical antecedent is perhaps the view of certain gnostic groups that the Hebrew Scriptures, being written in the interest of the world-creator, repressed and distorted the true history of salvation whose heroes are the serpent, Cain, and so on.

How do these enterprises compare with doctrinal criticism as envisaged and practised by Wiles? As to the former, it is not clear that we can analyse doctrinal statements quite so readily into genres, especially narrative genres. Evidently there are doctrinal utterances that have a loosely narrative form—the second article of the Creed is a case in point—and it is possible to say, as theologians have long granted, that some aspects of liturgical and hymnodic language have to be read in the light of more general and programmatic principles. Since at least the third century[7] theologians have appealed to various kinds of regulative pressure in Christian language reminding us of the risks of anthropomorphism or mythology.[8] As I shall try to show in more detail later on, the *doctrine* of the incarnation in the strictest sense is not identical with a simple narrative of a divine agent embarking on a fresh episode in his biography; nor is it simply a sort of explanatory device to make sense of unusual features in the life of Jesus. It may at times work in such ways, but they cannot be said to exhaust the scope of the doctrine overall or to be determinative for its interpretation. A similar point might be made about the doctrine in Catholic Christianity of a 'real presence' of Christ in the consecrated elements (an instance discussed in Wiles 1977: 2); piety and semi-theological rhetoric deploy a number of images and idioms (the highly materialist imagery of the 'Mass of Saint Gregory' legend or some of the byways of the Grail tradition, the Byzantine language of the descent of the heavenly Emperor borne up on the shields of the angels, like the earthly emperor and his guard at a coronation, the baroque metaphor of the 'Prisoner of Love' in the tabernacle, and so on) which, taken as they stand, offend against any number of wider theological concerns. But neither they, nor indeed the conceptualization of the belief in terms of a specific ontology (transubstantiation), tell us adequately what the doctrine claims and exactly how it works—nor have they been seriously thought to do so by theologians. To put it briefly: 'doctrine' is a text already differentiated, already showing cognizance of its own ambiguities.

Criticism here is not a matter of determining on analytic (literary and historical) grounds how to distinguish the information we appear to be deriving (from the 'surface' sense) from the information genuinely available. Our misunderstandings of the propositional content of doctrinal formulae cannot be put down to ineptitude in the reading of conventions with which we are no longer familiar; judgement on the lack of straightforward informational content must rest on other grounds—as indeed is the case in Wiles's 'Does Christology Rest on a Mistake?', where the procedure is in fact very much *unlike* that of the biblical critic in so far as it looks for a direct error in reasoning, thus questioning the legitimacy of the idiom it seeks to interpret. A better case could be made for the significance of cultural misunderstanding with regard to the alleged association of incarnational language with apocalyptic, where we might reasonably appeal to the inaccessibility of an idiom in arguing to the unintelligibility of a doctrine formulated in its terms; but more would then have to be done to show that the connection between apocalyptic and any statement of incarnationalism was such as to warrant this move. If apocalyptic is an element among others in the formation of the doctrine, an element which can recede without being missed, the argument is less telling. We could appeal to a sense of what *must* have been the initial and determinative impulse, but we are then speculating—and doing so in a way which runs all the risks associated with any search for a *single* explanation of a historical phenomenon.

The second aspect of the critical enterprise offers far better analogues. *Tendenzkritik* of scripture and of doctrine may well run along similar lines; and once again, feminist theology brings the issue into very clear focus.[9] Not only doctrines of creation, fall, and incarnation, but the very regulative principles of doctrinal talk about God (divine aseity and impassibility, in the traditional framework) come under question here in respect of the interests they serve and legitimate. Wiles has had relatively little to say of this kind of *Kritik*, but I suspect that it poses far more serious difficulties for doctrinal traditionalists than the rather nebulous idea that doctrine is a matter for conventional literary-historical decoding. One of the greatest positive elements in the programme Wiles sets out is, of course, the recognition, painfully slow to dawn on theologians, that doctrine really does have a history;[10] and

Tendenzkritik reminds us further that human history is a history of conflict, the contesting of the power to define situations and mould them accordingly. Doctrine is implicated in power if it is implicated in history.

What we have here is not so much the possibility of misjudging the sort of information offered by a text as the possibility of a reader's failure to derive from the text the information it actually carries, information about its own production and use. And what poses serious questions here for the student of doctrine is much the same point that Wiles makes in a rather different context: it becomes possible to see how factors extraneous to the business of Christian believing itself can shape the argument and direction of a doctrinal tradition. I do not think that there is any simple or general response which would blunt the edge of this sort of criticism. Any defence of the viability of a particular bit of doctrinal language in the face of a strong demonstration of its interest-laden character would have, once again, to argue against the propriety of single global explanations for a start; but that would mean demonstrating in any given case that a doctrinal idiom or formulation is 'underdetermined' by the interest it may serve—i.e. that it preserves themes and elements either irrelevant to or even subversive of that interest. There is also the epistemological consideration that the truth and sense of a proposition cannot be derived solely from an account of the purposes it is made to serve (and so its truth cannot be denied solely by arguing against the legitimacy or propriety of the interest in which it works unless that interest could be shown to be wholly and exclusively formative of its structure).[11] Thus the truth or falsity of Marxist claims about economic relations could not be settled by reference to the iniquities of Eastern European state socialism; and the truth or falsity of incarnational doctrine could not be settled by reference to the oppressive patriarchalism of a Church which explicitly or implicitly deploys the maleness of the person of Jesus in defence of its practice. So long as it can be shown that other trajectories are possible, that other motifs are embodied in the tradition which make for its *self*-critique, the analysis of doctrine as simple and monolithic ideology is inadequate.

Tendenzkritik alerts us to the questionable character of a text rather than displaying directly and incontrovertibly the non-sustainability of its claims—that is to say, it begins rather than ending critical discussion. It underlines the hybrid nature of texts, their determination by factors beyond what the first, 'innocent' reading shows, and so prompts consideration of questions that seem both futile and compulsive about 'essential' meanings. Where both scripture and doctrine are concerned, this can produce a search for pure sources, religion uncorrupted by the world,[12] the gospel before culture. But the lesson of criticism is precisely that of the radically historical nature of all religious utterance: there is nothing untouched by culture and the contestation of power. This is acknowledged rather strikingly in an undeservedly neglected discussion of biblical hermeneutics by Karl Barth in the introduction to the third edition of his Romans Commentary (Barth 1933: 16–19). Here he dismisses Bultmann's efforts to identify *in* the text the authentic Word of God differentiating itself from the products of the human spirit: *all* the words of scripture are human, compromised, and inadequate, and *all* are potentially the vehicles of the Word. 'There are in the Epistle no words at all which are not words of those "other spirits" which he calls Jewish or Popular-Christian or Hellenistic . . . Rather it is for us to perceive and make clear that the whole is placed under the KRISIS of the Spirit of Christ' (ibid. 16–17). What might this mean in the study of doctrinal history? The conclusion might still be a Wilesian one; but if so some other difficulties would also need to be dealt with. In particular (as we shall see later), the question has to be resolved of how to avoid the kind of historicizing and relativizing of doctrine that simply replaces traditional formulations by some unthematized commitment to the developing stream of Christian life and reflection in a way which makes the self-critique of the tradition practically impossible to articulate (a position which I do not think Wiles would find congenial). For the moment, it is enough to recognize that *Tendenzkritik* is quite as grave a challenge to doctrinal assertion as it is claimed to be—indeed, arguably more serious than Wiles's very muted version of it might suggest; but that neither it nor the simpler styles of genre critique can settle the truth and intelligibility, the intellectual legitimacy, of doctrinal propositions with any decisiveness.

2.   *What counts as a doctrinal statement?*

In his London inaugural, Wiles takes as his example of material for the doctrinal critic 'the church's conviction about the uniqueness or finality of Christ' (Wiles 1976: 154). Here and elsewhere, it is reasonably clear that he means the whole complex of strategies by which Christians have tried to latch their sense of Jesus' significance on to a reality beyond what is tangibly and historically given, so as to *ground* the apprehension of that significance in a statement of how things are with the universe. This covers, of course, a great variety of statements: as the Christology essay of 1970 implies, it includes the 'second Adam' typology of Paul and Irenaeus; but it extends equally to the very formal and abstract idiom of Chalcedon. It would be appropriate, surely, to spell out the sorts of *Kritik* suitable to the different idioms involved here, and this has not, I think been fully carried through in Wiles's work. In respect of the 'second Adam' language, or perhaps the transferring to Christ, in Colossians 1, of attributes associated in Jewish speculation with the pre-existent Torah, we can quite evidently and properly discuss the context in which metaphors develop and shift: in Paul's universe there are indeed a number of available schemes for ascribing to something supreme and decisive meaning, generative and authoritative import. He (and the author of Colossians if it is not Paul) works at least partly in a context in which primordiality is one such scheme: if the Law is the decisive communication of God's purpose, it must be 'with' God at the beginning of all things. It cannot be a contingent event in the world. In a different context, different strategies would be appropriate (as with those Chinese Christians who have proposed identifying Jesus as the embodiment of Tao). These moves are informal, pre-dogmatic, and it is not in dispute that the intelligibility of certain metaphorizations depends on the intelligibility of their context. Good critical reading of a text like Romans 5, 1 Corinthians 15, or Colossians 1 will show how a metaphor works in greater depth than any reading which merely takes the language for granted—let alone the sort of reading which does not even spot the presence of a metaphor at all. Similarly, a critical reading of a text like Anselm's *Cur Deus homo?* will display the ways in which a metaphor shapes the argument—and perhaps how problems arise in interpretation when neither author nor pre-critical reader acknowledges the metaphorical character of certain premises or moves in the argument. This, I think is very much how Wiles sees the paradigm of doctrinal critique at its most basic.

But this could be taken to imply that all doctrinal utterances are,

or are reducible to, rhetorical strategies (metaphor as a communicative device), and that doctrinal formulation, credal or conciliar
as well as systematic or 'descriptively didactic', to borrow
Schleiermacher's term (cf. Schleiermacher 1928: §§ 15 and 16), is
generally characterized by a misprision or forgetfulness of its
metaphorical origins (understood in terms of vivid communicative
strategy). Yet the history of doctrinal controversy in the early
Church is in large part a record of the struggle between metaphorical
or narrative modes of tracing and evoking God's action and a set
of diverse considerations, some philosophical, some soteriological,
which pointed up the tensions within these modes and sought to
resolve them, or at least contain them by surrounding them with
warning signs and insisting on their rigorous purging from anthropomorphism (cf. n. 8 and Wiles 1977: 2). Thus: the generation
of the Word is not an event in the life of God preceded by some
other state of affairs; the Word of God does not supply the missing
motor in a defective human vehicle; the story of Jesus is not one
in which a human individual collaborates with a divine individual,
intermittently yielding full control to the latter—although all these
notions were respectably current in the idiom of Christian rhetoric
up to 451 (and beyond). In short, while Christological language
may employ metaphor, it also carries a measure of 'immanent
critique' of the unexamined metaphor and an awareness of the
potential contradictoriness and inadequacy of metaphor when
treated either as an explanation in its own right or as a mere
illustration of a simpler and more primitive idea. As I put it earlier,
this is a 'text' already cognizant of its own ambiguities.

   The church's conviction about the uniqueness or finality of
Christ is thus, as already intimated in (1) above, a manifold,
nuanced, and self-reflective business. Early and diverse metaphorizations of this conviction are not superseded or crudely
translated into 'literal' language, but qualified by the application
of regulative considerations: doctrinal definitions, Chalcedon
above all, and the subsequent Christological clarifications of the
Byzantine period, are indeed not *simply* regulative stipulations (no
more ontologically bold than the rules of tennis), but the result of
applying regulative principles to the more chaotic language of pre-
dogmatic *doctrina*. Given a commitment to the truthfulness of
the whole complex of practices, verbal and non-verbal, moral,
imaginative, devotional, and reflective, which embody 'the church's

conviction' about Jesus, dogmatic Christological definition sets out to establish the conditions for telling this truth in the most comprehensive, least conceptually extravagant, and least idly mythological language. *Pace* Wiles and many others, including nearly all of the contributors to *The Myth of God Incarnate*, incarnational doctrine is not to be reduced to the narrative of a heavenly being coming down from his native habitat, uneasily combined with an undifferentiated assertion of *identity* between Jesus of Nazareth and the divine Word. No professional theologian from 451 to (say) 1850 would have recognized that as an account of what the doctrine claimed.[13]

Now the Wilesian doctrinal critic might well respond that the critical element in doctrinal formulation is neither here nor there: it is simply the sophisticated articulation of a basic misconception, which vitiates any attempts at refinement. If the fifth-century theologian acknowledged the need to qualify the metaphors of piety, he was still under the illusion that these metaphors were part of the process of bringing to speech a single focal truth about Jesus' relation to God, a truth not to be stated in any way except one that expressed the unsurpassable character of that relationship. Everything rests on the belief that the 'impact' of Jesus is to be construed in a certain way; and if the critic is right to see this construal as dependent on a set of cultural and intellectual assumptions we can no longer make, the refinement of the initial belief by 'immanent critique' will not help us. This at once raises a point of the most fundamental importance as to how we are *now* to identify or to characterize the initial experience of Jesus' 'impact' in such a way as to make it clear that the traditional construal is in some sense a mistake. I shall return to this in a moment; but before leaving the question of how 'doctrinal statements' are being defined in Wiles's argument, it is, I think, worth registering that his account of the doctrinal critic's task depends quite heavily on what looks like a reductive and undifferentiated view of what doctrine consists in, a view that, on the showing of his various essays in Christology, tends repeatedly to search for some originary miscalculation or wrong turning, some category error about the status of the language used. What I have been trying to suggest in this section is that, if the history of doctrine is in fact both messier and more self-reflective than Wiles appears to allow, the critic needs to query whether this kind of search is really the essence of the job, and attend more to how exactly the tensions between dogma and metaphor are negotiated under different kinds of pressure from different historical contexts.[14] It is not enough to assimilate all doctrinal utterance to metaphorical elaboration unconscious of its own questionable status, as though 'Once in Royal David's City' and the beginning of Duns Scotus' *Opus Oxoniense III* were comparable enterprises.

3. Doctrine and experience

The most problematic area of Wiles's discussion lies in his attitude to the relation between the fundamental (or, better, foundational— not just a nit-picking distinction) moment of Christian experience and its articulation in terms of what is truly the case in the universe. There can be no doubt at all of Wiles's own commitment to the belief that Jesus—the Jesus of flesh and blood, ministering and crucified—makes a decisive, perhaps even uniquely authoritative, difference to how we speak of God and God's relation to the world (the human world at any rate): this is expounded eloquently and movingly in the chapter on 'Jesus and the Way of Faith' in *Faith and the Mystery of God* (Wiles 1982: esp. 60–3) but it is in evidence in all that Wiles has written on Christology. Jesus is the (or 'a'?) supreme case of an event in which God is active in the only way we may properly expect God to be active: in the creation of 'new possibilities', and in summoning men and women to transforming decisions. His life functions as a parable, in so far as parable may be thought of (following Eta Linnemann) as 'an event which decisively alters the situation' (ibid. 70).

However, as Wiles elaborates the point, it seems that the parabolic quality of the story of Jesus, above all the death of Jesus, amounts to something rather less than Linnemann's words might suggest. The narrative of the crucifixion, taken together with the whole record of the ministry, shows us how God deals with evil: 'the parable of the cross points the human imagination to a vision of God as participant in the continuing conflict with evil, identifying himself at whatever cost with both the perpetrators and the victims of that evil. It is through the cross that he is most clearly seen as the God for whom nothing is expendable except himself' (ibid. 72). This insight invites us to decision—to recognize the evil in ourselves and to begin the work of our own transformation. This is very finely said indeed; but is it all? It seems here as if *the* basic Christian experience were that of acknowledging an insight into the divine character. But this is some way short of Linnemann's idea of a moment in human language which concretely alters the possibilities in a situation by (at least) reconstituting our sense of ourselves, our responsibility, our guilt or complicity, our hope. And how exactly do we move from the story of Jesus to the language Wiles uses about divine involvement and divine cost— language which is in fact dramatically anthropomorphic, even mythological? What does the powerful phrase about God's 'expendability' actually *mean* for a theology which has elsewhere entered severe proscriptions against presuming to talk about the divine life in itself? It might be said, in the light of Wiles's excellent discussion of metaphor earlier in the same book, that there are matters which can only be spoken of in metaphorical idiom, and that we can and must not press for an answer to the question of what 'exactly' such a turn of phrase as this refers to. This is entirely correct; but I do not think it answers the difficulty here, which is that in Wiles's own terms we have no grasp of how the metaphor is generated or how the move to a strong narrative statement about God can be explicated (let alone legitimated). God's 'expendability' is a good instance of a robust metaphorical move standing in profound tension with (Wiles's) regulative principles for talk of God: it is, to use the terms I proposed earlier, pre-dogmatic and informal, an agendum for reflection.

We could deal with this, perhaps, by saying that the story of Jesus somehow confirms and deepens what we already know of the nature of God's action from thinking about the world in general or the lives and words of those who seem to live very close to God: Jesus 'lives out' the pattern of divine action and compassion, the divine denial of force, so radically, to the point of death, that we become aware as never before of what is involved in believing in a compassionate God. But if this is true, it is something of an overstatement to say that this story 'decisively alters the situation'. Should we say, then, that Jesus, by speaking for the love and mercy of God in his ministry, requires of us that we see the same love in his passion as in his action, thus introducing into our grasp of God's love the element of true vulnerability? This is more promising: but it still involves a considerable leap from the detail of Jesus' life and

death to ascribing to God a kind of cost or privation, let alone the
identification alike with perpetrators and victims of evil of which
Wiles speaks. We should need to spell out too why it is that Jesus'
speaking and acting for the mercy of God have sufficient distinc-
tiveness and authority to warrant the belief that this suffering
shows us a suffering in God *in a way that other martyrdoms in the
Jewish world did not or do not.* How is a story of unjust suffering
patiently and unresistingly borne transformed into a story of *God*?

I do not want to dismiss or dismantle Wiles's vision, only to
draw attention to its profoundly tantalizing character. Our situation, it is claimed, is changed by an insight about the nature of
God's action and love whose precise relation to the story of Jesus
is difficult to state with clarity. It could also be noted that the form
in which this insight is expressed is quintessentially twentieth
century, taking for granted the intelligibility of the radical vulnerability of the divine person in a way quite alien to all preceding
generations of belief, including the world of the New Testament
(a point elsewhere raised by Wiles in criticizing putatively orthodox
accounts of incarnational doctrine among some contemporary
theologians). Is the narrative of Jesus *constitutive* of this insight (and
if so, in virtue of what, and 'by what authority') or is it *illustrative*
of a more generally available understanding (in which case, can it
bear the full 'parabolic' weight of creating the conditions for a
genuinely transforming decision)? Then there is the question of
how the insight privileged in Wiles's account actually relates to
what we can say about the historically primary sense of the impact
of Jesus, to which implicit appeal is made in the critique of doctrinal
formulation. This is to bring into focus the distinction hinted at
earlier between foundational and fundamental experience: is the
historically primary sense, the foundational experience, demonstrably
one with the central insight afforded, in a modern theologian's
eyes, by the life and death of Christ, the fundamental, distinctive
contribution of the Christian vision? The New Testament falls
some way short of saying that the life and death of Jesus provide
a manifestation of the character of God's love in the sense of giving
us a supremely full human analogue, in death as well as life, of that
love: if they manifest God's love, it is because they *are* the action
of God, moving towards the restoration and the universalizing of
God's people, or the adoption of human beings as children of the
Father. In other words, for the New Testament writers overall, the

difference Jesus makes is *first* concerned with how and with whom God may be called upon, a difference in language and community, and only derivatively a difference in how God is to be thought about. It makes some sense to consider Jesus as constitutive of an understanding of God if Jesus is first the one who precipitates into existence the restored community of Israel, a community whose prayer and practice slowly and traumatically separate it from the historic Israel. Before we come round to reflecting on the difference Jesus makes to understanding God, he has made a difference encoded in the tangible difference of the *ekklēsia* from both Jews and Gentiles (Wiles 1982: 60). And this unmistakably suggests that the language of reconceiving God in the light of Jesus is irremediably parasitic on a prior apprehension of the life and death of Jesus as divine action, not on the basis of discovering analogues between the character of Jesus and the character of God, but in the light of the kind of transformation already begun in the social reality of those who called themselves God's people.

If the assumption is that the *essence* of the difference associated with Jesus is the provision of a new and undoubtedly challenging and radical picture of God, it is quite intelligible to conclude that doctrinal formulation focused on the person of Jesus is in an important sense misconceived. But such an assumption runs a real risk of foreclosing on the results of 'doctrinal criticism', importing into the understanding of the first believers a kind of 'pre-doctrinal' (not only pre-dogmatic) and innocent kernel of belief (Jesus shows us the truth about God) which is in fact dependent upon, the deposit of, a highly developed chain of reflection. Wiles does not claim that the essence of primitive Christian belief included the vision of a vulnerable God (the very vocabulary necessary for formulating this is only born in the course of complex and very robust incarnational debates in the fifth and sixth centuries); but his exposition in *Faith and the Mystery of God* suggests that this is a proper extrapolation from the 'vision' of God's action and purpose first conveyed through Jesus. There is a certain circularity at work here, not necessarily vicious, but not much easier to handle than the traditional doctrinal idiom. What can now be salvaged from a chastened doctrinal heritage must be something like what impelled the Christian enterprise in the first place; and the chastening of the doctrinal heritage is itself spurred by a recognition of the distance between foundational experience and its supposedly mythological articulation. It is a little bit as if the devout imagination could make us coeval with Jesus and the first believers, so that we can lay hold of the buried pearl of Jesus' 'impact' and yet remain free of those cultural pressures that lead inexorably towards the errors of doctrine. Remember that a *mistake* is something recognizable in a community of people sharing the same world-construction, the same rules: if Christology rests on a mistake, we must be able in some way to share the rules and aims and horizons, the definitions, of the first makers of Christianity, so as to be able to say, 'That is not a legitimate move (however predictable or intelligible in the light of circumstances)'. And that is possible only if our experience of Jesus is at least potentially on all fours with that of the first believers, if we can find an experiential essence in common (allowing, of course, for some measure of nuancing and development in the passage of time).

The problems here are manifold. We have to consider not only Troeltsch's critique of Harnack, but also Kierkegaard's argument in the *Philosophical Fragments* (Kierkegaard 1985: ss. IV and V, esp. pp. 99–105) that the experience of the believer contemporary with Christ furnishes the occasion or condition of subsequent faith, not its normative content. What prompts and forms belief is not the 'raw' event of the life of Jesus, but that event as witnessed to—as already mediated. If we have to make ourselves contemporary in imagination with the first believers, reconstructing an 'impact', our faith will constantly come to rest either in speculative projections or in inoffensive generalities. We have no way of saying what *we* would see as contemporaries of Jesus and the apostles: the 'impact' of Jesus is itself embedded in a world of image and expectation not our own, and we could not ever be in a position to evaluate this more satisfactorily than Jesus' contemporaries—having the experience (as Eliot might have said) but *not* missing the meaning. It is not simply that the importance of Jesus is misconstrued: what the experience of Jesus as significant actually amounts to is, as a historical question, answerable only in the terms of his contemporaries. He was important for first-century reasons, not important for timeless reasons distorted by confused first-century minds. I suspect that Wiles is here not enough of a historical relativist![15] It is difficult to work out how far he is really committed to the implied view that the first-century believer and the twentieth-century believer are engaged in the same task, making sense of the historical effect of another man's biography, but there is enough in what he writes to generate the difficulties I have tried to indicate. And my doubts about whether we should find Jesus significant *as a historical figure* for good twentieth-century reasons are not, I should add, a recommendation of some sort of programmatic scepticism about the Gospel record, or a dismissal of the theological importance of the Jesus of history, but merely a recognition that Christology is not *first* a task of historical assessment of a chronicled individual. A good deal of recent criticism of classical incarnational doctrine seems to be based on the complaint that there is not enough evidence to justify dogmatic conclusions, and Wiles's interpretation assumes such a gravamen. But what if the entire enterprise is not about *historical* evidence and (incommensurable) dogmatic conclusions at all?

The model of 'experiencing' Jesus discernible in Wiles and others in this connection is problematic. The New Testament writers and their congregations did not (as Wiles himself agrees) make deductions from an overview of the facts of Jesus' life and the impression made by him. What their language actually says is that, in his ministry *and* now, Jesus is the form which God's judgement takes; that he, then and now, makes real the welcoming mercy of God in the Lord's Supper; that the believer is united with him, that the death and resurrection of Jesus in particular constitute the condition of there being a new humanity of unrestricted *koinōnia* so that if we 'enter into' the dying and rising of Jesus by baptism and in daily conversion, we come to stand where he stands, in full intimacy with the Father, and the barriers separating us from other human beings fall away. The relation of the believer to Jesus here is not that of an observer, however deeply or lastingly impressed, but what Paul and John conceive as 'indwelling', being where he is. How exactly can we relate all this to the assessment of Jesus' significance as a historical human individual? For these are the words and images which say what the difference is that Jesus makes—what the 'experience' involved is. You may say that they are unintelligible, but not that they represent a simple misunderstanding. And both within and beyond the New Testament, the basic intra-Christian impulse to doctrinal reflection lies here: what is to be said of a human life that is creative and definitive of a new frame of reference in speaking of God and the world by establishing a new social reality in which God is spoken of—a human life which is believed, rightly or wrongly, to be present and active, still being lived, for and in the Christian, a life not perceived as something that can be talked of as an episode in the past?[16] If we want to say that the essential core of all this is still an *evaluation* of the impact of Jesus, we are saying that we understand the early Christians' experience so much better than they did that we can discount the greater part of what they concretely said not only as metaphor but as misplaced or dispensable metaphor. Is it enough to say, with Wiles, that the early believers had experiences which they 'associated' with Jesus as risen Lord (but which might in principle be intelligibly detached from that association)? To sustain itself in this connection, Wiles's thesis would need to be very much refined, to avoid either the Harnackian anachronism of thinking that what we find attractive and important in Jesus was itself the foundational experience, or the implication that we stand alongside the first believers, striving to interpret an experience not previously mediated.

4.   The nature of criticism

Very briefly: I have used words like 'legitimacy' and 'legitimation' quite frequently in this essay, partly as a reminder of how much critical activity is bound up with a kind of *legal* paradigm. What is allowed to count? Can we agree on what people have a right to expect will be accepted or understood as valid currency? In a very interesting passage of the first *Critique* (Kant 1933: 601), Kant spoke of his aim as being to deliver us from the 'natural' state of war, where assertions are contested and sustained by force alone, and to establish a quasi-legal authority: 'The critique . . . arriving at all its decisions in the light of fundamental principles of its own institution, the authority of which no-one can question, secures to us the peace of a legal order, in which our disputes have to be conducted solely by the recognized methods of *legal action*.'

Legal settlement is universally and eternally valid, in that it does not depend on the outcome of messy and protracted negotiations between arbitrarily distinct interests (as between nations in the aftermath of war). We are delivered from the Hobbesian 'injustice and violence' of pre-rational nature[17] by the establishing of an authority whose credibility and legitimacy are beyond the disputes of mere interest and locality and are accessible to all reasoning

minds. The hope of being able to settle disputes without recourse
to contests of power is a noble and persistent one (most recently
and fully defended by Habermas); but it is a hope that is easily
confused with the fantasy that there might be a form of human
discourse free from local and personal pasts, from standpoints. The
universal tribunal envisaged by Kant is meant to be in everyone's
interest and to be distorted by no 'local' constructions of reality.
But the history of post-Enlightenment thought has left us, at the
very least, a legacy of scepticism about these universal juridical
claims, and a tendency to think more about how different local
constructions can engage 'critically' with themselves and each other
in the purging of violent and untruthful exclusivisms and the
negotiating of the tensions between real difference and possible
new forms of communality.

These are the commonplaces of recent epistemology (and anti-
epistemology). To say that there is no universal tribunal, that
pluralities of perception cannot be settled by 'legal action', is not
necessarily to doom ourselves to irrationalist relativism. It is,
though, to acknowledge that what is sustainable, what can be
asserted without arbitrariness (if that is a proper paraphrase of what
legitimacy means), has more to do with how particular perceptions
cope with and absorb contesting claims and maintain elements of
critical 'listening' provisionality within their own frameworks than
with meeting foreordained universal conditions of legality. In our
specific case, I am uneasy that Wiles follows Woods so faithfully
in assuming that the 'truth and adequacy of doctrinal statements'
can be tested in a fundamentally historical and analytical discipline.
Wiles here comes curiously close to Pannenberg—not usually
his favourite theologian—in implying that the truth of revelation
should be accessible to supposedly neutral study (see e.g. Pannenberg
1969: esp. 135–9); or to Lonergan's confidence that 'dialectics' can
deal with the truthfulness of doctrinal propositions as part of a
continuum of analysis slipping easily from history to systematics
(Lonergan 1972: ch. 10). Wiles's appeal (Wiles 1974: 17) to
'economy and coherence' in the assessment of doctrinal validity or
viability makes little allowance for how *transitions* in understanding
extend and outgrow (in his own words) currently available
conventions of making sense within an existing tradition, let alone
within the canons of some general normative rationality.

To the task of doctrinal criticism, the following, I believe, may be granted: the rigorous exploration and testing of conceptual structures for points of strictly logical inadequacy, the attempt to identify concepts imperfectly defined or focused; the examination of the role of metaphor, and the attempt to discern places where it might be leading an argument by the nose in unconscious (uncriticized) ways; and the search for interest or *Tendenz* in doctrinal utterance. All this is more or less included in Wiles's basic proposals. But I have tried to suggest in these pages that dealing with these issues can easily be tied in with settling issues of truth if we are not careful, in ways which are actually inattentive to the concrete history and operation of doctrinal formulation. Such a connection can only be defended by recourse to a very full-blooded abstract universalist rationalism, which I do not think Wiles really professes, though he may come pretty near it at times. Our disagreement is ultimately, I should say, about how to 'read' the difference made by Jesus. If Jesus is finally *illustrative* of truths about God which are in principle independent of this particular life and death, doctrine will be above all the process of transmitting these truths (with all the resources of image and symbol to which Wiles grants increasing importance), and the exact place occupied by Jesus may quite properly vary from one bit of Christian pedagogy to another. If Jesus is *constitutive* for Christian language about God and for the present reality of the believer's relation to God, in such a way that what is said, done, and suffered is strictly unintelligible without continuing reference to Jesus in a more than historically explicatory way, doctrine will be an attempt to do justice to the way in which the narrative and the continuing presence (or presence-in-absence, if you want to nuance it further) of Jesus is held actively to shape present horizons, in judgement and in grace. The disagreement is not over whether doctrinal utterances are or are not to be received uncritically, but over whether any kind of critical method can settle the legitimacy of the distinctively *doctrinal* enterprise itself as generally conceived by Christians, an enterprise resting as it does on the conviction, variously and often very confusedly articulated in our primary texts, that our world of speech and corporate life has been comprehensively remade, so that new conceptualities are brought to birth. *Kritik* can look hard at those conceptualities, with a wide variety of suspicions; but not all Wiles's reasoned eloquence should persuade us that it is in a position to disallow the underlying unsettlement of our thought:

the question, 'What is it that is true of Jesus of Nazareth that would make some sense of the Church's commitment to new imaginings of God and humanity and of the possibility of new relation to God and humanity?' I believe that this is in fact the question that arises from taking with full seriousness the notion of parable which Wiles finds so attractive—an event which interrupts us and compels us to take up new positions by showing us quite unexpectedly where and what we are in respect of an unforeseen reality set down before us; something more than an extended simile. Wiles is far from insensitive to this priority of *krisis* over *Kritik*; but how can his model of doctrinal criticism allow it its proper weight?

NOTES

1. This is the conclusion of a very early (1957) paper, 'Reflections on the Origins of the Doctrine of the Trinity' (Wiles 1976: 1–17), and the point is reiterated in Wiles's first essay in *The Myth of God Incarnate*, which is entitled 'Christianity without Incarnation?' (Wiles 1977: 1–10, esp. 3–6, 8–9).

2. This position is now associated with George Lindbeck, in the wake of his book on *The Nature of Doctrine* (Lindbeck 1984). For Wiles's views on this, I am dependent on conversation with him, and on an unpublished paper delivered to the late Hans Frei's seminar at Yale.

3. There is actually some confusion here: Wiles does not distinguish between the idea of creation *ex nihilo* as an absolute and unrepeatable beginning (i.e. creation in the strict traditional Christian sense), creation as a punctiliar 'event' in the sense of something occurring in time (a view generally rejected by theologians at least since Augustine, and the subject of considerable philosophical discussion in late antiquity (see Sorabji 1983; Williams 1987: 181–98)), and the creation of the human species by special intervention (a more thorny point, on which it is difficult to pin down many classical theologians, because they are capable of using both the language of a discrete act of creation and something more like a doctrine of the divine simultaneity of the entirety of the creative process). Only in respect of the third is Wiles's argument strictly pertinent, and this uncharacteristic unclarity makes the article in some ways hard to evaluate.

4. Cf. Wiles 1982 on the uses of metaphor.

5. See e.g. Wiles 1977: 161 on 'the union of human and divine at the heart of the human personality' as the ontological substrate for the myth of the Incarnation. This is a far from straightforward statement: it clearly

has little to do with the primitive connection of incarnational language with the perception of an event of global change in the world (a connection which Wiles regards as the effect of the apocalyptic milieu); how then does it relate to the initial experience of Jesus by his contemporaries, and how could we know or guess that this was what the doctrinal language was 'really' trying to say? I return to this problem later in the present essay. And what precisely is the nature of the 'union' here spoken of? The union with God of which the New Testament speaks is almost uniformly a union whose character depends on the notion of a relationship defined by and communicated in the person of Jesus and the Spirit of Jesus, a relation to the source of the world as to a father. Is Wiles talking about this, or about something more monistic?

6. This is the burden of Augustine's *De doctrina Christiana* (especially book 2); cf. also Aquinas, *Summa theologiae*, 1. 1. 9 and 10.

7. See e.g. Origen's discussion of what it means to call God 'spirit' (*pneuma*) in an intellectual culture where the word had highly specific philosophical (materialistic) connotations, in his *De principiis*, 1. 1.

8. A very significant example would be Athanasius' insistence that the language of begetting or sonship used of the relation of the Logos to the Father must be carefully purged of any suggestion of the temporal, physical, and mutable associations of the terms in ordinary use; see e.g. *Contra Arianos*, 1. 26–7.

9. For a recent analysis of Christology in the context of feminist critique, see Hampson 1990, 1 and 2—a very nuanced querying of the possibility of salvaging Christology from patriarchy, granting, paradoxically, that such a task would be easier with patristic than with much modern Christology, but assuming that the intellectual structure of the former is now not available to us.

10. For a discussion of how this issue was seen by some in the Church of England in the early 19th century, see Williams 1990.

11. A good discussion of the issues arising here may be found in McLellan 1986.

12. See e.g. Schüssler Fiorenza 1983 for a very sophisticated essay in this genre. This learned, moving, and profoundly creative work does not quite, finally, escape the temptation of setting up a primitive and 'innocent' Jesus-movement as that against which the corruptions of the canon and the later churches may be judged, despite the disclaimer on p. 92. But it must also be granted that Schüssler Fiorenza's understanding of the task of historical reconstruction is a complex one, and does not necessarily involve any claims about a primordial community *achieving* the emancipation it presages on its structure and language.

13. Some defenders of the doctrine of the Incarnation have apparently assumed that what has to be vindicated is precisely something like an identity statement, and have produced accounts of the doctrine quite considerably removed from, say, the major medieval discussions of it. The most striking recent example is Morris 1986.

14. E. A. Peterson's celebrated *Der Monotheismus als politisches Problem* (Peterson 1935) begins to do something like this. Recent years have seen several studies of Marian doctrine and eucharistic practice which have raised these sorts of question; an application of this method to Christology on a wide historical front, setting side by side the characteristic metaphors and visual images of a period with the language of doctrinal debate, would be of great significance.

15. He may be contrasted in this respect with Dennis Nineham whose essay in *The Myth of God Incarnate* (Nineham 1977) and discussion of the wider issues of history and faith in *The Use and Abuse of the Bible* (Nineham 1976) take for granted the radical historical inaccessibility of Jesus, and concentrate on elaborating a theology of the Church as carrier of an experience of God *occasioned* in some sense by Jesus, but not given specification by any particular facts about him. Wiles is sometimes quite close to such a position (for example, his paper of 1978 'In What Sense is Christianity a "Historical" Religion?' (Wiles 1978) appears to imply this), but in practice (as in Wiles 1982) he continues to see the narrative of Jesus as having some kind of normativity for faith in a way which is not obviously entailed by Nineham's account.

16. See Herbert McCabe's discussion of *The Myth of God Incarnate* and subsequent correspondence with Wiles in his collection of essays and sermons *God Matters* (McCabe 1987), and in particular his statement on p. 71: 'It is in the contact with the person who is Jesus, in this personal communion between who he is and who I am, that his divinity is revealed in his humanity, not in any, as it were, clinical objective examination of him.'

17. On the philosophical and theological problems of the assumption that the state of nature is a state of violent conflict, see most recently Milbank 1990: 278–325.

REFERENCES

Barth, Karl (1933), *The Epistle to the Romans* (Eng. trans. of 6th edn. by E. C. Hoskyns), Oxford.

Hampson, Daphne (1990), *Theology and Feminism*, Oxford.

Kant, Immanuel (1933), *Critique of Pure Reason*, trans. Norman Kemp Smith, London.

Kierkegaard, S. (1985), *Philosophical Fragments/Johannes Climacus*, ed. and trans. Howard V. Hong and Edna H. Hong, Princeton, NJ.

Lindbeck, George (1984), *The Nature of Doctrine*, Philadelphia.

Loades, Ann (1990) (ed.), *Feminist Theology: A Reader*, London.

Lonergan, Bernard (1972), *Method in Theology*, London.

McCabe, Herbert (1987), *God Matters*, London.

McLellan, David (1986), *Ideology*, Milton Keynes.

Milbank, John (1990), *Theology and Social Theory: Beyond Secular Reason*, Oxford.

Morris, Thomas V. (1986), *The Logic of God Incarnate*, Ithaca, NY.

Nineham, Dennis (1976), *The Use and Abuse of the Bible*, London.

—— (1977), 'Epilogue', in John Hick (ed.), *The Myth of God Incarnate*, London: 186–204.

Pannenberg, Wolfhart (1969), 'Dogmatic Theses on the Concept of Revelation', in Wolfhart Panneberg (ed.), *Revelation as History*, London.

Peterson, E. A. (1935), *Der Monotheismus als politisches Problem*, Leipzig.

Ricœur, Paul (1976), *Interpretation and Theory: Discourse and the Surplus of Meaning*, Fort Worth, Tex.

—— (1981), *Hermeneutics and Human Sciences*, ed. and trans. John B. Thompson, Cambridge.

Russell, Letty (1985) (ed.), *Feminist Interpretations of the Bible*, Philadelphia.

Schleiermacher, F. D. E. (1928), *The Christian Faith*, Edinburgh.

Schüssler Fiorenza, Elizabeth (1983), *In Memory of Her: A Feminist Theological Reconstruction of Christian Origins*, London.

Sorabji, Richard (1983), *Time, Creation and the Continuum*, London.

Wiles, Maurice (1974), *The Remaking of Christian Doctrine*, London.

—— (1976), *Working Papers in Doctrine*, London.

—— (1977), 'Christianity without Incarnation?' and 'Myth in Theology', in John Hick (ed.), *The Myth of God Incarnate*, London: 1–10, 148–66.

—— (1978), 'In What Sense is Christianity a "Historical" Religion?', *Theology*, 81 (Jan.): 4–14.

—— (1982), *Faith and the Mystery of God*, London.

Williams R. (1987), *Arius: Heresy and Tradition*, London.

—— (1990), 'Newman's *Arians* and the Question of Method in Doctrinal History', in Ian Ker and Alan G. Hill (eds.), *Newman after a Hundred Years*, Oxford.

Woods, G. F. (1966), 'Doctrinal Criticism', in F. G. Healey (ed.), *Prospect for Theology*, London: 73–92.

15

Paideia and the Myth of Static Dogma

FRANCES M. YOUNG

I

Modern theology often treats patristic doctrine as static on the grounds that it dealt in ontological categories, while modern historical scholarship traces the story of doctrinal development in the patristic period. Prima facie it might seem that these perspectives are contradictory, but in fact 'making and remaking' implies development to a fixed form, together with the suggestion of a need to unpick a finished tapestry so as to re-weave it, thus betraying the influence of both modern assumptions.

In so far as the hermeneutical process involves seeing the past in terms of current models of understanding, such perspectives may have some justification, and they provide the assumptions which have enabled the development of Maurice Wiles's stimulating programme of doctrinal criticism. It is a privilege to honour his challenging contribution to a field which too easily permits retreat into safe text-critical studies or neat but merely historical reconstructions.

However, the thesis of this essay is that both assumptions are modern 'projections', and both reflect a mistake about the nature of Christian dogma. This mistake goes some way towards accounting for the gulf between theology and religious experience, doctrine and spirituality, which is evident in Western Christianity. Both doctrine and theology tend to be regarded as 'second-order' activities, intellectual reflection on first-order religion (such a position is explicit in Richardson 1935). A perspective which is more true to much of the Christian tradition may be discovered if we investigate the patristic approach, reclaiming both the central place of exegesis and preaching for doctrine, and uncovering the roots of Eastern theology where doctrine and spirituality are inseparable.

The clue to this perspective is the realization that *dogmata* are simply teachings, and that teaching involved a whole process of education, a *paideia*, ascetic training in a spiritual way of life which involved both moral and intellectual progress. That is why heretics were treated as morally culpable as well as doctrinally deviant: their whole discipline was wrong. The kind of thing we modern Westerners tend to mean by doctrines emerged within the process of marking diversions from the correct direction as the journey or pilgrimage was pursued. They were never intended to provide the whole truth; nor was the truth a static object which could be possessed.

II

It might seem obvious that Origen's teachings were meant to be such a *paideia*. But that is only so because of the progress of Origen scholarship over the past one hundred years.

When in 1886 Charles Bigg produced his Bampton Lectures entitled *Christian Platonists of Alexandria*, it was still possible to treat the *De principiis* as a compendium of Origen's doctrine. Bigg recognized that Origen accepted a somewhat limited role for 'Tradition which handed down certain facts, certain usages, which were to be received without dispute'. Tradition did not explain 'the why or the whence', and so it was 'the office of the sanctified reason to define, to articulate, to co-ordinate, even to expand, and generally to adapt to human needs the faith once delivered to the Church' (Bigg 1886: 191). But he takes for granted that what Origen offers is his established doctrines, doctrines of God, the Logos, the Trinity, the Soul, etc. All that is necessary is to expound Origen's views on the classic doctrinal questions, taking *De principiis* as a kind of systematic theology in which Platonism has contributed to the intellectual formulation of dogma.

Strikingly different is the position of Henri Crouzel (Crouzel 1985). Crouzel has reached the view that Origen belonged to a time when discussion and hypothesis were still permissible, indeed that Origen as a true intellectual made alternative suggestions and that this is the explanation of our difficulties in knowing whether or not he taught such controversial doctrines as *metempsychōsis* (Crouzel 1985: 166). It was in the Origenist controversy that the attribution of 'doctrines' began, for this was a different era, and Origen's 'orthodoxy' was the issue.

Perhaps even more fundamental, however, has been the shift reflected in Crouzel's estimate of Origen's central concern. In evaluating Origen's thought as a whole, his spirituality had already come into sharper focus. Here too the influence of Platonism was explored, but attention had also been directed to his exegesis of scripture. So it is not doctrine derived from Platonist theorizing that is given priority in Crouzel's account of Origen, but rather his exegetical activity, which was indeed the predominant aspect of his life's work. Even more significant is the new approach to studying Origen's exegesis found in the work of Karen Jo Torjesen (see also Greer 1973).

In *Hermeneutical Procedure and Theological Method in Origen's Exegesis* (Torjesen 1985a) she subjects Origen's exegetical practice to careful analysis, and convincingly shows that for Origen the task of the exegete is to enable scripture to function pedagogically for the hearer, assisting the journey of the soul. The progression discerned in his homilies and commentaries corresponds with Origen's conception of that journey through three stages: the stage of purification, then knowledge of the Logos, finally union with God. This journey is the means of redemption, and the saving work of the Logos is essentially educative, leading from one step to the next, each being interconnected. There is progressive transformation through this process and *paideia* takes place through the ministerial task of the church in the exegesis of scripture.

So the hearer is to be drawn into the text, and the steps observable in Origen's exegesis correspond to the progression of the soul on this journey. The literal sense is the wording of the text and what the words meant to psalmist or prophet; the spiritual sense what it means to the Christian making the journey of faith and participating in the history of salvation. This may involve a simple universalizing of the text, the hearer appropriating the words fairly straightforwardly; or it may involve what we would recognize as allegory.

'The purpose of inspiration is paideia, the progressive perfection of the Christian through assimilation of the saving doctrines' (Torjesen 1985a: 42). Not all Christians are ready for every doctrine, and so a homily has teachings intended for different levels. There are saving doctrines for the beginner, for those advancing, and for those perfect. Through scripture and its exegesis these doctrines are taught and made effective for the hearer's salvation. This progression is for every soul. Torjesen argues (Torjesen 1985*b*) that Origen never intended his threefold classification to apply to different 'senses' of scripture, nor to separate classes of Christian. Rather they correspond to different stages on the journey, and the shape of each homily reflects the threefold advance.

Origen's procedure in dealing with the New Testament, she notes, is different from his handling of the Old. This she attributes to the fact that the Old mediates the Logos, whereas in the New the Logos teaches directly:

> The exegesis of the Old Testament prepares the reader or hearer for the exegesis of the gospel; unless he is properly prepared he cannot receive the truths of the gospel. This can also be seen in the arrangement of the liturgical services. A three-year catechumenate, during which the Old Testament was interpreted, prepared Christians for participation in the Eucharistic services in which the interpretation of the Gospel was presented. (Torjesen 1985*a*: 107)

The very diversity of doctrines in scripture makes it a perfect pedagogical instrument for the revelation of the Logos.

For Origen, doctrine is the means whereby the Logos communicates himself to the soul. There is a progressive disclosure of the Logos which makes possible a progressive comprehension of him, and that constitutes progress in the soul of the hearer (ibid. 120). The catechumen is at the beginning stage in which purification from sin, healing from the soul's physician, is required. Then there follows sanctification and redemption whereby, through moral and mystical pedagogy, the soul is prepared for perfection. The particularity of scriptural history becomes universal, as the journey of the soul becomes the allegorical meaning of, for example, the wanderings of Israel, and the text itself is taken to refer to these spiritual realities.

To assess Origen's Christology simply according to the categories supplied by the typical 'History of Doctrine' approach is therefore to lose its real dynamic. If it makes sense to speak of humanity and divinity and the relationship between them, it only does so in the context of the overall pedagogical accommodation of the Logos to the level of those who need healing and sanctification. Understanding the Gospels requires the penetration which discerns the divinity beneath the particularities of the earthly presence. There is a profound continuity between the two, a kind of sacramental relationship. What we would call 'correct doctrine' belongs to an entirely different realm of discourse from the transforming and progressive response to the Logos' teaching envisaged by Origen.

III

Maybe Origen can be dismissed as a kind of free-thinker who could float hypotheses, a philosopher rather than dogmatician whose ideas then became much more problematic several generations later as the Church defined and solidified its doctrinal position. After all his more speculative statements were rejected and he did become regarded as dangerous. But such a view is hardly fair to the later period.

Gregory of Nyssa, it is true, avoids mentioning Origen's name—he lived when the shadows had begun to fall. Yet he was much indebted to Origen, and the fact that the journey of the soul is fundamental to Gregory's spirituality takes little demonstration. Again exegesis provides the *locus* for spelling out the mystical progression to knowledge of God. The classic example is, no doubt, the *Life of Moses*.

Gregory produced this work in response to a request to send counsel on the perfect life, and his initial image is the highly dynamic one of a chariot race: as spectators encourage their favourites, so he cheers on his friend. He suggests that perfection in sensible objects involves limitation or boundaries; but virtue is not like that. Like the nature of the infinite God, perfection is boundless, and there is no stopping-place or final attainment. Growth in goodness constitutes human perfection. So examples to be followed are such as Abraham, or Moses. Gregory promises to outline Moses' life, and then, through contemplation of it, reach an understanding of the perfect life for human beings.

Moses' life was characterized by journeying, by watching the mysterious cloud that guided the people and teaching them to keep it in sight. Food was miraculously provided, enemies were overcome. At Mount Sinai he and the people were initiated, passing through purification to revelation. Moses had to ascend beyond the visible and enter the inner sanctuary of divine mystical doctrine. Gregory has summarized the story, yet 'amplified' it to bring out its spiritual intention (325M: Jaeger 33: 3–6). He goes on to probe its exemplary character more deeply.

Expounding details allegorically Gregory delineates both divine accommodation to the level of human weakness and the continuous progress upwards that constitutes perfection. If at first religious knowledge comes as light, further progress and deeper penetration discovers the invisible and incomprehensible, the darkness in which seeing consists in not seeing, for 'no one has ever seen God'. Moses enters the luminous darkness of the cloud of the presence. He is transformed by God's glory so that no one could look at him; he speaks with God as one speaks to a friend. Yet to see God is not attainable, and God hides him in a cleft in the rock, allowing him only to see his back-parts—the point being not just the absurdity of a literal seeing of the invisible, but the recognition of God's infinity. For 'this truly is the vision of God: never to be satisfied in the desire to see him' (404M: Jaeger 116: 17–19), and Moses 'is now taught how he can behold him: to follow God wherever he might lead is to behold God . . . He who follows will not turn aside from the right way if he always keeps the back of his leader in view' (409M: Jaeger 121: 4–6).

In Gregory's spirituality, then, there are no static conceptions, as many important studies have shown. But the relevant point here is the significance of the journey motif, not just in exegesis and in works we might treat as spiritual guides, but also in those we might regard as Gregory's 'dogmatic' works.

The *Great Catechesis* is intended to equip catechetical teachers for their job of training converts for initiation, so it is an object lesson in Christian *paideia* and leads to a consideration of what baptism is about. The crucial point about it is that there is a likeness between the journey made by Christ through death to life and the journey made by those who follow:

it is necessary for those with equal commitment to the Good, to follow by imitation the one who leads the way to our salvation, bringing into effect what he demonstrated. It is in fact impossible to reach the same goal without travelling by the same route. Should those puzzled as to how to thread the turns of labyrinths, happen to meet someone with experience of them, they pass through those various misleading turnings in the chambers by following him behind, which they could not do, without following their leader step by step; so, please note, the labyrinth of this life cannot be threaded by human nature unless one takes that same path as the one who, once in it, got beyond the difficulties surrounding him. Using labyrinth figuratively, I refer to the inescapable prison of death which encircles the wretched human race. (*Oratio catechetica magna*, s. 35, PG 45. 88B)

In this context Gregory stresses the moral character of this journey: it is not just in 'doctrines' but in actions that the way is to be pursued, as was the case with Christ. However, if we return to the beginning of the work, we find that the very procedure of this introductory account of the Christian faith is to encourage catechetical teachers to lead converts on an intellectual journey from their initial notions to a more transcendent conception. This is done by *anagōgē*, moving from human analogy by induction or abstraction to an appropriate conception of God. But while one who engages in this depth of study gains a certain amount of apprehension of God's nature, secretly in his spirit, yet he will never be able to articulate clearly in words the ineffable depth of this mystery. For Gregory the incomprehensibility of God is a 'doctrinal' necessity (*Oratio catechetica magna*, ss. 1–3, PG 45. 13–20).

This is true also in his controversial works against Eunomius, and that presumably has greater significance for our argument: the *Great Catechesis* is after all a work of *paideia* and we might expect a certain emphasis on the process of salvation. The controversy with Eunomius, however, was about the nature and identity of God and the Being known as God's Son. One might expect the 'static ontological categories' to dominate. But in practice the journey into understanding is as fundamental here as anywhere— it is indeed a doctrinal necessity.

For Eunomius' fundamental flaw is cleverness and over-wise philosophy which fixes a gulf between him and the saving faith of Abraham (*Contra Eunomium*, 2. 84–5: Jaeger 251–2), who

went out by Divine command from his own land and kindred on an 'exodus' befitting a prophet set on understanding God . . . For going out from himself and his country, by which I understand his lowly and earthly mind, he raised his conception as far as possible above the common bounds of nature and forsook the soul's kinship with the senses, so as to be troubled by none of the objects of sense and blind for the purpose of contemplating invisible things, there being neither sight nor sound to distract the mind; so walking, as the Apostle said, by faith not sight, he was lifted so high by the sublimity of his knowledge that he came to be regarded as the acme of human perfection, knowing as much of God as it was possible for finite human capacity at full stretch to attain.

That is why, according to Gregory, God is called the 'God of Abraham'. Abraham was able to soar above sense-objects and the beauty of objects of contemplation to behold the archetype of all beauty. He could use various human conceptions, such as God's power, goodness, being without beginning, infinity, or whatever, as stepping-stones for the upward course, and yet recognize that all fall short of what he was seeking, so that

when he had outstripped every supposition with respect to the divine nature, every single conception of God suggested by any designation, when he had thus purged his reason of all such fancies and arrived at a faith unalloyed and free from all prejudice, he produced an evident and unmisleading sign of the knowledge of God, namely the conviction that God is greater and more sublime than any known signification. (2. 89)

For Gregory, Abraham is the type of a faith which recognizes it is but dust and ashes, and that the curiosity of human knowledge betrays an inappropriate empirical disposition. 'Knowing, then how widely the Divine nature differs from our own, let us quietly remain within our proper limits' (2. 96). Dogmatic formulations issue from heretics who offer the figments of their own imaginations. 'Whoever searches the whole of the inspired Word will find there no doctrine of the Divine nature' (2. 106).

Indeed, there is accommodation to human understanding through analogies, but 'the object to be aimed at, in discourse about God, is not to produce a pleasant and harmonious melody of words, but to work out a reverent conception, whereby a worthy notion of God is safeguarded' (*Contra Eunomium*, 2. 136: Jaeger 265). For Gregory a discernment that proceeds beyond language, indeed beyond knowledge, is required; but since there is no suitable word to encapsulate the divine being, human expressions need to be manifold, and the process of questioning and discussing and 'word-building' is essential to maintain the necessary relativizing of religious language. This is a kind of pilgrimage:

we apply such appellations to the divine essence which surpasses all understanding, not seeking to glory in it by the names we employ, but to guide our own selves by the aid of such terms towards the comprehension of the things that are hidden (*Contra Eunomium*, 2. 154: Jaeger 270) according to my account, conception is the method whereby we discover things that are unknown by finding further consequences through what attaches to or proceeds from our first perception of the matter pursued. (*Contra Eunomium*, 2. 182: Jaeger 277)

For Gregory the intelligence to do this is a gift of God. God is not the creator of words but of things made known to us through the signification of words. So 'the scriptural account of the Creation is the learner's introduction, as it were, to knowledge of God, representing to our minds the power of the Divine Being through what is more ready to our comprehension' *(Contra Eunomium*, 2. 228: Jaeger 292). Just as *we* have to build a house, even though the ability to do so is God's gift, so *we* have to invent particular words, even though the power of speech is God-given. There are lots of different languages, precisely because language is a human invention. Gregory's conclusion is that 'if certain of our accustomed expressions are attributed by Holy Scripture to God's person, it should be recognized that the Holy Spirit is addressing us in language of our own' (*Contra Eunomium*, 2. 238: Jaeger 296), and naturally he refers to the story of Pentecost where each heard the Gospel in his own language.

So like Origen he paints a picture of a divine accommodation to our level, which provides guides for us to follow as we progress towards knowledge of God. He refers to Paul's adaptation of his speech to the capacity of his hearers, offering milk not solid food where appropriate. The fundamental image, then, is of a process of *paideia*, a two-way dynamic, a synergism, in which divine Teacher and human disciple respond to one another. The very possibility of this is grounded in God's being as love. What is by nature finite cannot ascend above its prescribed limits:

on this account, bringing his loving power down to the level of human weakness, he dispensed on us, so far as it was possible for us to receive it, grace and assistance from himself . . . though transcending our nature and inaccessible to human communion, yet like a tender mother joining in the inarticulate gurglings of her baby, the divine power gives our human nature what it is capable of receiving; and thus in diverse theophanies, he adapts himself to humanity and speaks in human language, assuming wrath and pity and such-like emotions, so that through feelings corresponding to our own infantile life we might be led by the hand, and grasp the divine nature by means of the words which his foresight has provided. (*Contra Eunomium*, 2. 417–18: Jaeger 348)

Doctrine is indistinguishable from spirituality, for both are about 'teaching' and 'learning' in a cosmic process of *paideia*.

The significant point here is that this account of doctrine was vital for the confrontation with what was indeed a static and limited view of truth. The notion of dogma as a set of propositions or a fixed credal formula is entirely foreign to Gregory's thought, though the language of scripture and traditional belief is important for guidance on the journey.

IV

At this point, the voice of the objector may be heard. Granted that this is true for the Origenist tradition, and indeed for the Cappadocians in general, it surely cannot be generalized to the whole Greek patristic tradition, or be taken to mean that there is nothing in the modern attribution of fundamentally static categories to patristic thought. Given that the converse attitudes are reflected in the very opponents Gregory was dealing with, they are unlikely to have been absent from Church tradition—indeed, can surely be documented: do not Eusebius and Epiphanius have a view of pristine original truth from which there was subsequent deviation?

The case of Eusebius is particularly interesting. He too was an Origenist, and the Origenist picture of the soul finding salvation occasionally surfaces in his writings. For Origen, however, the process of fall and return was seen not just at the individual level, but also at the cosmic level: the very creation of the material order was part of God's providential *paideia*, the foundation of a kind of 'school' to educate God's fallen creation back to comtemplative union with God's self. Eusebius transported this fundamental conception to his understanding of history.

In his *Praeparatio evangelica* we can see him working this out. Fundamentally this is an apologetic work, but Eusebius recognizes he is charting a path rather different from that of his predecessors. Like them, however, he has to answer those critics who object to Christianity because it neither upholds the ancient religious traditions of the Graeco-Roman world, nor embraces Judaism properly.

In offering his critique of religion, Eusebius exploits accounts given by Plutarch, Porphyry, and many others, accepting a progressive degeneration from primitive worship of heavenly bodies to the superstitious and idolatrous practices of later times. But all alike were deviations from true religion, since they worshipped the creature rather than the Creator. True religion was practised only by the Hebrews, by which he meant the patriarchs prior to Moses. Moses gives a true account of these pioneers, but then introduces polity and legislation to keep their deviant descendants, the Jews, on the true path, providing symbols and prophecies of the truth once more to be revealed in Jesus Christ. Both Jewish and pagan religion is therefore degenerating. The pattern of fall is traced in world history, and the return begins with the incarnation.

The function of the Logos is educative, restoring true religion, which is proper worship of the one true God, not a set of credal propositions, and teaching the true way of life. The Gospel is about 'friendship' with God, and this is what the Logos came to preach. It had been promised in the prophetic oracles, and the way providentially prepared for its revelation. The truth about the Sovereign of the universe wins the world from its delusive worship of daemons, brings peace and justice, restores rationality. Thus the teaching of Jesus in the Gospel and the providential activity of God cohere in the historical provision of *paideia* for the fallen human race, and Eusebius delights in pointing to the growing success of Christianity in his world as proof of his claims.

Book 7 provides a summary focus of this overall conception. The Hebrews alone deduced from the created order the existence of a Creator, and their own place within creation as rational beings charged with the privilege of rule and royalty over all things on earth. Eusebius credits them with realizing that the soul's rational and intellectual faculty should therefore be cultivated rather than the body, since it bore the likeness of God. Knowledge of God and his friendship they recognized as the consummation of all happiness, and they lived (before Moses) a free and unfettered life according to nature. The models of the righteous beloved by God are then sketched, Enos, Enoch, and Noah, then Abraham, Isaac, Jacob, and Joseph. They are called Hebrews, according to Eusebius, because 'they are a kind of "passengers", who have set out on their journey from this world to pass to the contemplation of the God of the universe. For they are recorded to have travelled the straight path of virtue aright by natural reasoning and by unwritten laws, and to have passed beyond carnal pleasures to the life of perfect wisdom and piety' (*Praep. evang.* 7. 8. 309b–c).

Eusebius may have a conception of a pristine faith, indeed of the original true religion, but it is not framed in terms of credal formulae or static ontological categories.

So what about the anti–Origenist, Epiphanius? What we know of Epiphanius is largely related to his campaign to eradicate heresy on all sides. But what did he mean by 'heresy'? The word is not confined to Christian deviations. It embraces also Greek philosophical schools and Jewish parties like the Pharisees and Sadducees. In other words it retains its original meaning of 'options'. What is wrong with options? As far as Epiphanius is concerned, the existence of options implies division, splinter-groups, factions, and is symptomatic of the breakdown of the original unity purposed by God. This unity is now restored in the one, holy, catholic, and apostolic church. Anything that rends that unity is rebellion, adultery, idolatry. Any kind of deviation belongs *outside*. Hence Epiphanius' hostility to anything he saw as false doctrine.

Adam was neither an idolater nor circumcised, but held the faith of the holy catholic church of God which existed from the beginning and was later to be revealed again. Because of Adam's sin, there appeared the opposite of the true faith. Piety and impiety, faith and unfaith coexisted, with the great biblical figures like Abel, Enoch, Methuselah, and Noah representing the former, which was the image of Christianity; Abraham in particular is presented as the type of the Christian, prefiguring, in his departure from his father's house, the call of the first disciples. To some extent Epiphanius shares Eusebius' historical perspective.

However, Epiphanius' main interest is to produce a genealogy of heresy, and his underlying conception seems to be a contrast between unity and multiplicity, heresy necessarily breeding further heresy, and compounding error. His schemata are not entirely consistent, and his material is artificially contrived to suit certain biblical texts (Young 1982), but the notion of the breakdown of pristine unity is clearly fundamental to his conceptions.

For Epiphanius, unity implies simplicity, and he mistrusts all kinds of 'speculation'. There are some things about which enquiry should not be made. Scripture speaks the truth in everything;

heresy is false because it does not receive the Holy Spirit according to the traditions of the Fathers of the holy catholic church. Wandering from the truth means being tossed on the storms of heresy. So good anchorage is required. So far from voyaging, Epiphanius prefers not to leave safe harbour and the security of truth given.

The well-anchored person (*Ancoratus* is the title of a work which preceded the *Panarion* or *Haereses*) knows the right formulae. When Epiphanius expounds the faith he piles up ecclesiastical jargon, scripture and tradition providing him with his tools: Christ is 'the only-begotten, the perfect, the uncreated, the immutable, the unchangeable, the unknowable, the unseen, become man among us . . . the one who though rich became poor for us . . . one Lord, King, Christ, Son of God, seated in heaven on the right-hand of the Father . . .'. Epiphanius not only quotes creeds, but writes in credal style. His fundamental concern is the avoidance of error.

No doubt this attitude is both perennially tempting and particularly understandable in the confusing maelstrom of fourth-century ecclesiastical controversy. No doubt Epiphanius was not the only one with this approach. But was he really typical?

The thrust towards unity is one thing he and others, even Origenists, had in common, and he was not alone in seeking to achieve it by a process of exclusion. To the extent that every philosophical sect had developed a tradition to be imparted to disciples and followed, Epiphanius' outlook reflected contemporary custom, and Christian practice in training catechumens and drilling them in a creed might seem to envisage the same fundamental outlook. This too was a kind of *paideia*, and it was geared to producing loyal adherents to a common stance. Deviation was suspect. But to deduce that catechetical instruction simply concentrated on imparting what we mean by correct doctrine is soon exposed as inappropriate by examination of examples of Catechetical Lectures which are extant from this period.

Catechumens were preparing for baptism, and Cyril of Jerusalem explains that baptism involved a melting-down and a re-moulding —it was quite realistically seen as transformation, as new life, as a dying and rising with Christ (e.g. *Orat. cat.* 3). Justifying the brevity of the Creed on the grounds that all cannot read the scriptures, some being hindered by lack of education, others by want of leisure, Cyril admits (*Orat. cat.* 5. 12) that the Creed comprises the whole doctrine of the faith in a few lines. It is a summary of scripture, but it needs filling out, it is simply the foundation on which the new convert is to build. Cyril of Jerusalem tells his class that they are standing at the gates of the heavenly mystery.

Memorizing the Creed was ensuring that the new covenant was written on the heart and not on tablets of stone: 'He gave us this new covenant . . . and because of this covenant we receive knowledge of these mysteries so that we should put off the old man and put on the new man who is renewed after the image of him who created him' (*Orat. cat.* 1), claimed Theodore of Mopsuestia. Entry to the future kingdom of heaven depends on adoption as sons of God; as the new-born baby is weak, so the newly baptized one cannot expect to be perfect, and needs suitable food for spiritual nourishment (*Orat. cat.* 16).

The Creed, then, proclaims the new creation, the gift of the Spirit, the future hope; a sense of wonder and mystery permeates Theodore's exposition of it. The Creed belonged to the process of commitment, of response to the Gospel proclaimed. It belonged at the beginning of the Christian life and was no mere assent to certain propositions. Converts were certainly warned against erroneous doctrines, but the teaching they received was more holistic, more transforming and dynamic than either Epiphanius or our preconceptions about doctrine might have suggested.

As for Gregory of Nyssa, so for Theodore, an essential component of doctrine is that 'dogma' is impossible: 'Human minds and human words are altogether unequal to the grandeur of the things I have to talk to you about. No language is really capable of explaining the sacred mysteries of our religion' (*On the Nicene Creed*, 1).

Epiphanius, it would seem, represents one persistent tendency in Christianity, reflecting the need for secure anchorage, but he cannot be regarded as typifying the attitude of his own time. The more persistent symbol of the Christian faith is a spiritual journey, or growth to maturity. Indeed, space permitting, it would be possible to show that this is true even for the participants in the Christological controversy. Both the exegesis, and indeed the Christology, of Cyril of Alexandria falls into the same pattern of *paideia*: for the Pentateuch is essentially understood as exemplifying exile and spiritual famine, followed by repentance and renewal, both Abraham's migration and the exodus being paradigms of God's grace effecting conversion, while the dynamic of *kenōsis*, or divine accommodation to humanity, lies at the heart of his Christological concerns. Furthermore the interest of the Antiochenes in the exemplary synergism of divine and human natures in Christ, who as high priest learned by what he suffered, is well documented (Greer 1973).

V

Yet, our objector might retort, appeal to the Fathers as well as scripture in the fifth-century controversies does seem to suggest that the notion of a 'pure deposit' or an original 'orthodoxy' from which deviation took place was a persistent view. Innovation and novelty were charges brought against heresy. Furthermore, the very Platonic notions behind Origen and Gregory of Nyssa imply that even if we are unable to grasp it or express it in propositional form, even if we have to progress towards it, behind the changes and chances of this life is an eternal unchanging reality. So surely the perception that the Fathers believed in static dogma cannot be wholly misguided. And were not the Christological controversies dominated by 'substance' categories?

The character of Platonism can hardly be tackled within the compass of this essay: suffice it to say that it is too easy to caricature ancient philosophy, understanding its concerns and doctrines in an overly simplistic way. An examination of late fourth-century discussions of human nature soon reveals a much more sophisticated sense of the complexity of the soul–body relationship than is generally attributed to this period—the soul is almost what we call the central nervous system, as well as the 'person' who transcends bodily existence (Young 1983). In the Platonist tradition life and motive power were associated with soul, and even the Ideas were regarded as intelligences, living beings. For Origen the eternal world was peopled by *logikoi*. There is a deep tension in Platonism between the attribution of changelessness and impassibility to spiritual realities like God and the soul, and the recognition that spiritual realities are both living and the source of life, movement, and power. Impassibility was not impassivity.

The 'substance' categories were to do with discussion of identity

as enduring reality. In the Trinitarian and Christological controversies the issue of identity, and therefore of substantial reality,
became the subject of debate, and it was inevitable that ontological
terminology should dominate the discussion. This may give a static
'feel' to much of patristic thinking, but this terminology was
employed to identify the living subject(s) of God's *oikonomia*.

By the time of the Cappadocians the dynamic of the divine
oikonomia, God's creative and redeeming activity as self-revealing
love, was recognized to be the known aspect of a triune God whose
essential being was unknowable:

> God is Light: the highest, the unapproachable, the ineffable, that can
> neither be conceived in the mind nor uttered in speech, that gives light to
> every reasoning creature. He is in the world of thought what the sun is in
> the world of sense; in proportion as we are cleansed, he presents himself
> to our minds; in proportion as he is presented to our mind, he is loved;
> and again in proportion as we love him, he is conceived; himself
> contemplating and comprehending himself, and pouring himself out upon
> what is external to him. I mean that Light which is contemplated in the
> Father and the Son and the Holy Spirit, whose wealth is their unity of
> nature and the single outburst of their brightness. (Gregory Nazianzen,
> *Orat.* 40. 5. p. 204)

This is the language of dynamic relationship, of response and quest,
of mind and heart. It is the language of liturgy and devotion
as well as of doctrine; and doctrine informs the religious life of
the community in such a way that it is indistinguishable from
spirituality.

There is, of course, a sense in which the truth is there in advance
of the journey: for the priority lies with the reality of God and
God's self-disclosure. The pride of the intellectual athlete who
presumes to use human reasoning to comprehend God is certainly
to be exposed. Bold innovation is rebellion against the truth. So,
as Gregory insists (*Orat.* 27), the true theologian has to submit in
humility and obedience to the discipline of purification and meditation. On the other hand, God, like a schoolteacher facilitating a
pupil's progress, has to accommodate the *paideia* to the level of the
human recipient: there must be a mutually interacting dynamic for
the teaching to effect growth in understanding.

VI

The consequences of this study are, I suggest, threefold:

1.   That the current tendency, initiated by Maurice Wiles, to see soteriological concerns as underlying the doctrinal debates of the early centuries should be affirmed, and even radicalized in the sense that the distinction between soteriology and doctrine be recognized as false. Since both are about *paideia*, and the education involved is true religion, our Western distinctions, especially that between the head and the heart, have come to distort what lies at the heart of Christianity, which is a process of personal, social—indeed global —transformation effected by getting to know God and being reunited in the divine life.

For that process to be true to the reality of the way things are requires the nearest approximation possible in human terms to a true perspective on the identity and purpose of God, but this can only be attained through response to God's creative and educative activity (another way of characterizing what used to be called 'revelation'). That means doctrine is more than what we now mean by dogma or credal formula, and more than 'second-order' reflection on religious experience. It constitutes the religious life.

2.   That the projection of 'static' received dogma on to the teachers of the early Church should be repudiated as a distortion of their fundamental outlook. It is true that they had sufficient humility to revere the common heritage and to seek to honour what had been received from the past. It is also true that innovation and indeed diversity of opinion was distrusted and associated with heretics. But the Fathers were not afraid to enter into argument to spell out the implications of the revelation received, and they largely envisaged this life in terms of a process of response to God's attempts to educate the human race.

This, I would suggest, is the appropriate way of discerning some sense of 'doctrinal development' or 'progressive revelation' in the thinking of the Fathers. Such notions have been attributed to Gregory Nazianzen, who was forced to respond to the charge that the divinity of the Holy Spirit was an innovation: 'The Old Testament proclaimed the Father openly and the Son more obscurely. The New manifested the Son, and suggested the Deity of the Spirit. Now the Spirit himself dwells among us, and supplies a clearer demonstration of himself' (*Orat.* 31. 26). However, this seems at first sight much closer to 'dispensationalism' than any modern notions of historical evolution.

In fact it is precisely because doctrinal development and progressive revelation are notions of modern culture, triggered by Reformation controversies, nineteenth-century scientific theories, and the development of historical consciousness, that I have not hesitated to call them 'projections'. They are ways of thinking which help us to understand the past, and not ideas we should expect to find in past literature.

But having said that, in the passage referred to Gregory affirms gradual progress from glory to glory, the light of the Trinity shining upon the more illuminated—indeed, he appeals to John 14: 16–17 and speaks of the Spirit gradually coming to dwell with the disciples, measuring himself out according to their capacity to receive him. It is clear that progress in understanding, for the individual, for the human race, and for the cosmos, is envisaged in patristic thinking, and this process of *paideia* is the framework in which the equivalent of our idea of 'development' may be discerned. Gregory was not alone in being conscious of spelling out the implications and discerning new depths in the faith once delivered to the saints. History was seen as the arena of process and change, and as the journey of the soul was progressive apprehension of truth, so under the guidance of God tradition would realize its 'potential' meaning under changing circumstances.

3. That the idea should be laid to rest once and for all that patristic theological discourse was conducted in static ontological categories. We ourselves necessarily use such categories when discussing issues of enduring identity, nature, or even character. Such were the questions Church leaders found themselves debating, and which our histories of doctrine have fastened upon. But 'doctrine' was not confined to those issues, and Christian teaching was obliged to affirm change because it was about fall, repentance, and return, about transformation, indeed about deification.

Exegesis spelled out the doctrine contained in scripture, doctrine was doctrine because it was educative, and so it was about spiritual growth, about God's saving *paideia*.

REFERENCES

Editions

Cyril of Jerusalem, *Catechetical Orations*: Migne, *Patrologia Graeca*, vol. 33. 331–1128.
Eusebii Praeparatio Evangelica, ed. E. H. Gifford, text and trans. in 4 vols., Oxford 1903.
Grégoire de Nazianze: Discours 27–31 (*Discours théologiques* = *Orations*), ed. P. Gallay, text and French trans., Sources Chrétiennes 250, Paris 1978.
Grégoire de Nazianze: Discours 38–41, ed. C. Moreschini, text and French trans., Sources Chrétiennes 358, Paris 1990.
Gregorii Nysseni opera, ed. W. Jaeger and Hermann Langerbeck, Leiden. vol i, *Contra Eunomium libri*. ed. W. Jaeger, 1960; vol. vii. 1, *De vita Moysis*, ed. H. Musurillo, 1964.
Gregorii Nysseni: Oratio catechetica magna: Migne, *Patrologia Graeca*, vol. 45. 9–106.
Theodore of Mopsuestia, *Commentary of Theodore of Mopsuestia on the Nicene Creed*, and *Commentary on the Lord's Prayer and the Sacraments of Baptism and the Eucharist*, ed. A. Mingana, Syriac text and Eng. trans., Woodbrooke Studies v and vi, Cambridge, 1932.

Secondary Literature

Bigg, Charles (1886), *The Christian Platonists of Alexandria*, Oxford.
Crouzel, Henri (1985), *Origène*, Paris (Eng. trans. Edinburgh 1989).
Greer, Rowan (1973), *The Captain of our Salvation: A Study in the Patristic Exegesis of Hebrews*, Tübingen.
Richardson, Alan (1935), *Creeds in the Making*, London.
Torjesen, Karen Jo (1985a), *Hermeneutical Procedure and Theological Method in Origen's Exegesis*, Berlin.
—— (1985b), '"Body", "Soul", and "Spirit" in Origen's Theory of Exegesis', *Anglican Theological Review*, 67/1: 17–30.
Young, Frances M. (1982), 'Did Epiphanius Know what he Meant by Heresy?', *Studia patristica*, 18: 199–205.
—— (1983), 'Adam and Anthropos: A Study of the Interaction of Science and the Bible in Two Anthropological Treatises of the Fourth Century', *Vigiliae Christianae*, 37: 110–40.

Bibliography of Writings by
Maurice Wiles

Books

The Spiritual Gospel (Cambridge: Cambridge University Press, 1960).
The Christian Fathers (London: Hodder & Stoughton, 1966).
The Divine Apostle (Cambridge: Cambridge University Press, 1967).
The Making of Christian Doctrine (Cambridge: Cambridge University Press, 1967).
The Remaking of Christian Doctrine (London: SCM Press, 1974).
What is Theology? (Oxford: Oxford University Press, 1976).
Working Papers in Doctrine (London: SCM Press, 1976) (reprinting of articles marked ★).
Explorations in Theology 4 (London: SCM Press, 1979) (including a reprinting of articles marked †).
Faith and the Mystery of God (London: SCM Press, 1982).
God's Action in the World (London: SCM Press, 1986).
Christian Theology and Interreligious Dialogue (London: SCM Press, 1992).

Co-author with Mark Santer: *Documents in Early Christian Thought* (Cambridge: Cambridge University Press, 1975).

Editor: *Providence* (London: SPCK, 1969).

Articles

1. Published separately

'Jerusalem, Athens and Oxford' (Inaugural Lecture) (Oxford: Oxford University Press, 1971).
'Faith , Doubt and Theology' (The Maynard–Chapman Divinity Lecture, Westfield College, 1975).

2. Contributions to books

'Miracles in the Early Church', in C. F. D. Moule (ed.), *Miracles* (London: Mowbray, 1965), 221–34.
'The First Centuries', in L. Bright (ed.), *The People of God* (London: Sheed & Ward, 1965), 59–74.
'The Doctrine of Christ in the Patristic Age', in N. Pittenger (ed.), *Christ for us Today* (London: SCM Press, 1968), 81–90.

286 · Bibliography: Maurice Wiles

'The Study of Christian Doctrine', in F. G. Healey (ed.), *Preface to Christian Studies* (London: Lutterworth, 1971), 155–69.

'Does Christology Rest on a Mistake?', in S. W. Sykes and J. P. Clayton (eds.), *Christ, Faith and History: Cambridge Studies in Christology* (Cambridge: Cambridge University Press, 1972), 3–12 (repr. of paper first pub. in *Religious Studies*, 6 (Mar. 1970)).

'Eucharistic Theology: The Value of Diversity', in *Thinking about the Eucharist: Essays by Members of the Archbishops' Commission on Christian Doctrine* (London: SCM Press, 1972), 115–22.[†]

'Sacramental Unity in the Early Church', in J. Kent and R. Murray (eds.), *Church Membership and Intercommunion* (London: Darton, Longman & Todd, 1973), 35–49.[†]

'The Holy Spirit and the Incarnation', in Dow Kirkpatrick (ed.), *The Holy Spirit* (Nashville: Tidings, 1974), 90–104.

'The Uses of "Holy Scripture"', in M. Hooker and C. Hickling (eds.), *What about the New Testament?* (Festschrift for Christopher Evans) (London: SCM Press, 1975), 155–64.

'Christian Believing', a contribution to a report by the Doctrine Commission of the Church of England (London: SPCK, 1976), 125–32.

'Christianity without Incarnation?' and 'Myth in Theology', in J. Hick (ed.), *The Myth of God Incarnate* (London: SCM Press, 1977), 1–10 and 148–66.

'A Survey of Issues in the *Myth* Debate' and 'Comment on Lesslie Newbigin's Essay', in M. Goulder (ed.), *Incarnation and Myth* (London: SCM Press, 1979), 1–12 and 211–13.

(in collaboration with R. C. Gregg) 'Asterius: A New Chapter in the History of Arianism?', in R. C. Gregg (ed.), *Arianism: Historical and Theological Reassessments* (Philadelphia: Philadelphia Patristic Foundation, 1985), 111–51.

'The Reasonableness of Christianity', in W. J. Abraham and S. W. Holtzer (eds.), *The Rationality of Religious Belief* (Festschrift for Basil Mitchell) (Oxford: Oxford University Press, 1987), 39–51.

'Person or Personification? A Patristic Debate about Logos', in L. D. Hurt and N. T. Wright (eds.), *The Glory of Christ in the New Testament* (Festschrift for George Caird) (Oxford: Oxford University Press, 1987), 281–9.

'Scriptural Authority and Theological Construction: The Limitations of Narrative Interpretation', in G. Green (ed.), *Scriptural Authority and Narrative Interpretation* (Festschrift for Hans Frei) (Philadelphia: Fortress Press, 1987).

'On Being a Theologian in Today's Church', in *Het Leven is Meer Dan Ethiek* (Festschrift for Gerard Rothuizen) (Kampen: J. H. Kok-Kampen, 1987), 73–82.

'In what Contexts does it Make Sense to Say, "God Acts in History"?', in P. Devenish and G. Goodwin (eds.), *Witness and Existence* (Festschrift for Schubert Ogden) (Chicago: University of Chicago Press, 1989), 190–9.

'Eunomius: Hair-Splitting Dialectician or Defender of the Accessibility of Salvation?', in R. Williams (ed.), *The Making of Orthodoxy* (Festschrift for Henry Chadwick) (Cambridge: Cambridge University Press, 1989), 157–72.

'The Incarnation and Development', in R. Morgan (ed.), *The Religion of the Incarnation* (Bristol: Bristol Classical Press, 1989), 74–84.

'The Philosophy in Christianity: Arius and Athanasius', in G. Vesey (ed.), *The Philosophy in Christianity* (Cambridge: Cambridge University Press, 1989), 41–52.

'Orthodoxy and Heresy', in I. Hazlett (ed.), *Early Christianity* (Festschrift for William Frend) (London: SPCK, 1990), 198–207.

'What Christians Believe', in J. MacManners (ed.), *The Oxford Illustrated History of Christianity* (Oxford: Oxford University Press, 1990), 553–71.

'Puzzling Reflections of Truth', in D. Cohn-Sherbok (ed.), *Tradition and Unity: Sermons Published in Honour of Robert Runcie* (London: Bellew, 1991), 41–4.

'Worship and Theology', in D. W. Hardy and P. H. Sedgwick (eds.), *The Weight of Glory* (Festschrift for Peter Baelz) (Edinburgh: T. & T. Clark, 1991), 69–78.

'Can Theology still be about God?', in S. G. Davaney (ed.), *Theology at the End of Modernity* (Festschrift for Gordon Kaufman) (London: Trinity Press International, 1991), 221–32.

'The Authority of Scripture in a Contemporary Theology', in A. Linzey and P. Wrexler (eds.), *Fundamentalism and Tolerance* (London: Bellew, 1992), 3–9.

'Can we still do Christology?', in a Festschrift for Lee Keck edited by A. Malherbe and W. Meeks (forthcoming).

'The Meaning of Christ', in a Festschrift for John Hick edited by A. Sharma (forthcoming).

'Revelation and Divine Action', in P. Avis (ed.), *Divine Revelation* (forthcoming).

'Attitudes to Arius in the Arian Controversy', in M. Barnes and D. Williams (eds.), *Later Arianism* (forthcoming).

'Divine Action: Some Moral Considerations', in a volume edited by T. Tracy (forthcoming).

3. In journals

'More about Parables', *Theology*, 57 (Sept. 1954), 339–42.

'The Old Testament in Controversy with the Jews', *Scottish Journal of Theology*, 8/2 (June 1955), 113–26.

'St Paul's Conception of Law', *Churchman*, 69/3 and 4 (Sept. and Dec. 1955), 144–52 and 228–34.

'Some Reflections on the Origins of the Doctrine of the Trinity', *Journal of Theological Studies*, NS 8 (Apr. 1957), 92–106.★

'Letter from Nigeria', *Theology*, 60 (Nov. 1957), 455–60.

'Early Exegesis of the Parables', *Scottish Journal of Theology*, 11/3 (Sept. 1958), 287–301.

'The Enigma of Judas', *Ghana Bulletin of Theology*, 1/5 (Dec. 1958), 9–11.

'Gospel and Law', *Theology*, 62 (July 1959), 282–4.

'The Difficulties of Being a Theologian', *Theology*, 64 (May 1961), 181–4.

'An African University College', *East and West Review*, 27/3 (July 1961), 77–82.

'Eternal Generation', *Journal of Theological Studies*, NS 12 (Oct. 1961), 384–91.★

'In Defence of Arius', *Journal of Theological Studies*, NS 13 (1962), 339–47.

'The Holy Spirit and Christian Theology', *Theology*, 66 (June 1963), 233–7.†

'The Theological Legacy of St Cyprian', *Journal of Ecclesiastical History*, 14/2 (Oct. 1963), 59–66.★

'One Baptism for the Remission of Sins', *Church Quarterly Review*, 165 (1964), 139–49.★

"ΟΜΟΟΥΣΙΟΣ ΗΜΙΝ", *Journal of Theological Studies*, NS 16/2 (Oct. 1965), 454–61.

'The Nature of the Early Debate about Christ's Human Soul', *Journal of Ecclesiastical History*, 16/8 (Oct. 1965), 139–51.★

'Soteriological Arguments in the Fathers', *Studia patristica*, 9 (1966), 321–5.

'The Unassumed is the Unhealed', *Religious Studies*, 4 (Oct. 1968), 47–56.★

'Looking into the Sun' (An Inaugural Lecture in the Chair of Christian Doctrine in the University of London), *Church Quarterly*, 1/3 (Jan. 1969), 191–201.★

'Christian Doctrine in the 1960s', *Church Quarterly*, 2/3 (Jan. 1970), 215–21.

'Does Christology Rest on a Mistake?', *Religious Studies*, 6 (Mar. 1970), 69–76★ (also repr. in S. W. Sykes and J. P. Clayton (eds.), *Christ, Faith and History: Cambridge Studies in Christology* (1972)).

'Religious Authority and Divine Action', *Religious Studies*, 7 (Mar. 1971), 1–12.★

'The Consequences of Modern Understanding of Reality for the Relevance and Authority of the Tradition of the Early Church in our Time', *Œcumenica Jahrbuch* (1971–2), 130–43.★

'Psychological Analogies in the Fathers', *Studia patristica*, 11 (1972), 264–7.

'The Central Concepts of Judaism, Graeco-Roman Paganism and Christianity', *Didaskalos*, 4/2 (1973), 226–33.

'The Criteria of Christian Theology', *Theology*, 76 (Dec. 1973), 619–28.

'Theology and Unity', *Theology*, 77 (Jan. 1974), 4–6.

'The Remaking Defended', *Theology*, 77 (Aug. 1975), 394–7.

'"Myth" in Theology', *Bulletin of the John Rylands Library*, 59/1 (Autumn 1976), 226–46.

'The Relation between Psychology and Religion', *Harvest*, 23 (1977), 89–95.

'The Incarnation: An Exchange with Herbert McCabe O.P.', *New Blackfriars*, 58 (Dec. 1977), 542–53.

'In what Sense is Christianity a "Historical" Religion?', *Theology*, 81 (Jan. 1978), 4–14.

'Pilgrimage in Theology', *Epworth Review* 5/2 (May 1978), 68–74.

'Whither Theology?', *Modern Churchman*, 2 and 3 (Summer 1978), 64–71.

'The Language of Faith: A Christian View', *World Faiths*, 107 (Spring 1979), 5–10.

'Does Christianity Need a Revelation?', *Theology*, 83 (Mar. 1980), 109–14.

'Is Christianity Credible?', *Epworth Review*, 8/1 (Jan. 1981), 50–5.

'Farrer's Concept of Double Agency', *Theology*, 84 (July 1981), 243–9.

'Reflections on James Dunn's *Christology in the Making*', *Theology*, 85 (Mar. and Sept. 1982), 92–6 and 324–32.

'Ignatius and the Church', *Studia patristica*, 18 (1982), 750–5.

'John Robinson', *Theology*, 87 (Mar. 1984), 84–5.

'Marching in Step?', review article on the C. of E. Doctrine Commission Report '"We Believe in God"', *Theology*, 90 (Nov. 1987), 460–4.

'Christianity and Other Faiths', *Theology*, 91 (July 1988), 302–8.

'The Theology of Eusebius of Emesa', *Studia patristica*, 19 (1989), 267–80.

'A Textual Variant in the Creed of the Council of Nicaea', *Studia patristica* (forthcoming).

Index of Names